Dating Your Character

A Sexy Guide to Screenwriting for Film and TV

Marilyn R. Atlas
Devorah Cutler-Rubenstein
Elizabeth Lopez

Dating Your Character
A Sexy Guide to Screenwriting for Film and TV

© 2016 Marilyn R. Atlas, Devorah Cutler-Rubenstein and Elizabeth Lopez All Right Reserved

Print ISBN 978-1-941071-09-0
eBook ISBN 978-1-941071-10-6

This book is sold subject to the condition that it shall not, by way of trade or otherwise, be lent, resold, hired out or otherwise circulated without the publisher's prior consent in any form of binding or cover other than that in which it is published and without a similar condition including this condition being imposed on the subsequent purchaser.

STAIRWAY PRESS—SEATTLE

Cover Design by Chris Benson
www.BensonCreative.com

STAIRWAY≡PRESS

www.StairwayPress.com
1500A East College Way #554
Mount Vernon, WA 98273 USA

TABLE OF CONTENTS

Dating Your Character Master Chart

Foreword by Dr. Linda Seger

CASTING YOUR IDEAL CHARACTER: THE "PREP"   3
—STEP ONE

Preparing for Your Character to Show up	13
Beginning Your *DYC* Research Journal	15
Zeroing in on Your Contender Protagonist	16
Waking up Your Senses	18
Differences between You and Her	19
Knowing What Works for You	21
Taking Personal Inventory	22
Why Only You Can Tell This Story	24
Crafting Your "Personal Logline"	28

THE MEET CUTE "THE SET-UP"—STEP TWO   35

Where Will You Meet Your Character?	37
The Geography of Genre	42
Genre Trap—Simple Protagonist	45
Genre Expectations and Secondary Characters	47
Genre and Conflict	51
What Kind of Personality Should She Have?	54
Genre Trap—Simple Plot	72
Sample Genre Workup—"Mystery"	76
Wrong Character, Right Genre	82
Genre and Inherent Pacing	83
Genre Checklist	85
Genre Checklist—Tone	87
Genre Checklist—Demographics	90

i

TABLE OF CONTENTS

THE FIRST DATE "THE INCITING INCIDENT" —STEP THREE   95

Setting the Scene	102
Getting in Her Headspace and Physical Space	117
The Pre-Date Prep	120
Dialogue/Action Checklist	125
Inciting Incident	160
Inciting Incident and Genre	165
The Critic	177

SERIOUS DATING "ACT I TURNING POINT" —STEP FOUR   180

The 10 Fundamentals of Script Coverage	190
Trust Walk	199
Trauma > Wound > Goal > Behavior	212
The Price of Admission—Making Sacrifices	221
Compatible Neuroses	229

MOVING IN TOGETHER "THE MIDPOINT" —STEP FIVE   237

Drumbeat—Listening to Her Rhythms	255
Making Your Character Likeable	269
Lend Her an Ear—Confronting Her Softly	276
Setting Boundaries	286
Pep Talk	293

THE FIRST FIGHT "BACK HALF OF ACT II" —STEP SIX   306

Deconstructing Negative Reactions	309
Fear as Fuel	310
Avoidance/Denial	311

TABLE OF CONTENTS

Devising Active and Passive Reactions	315
Overt Plan, Covert Intention, Action	324
Your Character Is the Sun	339

MAKING A COMMITMENT "ACT TWO TURNING POINT"—STEP SEVEN — 360

Location and POV	369
Antagonists	385
The Darkest Hour	405
The Third Act	417
Setbacks and Reversals as Revolutionary Evolution	420
Weaknesses as Strength	422

HITCHED OR DITCHED "CLIMAX/RESOLUTION"—STEP EIGHT — 427

Ground Zero	437
Third Act Anxiety Attack	444
The Other Side	462
Genre Wrap-ups	467
Loglines—Why Are They So Important?	470

ADDENDA

DYC Index: Book/Celebrity/Film/TV References	478
List of Works Cited	492
DYC Chapter Exercise List	494

FOREWORD

As we set out on a new journey, whether we are climbing a mountain or writing a script, the greatest risk is the lack of preparation. We expect a mountain climber to have checked her gear, to have made sure that there's enough water and food and warm gloves, and to have practiced on 14,000 foot peaks before attempting Everest. Similarly, it is hoped that the writer has done some preparation before starting to write a script. Just as there are risks for the climber, the writer can easily get stuck and have to restart the entire journey, possibly having wasted months or even years by getting on the wrong path before fully becoming familiar with the terrain.

Unfortunately, many new writers simply begin in a random fashion catch-as-catch-can. Even experienced, working writers often try to shortcut the process and don't spend the time necessary to deepen their characters while focusing on a strong and original storyline.

So, what is really needed in order to create a great character? Setting out on the journey, it may be to your benefit to have guides as knowledgeable as Marilyn, Devorah, and Elizabeth, who provide an exceptionally workable and detailed map to follow. They show you how to look around you at all the possibilities, and are encouraging throughout the creative process.

When you stumble, you hope your guide emboldens you. Shows you how to take a deep breath, how to choose the right fork in the trail, and how to make sure you don't become irretrievably lost along the way. These guides hint at details you may not have noticed as you first walked the trail, pointing out important signs and markers, as well as reminding you to appreciate the beauty of the vistas. It's clearly vital that you make a serious effort and have the equipment you need, so at every step of the way, you have the essentials to make your trip special.

They'll give you a push at times, so you're not simply trudging, but are energetically moving through the journey with hope and fortitude—and determination and clarity—toward the goal. It's key that you understand where you have come from and where you are going. So, they'll help you take a kind of personal stock now and then.

At the same time, you will not only learn how to create multilayered characters, but you will become grounded in other screenplay fundamentals: structure, conflict, stakes, theme, twists and turns, and you may gain insight into movies you're already familiar with. Hopefully, your imagination will be reinvigorated and your creativity reawakened.

Through accessible concepts and exercises during each leg of the journey, you will get to know and form a stronger commitment to your character. As you conscientiously make your way through this book, I expect you will enjoy every step of this amazing journey and even feel a sense of exhilaration.

Dr. Linda Seger
Author of *Creating Unforgettable Characters*

THE DATING YOUR CHARACTER CHART:

1. CASTING YOUR IDEAL
   CHARACTER
   (PREP PHASE)
   ♥ Getting ready for love

   Why do *you* want to write this?
   Making mental notes on who *you* want to date.
   What can *you* use from *your* own life?

2. THE MEET CUTE
   (THE SET-UP)
   ♥ The Story begins

   Locating *your* character in time and space; eyeing what attracts *you;* first impressions.

3. THE FIRST DATE
   (INCITING INCIDENT)
   ♥ Opening up for change

   Finding common ground; noting likes and dislikes; being nosy, getting in *your* character's face.

4. SERIOUS DATING
   (ACT I TURNING POINT)
   ♥ Deepening the connection

   Listening as *your* character's embarrassing flaws, foibles and idiosyncrasies seep out; hearing what's under her words. How are *you* different from her?

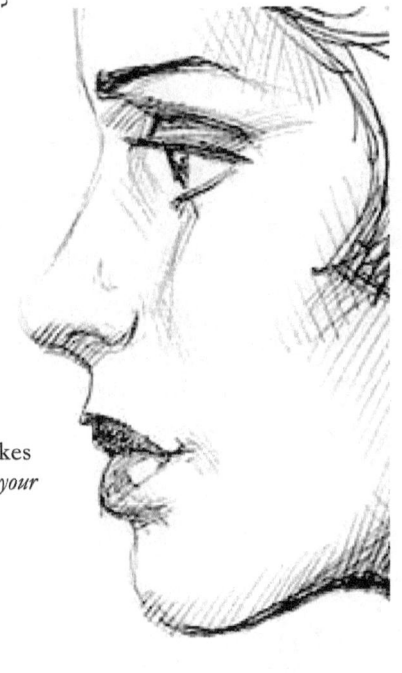

Dating Your Character

5. MOVING IN TOGETHER
   (MIDPOINT)
   ♥ Cracking open the relationship

   Blending *your* "shit": *your* history with *your* character's back-story; slapping the character on the cheek, making her admit to *hard* truths.

6. THE FIRST FIGHT
   (BACK HALF OF ACT II)
   ♥ The Truth comes out

   Catching the character in her lies; provoking her to mouth off about her needs, confessing ghosts and traumas at the root of her entrenched behavior.

7. MAKING A COMMITMENT
   (ACT II TURNING POINT)
   ♥ Total transformation is imminent

   Her deepest fears and limitations are unearthed moments before the final battle begins; encouraging her to keep her chin up, embrace her weaknesses as strengths.

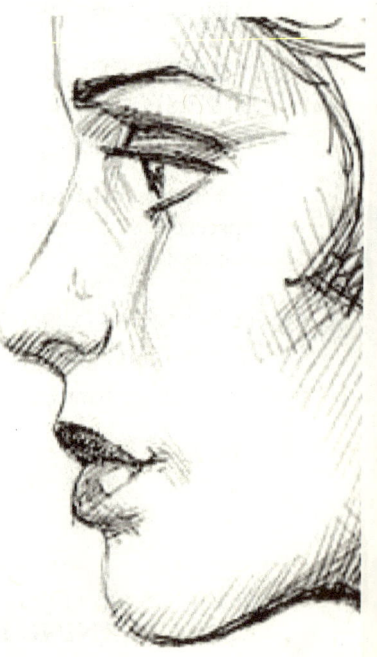

8. HITCHED OR DITCHED
   (CLIMAX/RESOLUTION)
   ♥ Clarifying your character's transformation

   You're holding your character's hand through the final beat, which can either be victory or defeat.

   If it's a victory: You've helped the character swallow the bitter pill of truth and go through necessary change; transformation is achieved,
   or
   If it's a defeat: The character remains trapped in her old system of being; it's a painful and tragic turn of events.

CASTING YOUR IDEAL CHARACTER

"THE PREP"—STEP ONE

> **Are you ready for a relationship…with your character?**

WHILE YOU MAY have never really thought about it, writing a compelling screenplay involves creating a dynamic relationship with your character.

Once in a while, the perfect character pops through the door of your imagination, without you thinking about it. You experience a giddy feeling akin to finding the love of your life. But more often than not, the wrong character stumbles in. It's kind of like the typical experience of meeting someone at a bar. You have that magical first night, but some of your important "must haves" are missing. And of course, the relationship doesn't work out for the long haul.

What if it were possible, from the very beginning of conceiving your character, to get exactly what you want from her?

> **Note:** For the purposes of our conversation with you, we'll be talking about your character as "she," but, obviously, your character doesn't have to be.

Dating Your Character

Settling for the first character that you think of can be a sign of laziness, habit, or naiveté. Whatever the reason, you don't want to choose the first arbitrary, clichéd choice in the assembly line of your mind. If you only had the equivalent of the right matchmaking checklist, you wouldn't just throw away your love on any old character. Then waiting for the right protagonist would be worth the wait, right?

The *Dating Your Character* system requires you to dig deep, from the very beginning, through exercises, questions and suggestive prompts; you'll know what you need and what you want from your character so you don't have to suffer through half-baked, unreliable characters, who'll only let you down.

For instance, what if you're excited by the possibility of a particular protagonist for an action flick? You've even gone so far as to write the first scene for *Guts and Gears* in your head. Maybe you've written for 20, 40, or 100 pages, rushing down a thrilling, but blind, alley, only to realize that you're about to come crashing into a dead end. And sadly, as you try to regain your balance and walk away from the wreckage, you acknowledge that your action flick is really more of an action-comedy hybrid. You would have gotten more story mileage if the Italian stud at the wheel of your story were, instead, a nervous hypochondriac who knows nothing about cars or the mechanics of women. So, you should have made a different choice from the get-go. But, who do you blame? Your… character?

That's why we recommend, during your character and story research before any real scriptwriting begins, that you ask yourself some soul-searching questions. We call this the **Prep Phase.** In this book we will continue to identify those key questions to help you achieve a more three-dimensional character. In the next eight chapters, we will be giving you our own *DYC* Criteria Checklist that helps you establish—and sustain—a relationship with the protagonist of your dreams. By the end of the process you should be in deep with your character and have created a truly viable and memorable character for your screenplay or teleplay.

The phenomenon of feeling as if you are in a relationship with your character is more common than not with many successful writers. But until our *DYC* story system, no one has looked into how that relationship even happens, and how to keep it going during the many twists and turns of writing a script. In interviewing hundreds of writers and carefully analyzing our own process, we saw that, during the writing, your relationship with your character mirrors the ups and downs of an evolving, intimate relationship.

As you commence thinking about your story, you will have ideas and questions about what will work for your character. You might ask, "Does my character serve my theme? Is the character going to grow and change? Will those changes impact the progression of my plot? Will my character undergo the necessary catharsis that marks a satisfying screenplay?" A satisfying script makes a real connection with its audience. If readers feel a real kinship with your character, they care about what happens to her. We call that the "relatability quotient," the character's "it" factor.

When you start out, your ideas about how to create a fascinating character can limit you. You may tend to settle for the first character type that drifts into your mind. We suggest, as part of this Prep Phase, that you really examine the ideas that you bring to the table before you decide on the protagonist worth dating for the entirety of your screenplay. Just like at the beginning of any potential relationship, you hope to find a connection, a spark of attraction, to the kind of character she may be.

Some of you may have been ruminating about your character for years and are just now sitting down to write. Others of you are a clean slate, ready and receptive for what—and who—might show up. Whatever the reason, today is the day you will begin to reel in the right person for your story—and the *DYC* system will help get you there. Congratulations!

For those of you who have been making mental notes on your character, we are going to examine and challenge the character you have been thinking about, to see if she's the best choice. Through these critical, initial exercises, whether you have your idea in place or not, you'll be able to further clarify your character. Your character will begin to snap into focus for your story and for the specific marketplace you're targeting.

Obviously, you may already know something about your character. You may have general ideas regarding her physically, mentally, sociologically, or emotionally. It might seem odd that we ask you to take stock of your character going into the process.

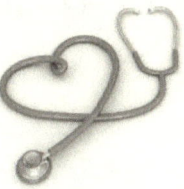

In order to find the best character out there, we need you to first acknowledge what you think you know. But just like in any relationship, you need to stay open to new possibilities. As you gather more information, you may decide to change your image of her or even dismantle it. Below is a way to check what you know about your character at this point.

For the first exercise, write out *one* (at the <u>maximum</u> *two*) *non-negotiable traits* you feel you absolutely must have for your character.

For *example*, if you're thinking of having your story deal with issues of domestic violence, at this point you might feel your only non-negotiable traits are that the protagonist is a *woman* who *becomes brave* over the course of the story.

(Though, wouldn't it be much more interesting if your drama features a male victim of emotional and physical abuse?)

For the purpose of this exercise, you are laying the basic groundwork. These details, which you feel comfortable attributing to your character, will probably not ever be in flux.

Dating Your Character

EXERCISE #1: CHARACTER CHECK-UP
WHAT DO YOU "THINK" YOU KNOW ABOUT YOUR CHARACTER?

Physically:
_____

Emotionally:
_____

Mentally:
_____

Sociologically:
_____

Exercise 1

Now let's see what you don't know…

> **EXERCISE #2: WHAT DO YOU REALLY KNOW?**
>
> Set a timer for *three minutes*. Have a red pen and a yellow highlighter, in addition to your pen and paper. Or be prepared to use different colored fonts on your computer.
>
> For this exercise, focus on everything that you feel you already know. As you write, some new ideas may occur to you; write those down, too. It does not need to be logical or orderly. Just let it all unfold.

> ***DYC* Example:**
>
> "Janet." She's a red-head, insecure about her body, 30-40 something, a closet chocoholic, 180-plus pounds but carries it well, a school teacher who works with autistic kids from an underserved group; maybe she teaches home economics or runs the chess club.

Exercise 2

> **EXERCISE #2-b: WHAT DO YOU REALLY KNOW?**
> If you're really in the flow, you may end up with a *page* of random images, thoughts, and feelings that come to you.
>
> Stop once the timer rings.
>
> First look at the list and *circle* all the items in red that resonate with you.
>
> Then, highlight your most important "must-haves."

Exercise 2-b

These details will work like paint on your palette, waiting to be used in the future. However, amongst them there will be one or two that are *indispensable* for your character. In other words, if you're heading towards choosing a particular character and her goal, there will be certain *obvious* requirements. And these are the only *key* traits that are critical to how your character behaves, and that will probably never change for you. These are not necessarily the most interesting or sparkly items from your excavation. Everything else that you've come up with may eventually all go by the wayside. While *DYC* celebrates the specific, at this stage, you are not locking down your decisions, but gathering information.

> ### *DYC* Example:
> For instance, the two non-negotiables for the previous example of the character tentatively named "Janet" are she's a teacher, and she works with some kind of fringe population. "Teacher" could be used more broadly—someone who doesn't necessarily work at a school but shares her knowledge in an unconventional way.

> ## EXERCISE #3: CHARACTER POINT OF VIEW (POV)
>
> Set your timer for *one minute*. Have your red pen ready. Your job is just to imagine *yourself* as your main character, and write continuously from the character's point of view. It might be about the kinds of problems and issues that challenge you now, *as the character*.
>
> Write down as many thoughts as you can. Don't over-think this. Write and let the ideas flow. Do not censor even the most seemingly ridiculous chatter. Keep your critic safely tucked in a box.

> **_DYC_ Example (Janet):**
> "I like cats. Always have. But my husband Darryl <u>hates 'em.</u> They have sharp little claws, which he doesn't approve of, but they need them <u>for protection</u>. I hate cleaning cat boxes, and Darryl won't go near them. He's afraid of the cats, maybe even a <u>little jealous.</u> Whatever. Those fluff-balls are worth it."

Exercise 3

A take away from the above example may be that the sample protagonist has a love-hate relationship with her husband and the animals are representative of that. Look for the subtext beneath the words that reveal important attitudes as you continue to mine your imagination and your research for rich details.

> **EXERCISE #3-b: CHARACTER POV**
> Although your exercise doesn't have to be this detailed, invariably there will be *one* or *two* relevant *words* you can *circle* and use for your character; specifics that somehow feel "spot on." You'll usually have a better understanding of one of the issues the character's

> facing.
>
> Note if something *feels* right and is worth further exploration. Is there *one detail* that you can use to help you begin to create a portrait of the character you would like to meet and "date" for the duration of your story? Write it down.

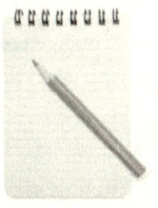

Exercise 3-b

PREPARING FOR YOUR CHARACTER TO SHOW UP

Prepare yourself right now to willingly spend a few weeks with the character you're going to be unleashing onto the world. The creative process doesn't start with you waking up, sitting at your computer, and end with you unplugging at night.

In the midst of organically evolving this relationship, you'll find you seem to be working around the clock: when you're showering, when you're biking…and it may even start to feel like you're on-call 24/7, completely devoted, as you acquire a working knowledge of your new main squeeze— your protagonist. Your world may take on a reflective quality, showing you people, places, and things you normally do not notice.

At this formative Prep Phase, observe, reflect on, and absorb the information coming at you. Your world will become a place with more spongy potential for your story. You may even experience an exciting preoccupation with your surroundings, scanning for details that serve your character's life. As often is the case, when you're dialed into your character, you may uncover a newfound interest in everything around you. People, animals, plants, colors, sounds, smells.

These specifics that grab your attention may seem new to you—objects, locations and insights—normally taken for granted within your world. For instance, while working on the Prep Phase, let's assume you noticed, tucked in the back of your cabinet, an old cup with some college logo on it. Something about it calls to you. Don't discard that detail as superficial—let it sit with you for a moment. As it ping-pongs in your mind, this process may lead you somewhere. You may find yourself overwhelmed with ideas, images flying at you. But, through simple questions, you can begin to dig deeper to uncover the details that could be keepers.

In this example, you might toy with the notion that your character went to this college. But then why would she keep this old cup hanging around at the back of her cabinet?

- Does she ever use it, or is it a forgotten part of her past?
- Did she buy it, or did someone give it to her?

Often a detail like this is what improv troupes call a "gift"—

something you can react and build upon, often revealing emotional or biographical information about your character. As is often the case, the detail is waiting to symbolically express some truth, at the very least engaging you and possibly deepening your understanding. In the Kenneth Branagh/Emma Thompson film *Dead Again*, the rare anklet that he gives symbolizes the love they share and their eternal bond; it helps the audience believe in their reincarnation.

Having read thousands of scripts, we've noticed that most writers seem to settle for characters that are stereotypical and generalized. Those scripts that have resonated with us embodied choice detail. Incorporating evocative details makes your characters and your scripts come alive.

WRITE IT DOWN—BEGIN YOUR DYC CHARACTER RESEARCH JOURNAL

As you walk around your world—or the world of your character—we suggest you keep a *DYC* character journal. This can be a physical notebook, or an electronic one, where you write down your character clues as you gather them. If you wanted to further explore the cup mentioned in the above example, you might ask *more* questions:

- Does this college souvenir create a fond memory or something akin to regret?

- Did she in fact go to college?
- Does the cup even belong to your character? Was it left behind by someone else? A former boyfriend who's just moved out and intentionally left the cup behind as a subtle reminder?

From our experience, getting really specific often takes you down roads that you've not thought about. You do not know, yet, how you will use these clues. You're creating a storehouse of seemingly diverse details that will eventually collapse into a tangible, three-dimensional protagonist as we get further into the *DYC* story system. The writer's mind—your mind—is good at ordering and identifying experiences, but it has to almost move aside for this gathering phase.

ZEROING IN ON YOUR "CONTENDER" PROTAGONIST'S UNIQUE POV

Living day-to-day, we don't often recognize opportunities to alter our own personal viewpoint. That's not to say that you've walked through the world in a self-centered daze. Sometimes a sudden loss will force you into seeing the world anew. But seeing the world from your "intended" protagonist's vantage point adds an important layer as you go forward into your story. It's absolutely necessary to have a sense of what *point of view* you'll need in order to laser-focus your premise.

If you're a gregarious people-watcher, you may not have thought about what it's like for your character to perceive the same surroundings through the eyes of someone who's very self-conscious or shy. Beginning to acknowledge that your character may need a different POV from *you* is important. Shifting *your* point of view is a big part of diving into the world of your character.

Because of your new whims of perception, the world may also assume a mirroring quality. Don't be surprised if this Prep Phase research—the unearthing process—suddenly draws you to people, places, or things similar to what you need for your character, supporting the notions swirling around in your head.

One of the authors was working on a story set at a racetrack. Never having frequented the track before, it was especially interesting to go behind the scenes and meet the quirky and unlikely characters that make up that community. Like Bess, the woman who tailors the "colors" the jockeys wear, which reflect the history and emotion of a particular owner or jockey.

As often happens, in the midst of researching a character, you could be sitting somewhere and the perfect expert you need is in the seat right next to you. Keep your mind and heart accessible. Curiosity may have killed the cat, but for a writer, it is what keeps our stories fresh and alive.

Dating Your Character

WAKING UP YOUR SENSES

EXERCISE #4: SMELLING THE ROSES

Choose a location that you might find your character lounging in. No need to set a timer. Write as long as you want and lounge, too!

Choosing <u>one</u> of your *five senses,* write about the location from the point of view of your character. Scents, visuals, sounds, textures, tastes that captivate you can later lead to bigger character clues. For instance, if you choose *smell*, which is a particularly powerful memory sense, you may be able to drill down deeper ("DDD").

DYC Example:

Perhaps you notice roses, where you, yourself, haven't in the past. Take care in describing how they smell. Is the smell pleasant? Are there any other smells competing with them? Do the roses remind you of anyone?

Then analyze the feedback from this exercise…

> ### *DYC* Example:
>
> - Could your character like roses?
>
> - She may adore roses, but does she unfortunately have a "black thumb" and manage to kill them all off?
>
> - Is she allergic to flowers in general? But, in spite of her allergies, is she an avid gardener?
>
> While these observations may seem random or irrelevant at first, we've found these sensory choices reinforce the all-important "relatability quotient" we referred to earlier.

Exercise 4

HOW DIFFERENT ARE YOU FROM YOUR MAIN SQUEEZE?

Of course, some of what you notice may be a part of your own personality that you're allowing, or choosing to incorporate, into the fabric of your emerging character. One of the greatest secret weapons that a screenwriter has is using facets of himself to fashion the cloth of his character. So you may wish to borrow from yourself, reinterpreting your own traits, hobbies, and family history.

Dating Your Character

Maybe your interests lie in politics or the arts, and you regularly go to a local museum. You may choose to have your character appreciate art with the same kind of fervor as a museumgoer or a docent. Or have that character relate to art in a completely sacrilegious way—as a forger or as a villain who desecrates art.

As things mesh together from your personal resources—your life, your research, and your imagination—what you *need* for your character, not just what you can recycle, begins to take form. And if you were to look into a figurative mirror, a truly unique character would be staring back at you, even though you may have largely based the character on yourself. As part of this process, you'll be identifying with her struggles to get a sense of what is at stake for her. You will begin to feel a real natural empathy as your relationship unfolds. Write down everything that you feel is worth remembering; even if there is only an inkling that you *might* use it, write it down!

One of the exciting virtues of being a writer is using the journey of creation to discover more about who you are. It's important to remember that, though you may be using bits of yourself to create your character's specific DNA, your character isn't a clone. What you want is an objective empathy with your character, like the sort you have with a friend.

KNOWING WHAT WORKS FOR YOU

However your process to get to know your character unspools, it is important to assess what works for you. You may find some of our *DYC* exercises and prompts inspiring, while others seemingly reap no rewards. Just keep an open mind; you may be surprised when your character comes together and snaps into focus.

In order to write authentically, a writer may well wonder how close his character should be to: A) himself, B) someone he's met in the past, C) someone he's researched, or D) someone he's completely forged from his imagination. That's up to you, as your character evolves. At this point, your character is still very much wet clay, and as you shape your ideas about what you need her to be for your specific scenario, expect many modifications as the character you're designing for your story reveals herself.

Don't review any previous lists you may have drawn up. But if information from that work crops up, then it's stuck with you for a reason. Rather than getting cozy in a cocoon of *facts* about your character that you've thought about in a purely intellectualized way, let your character inform her own creation. The following exercise can help you befriend your character by having you approach her from a nonjudgmental, even playful, place.

EXERCISE #5: RIP & SNATCH

Grab an old magazine. We suggest a travel, fashion, or city magazine with loads of pictures. Ask yourself as you flip through the magazine: *What are the kinds of people, places, and things that my character would gravitate to or hang out with*...and rip out those pictures. After you've done your "rip and snatch," grab a piece of paper (or talk into a tape-recorder) and write out the reasons why these images would resonate with your character. What in the pictures gives you clues to what your character likes, dislikes, does, or doesn't do?

Exercise 5

TAKING PERSONAL INVENTORY...

Knowing Who You Are & What You Want Pays Off

As you begin to imagine the faint outlines of the character you'd like to "date" for the next few weeks, be sure to look at your own motivation. Roll back time to recall your very first impulses to write *this particular* story. Don't underestimate the staying power of these first impulses. Ultimately, your intuition should be reinforced and clarified by your thoughtful investigation.

One important side benefit of this work is staying true to your vision through the collaborative process of filmmaking. The passionate gut connection you feel for your character not only sustains you in the process of writing your script, but it translates to a possible connection with your eventual buyers. And having that deep bond will serve you as you go forward by keeping you stoked. Even if you go through a period of dismissals and rejections from the fickle entertainment industry, those early embers will still glow and burn.

Writers have to wade through countless development meetings, memos, and drafts of the script if seeking substantial financing from production companies. While you may be lucky enough to tap into private equity to fund the production of your screenplay, you will still be required to succinctly pitch your story. What can often happen is that you aren't able to access your real reasons for writing the script in the first place. Because the film medium costs more than most artistic expressions to realize, you may start pressuring yourself to create from the outside, caught up in the push-pull to drastically rework your story. The danger in being agreeably accommodating is that you may subvert the very basis for an important meeting, your being hired for an open assignment, or your project being greenlit.

However, it's possible to make any compromise a win-win. It's possible to rewrite with integrity and not diminish your inspiration. The essence of your main character—the engine that drove the story in terms of the main character's internal conflict—will remain the same. And your character is an indelible part, who should never be discounted.

Following the steps in our *DYC* story system will help you stay true to your passion during the gauntlet of the development process. We encourage you to keep a *DYC* shoebox for your research data, like the magazine snapshots. And then, when creative executives supply you with development notes that unwittingly sap the story of its original power, the Prep Phase will give you the ammunition to share the emotional logic underlying your choices. It can help "lock you into" the rewrite stage, if your undeniable passion provides a thoughtful, persuasive argument to producers for why *only you* can gently refashion the story.

WHY YOU—AND ONLY YOU—CAN TELL THIS STORY

Let's get a picture of who *you* are. We're not talking heavy therapy here, just some helpful insights into your history. What we'd like you to do is sit down and basically interview yourself about your reasons for writing (which are separate from your ambitions), as well as any emotional pay-offs for you.

You may be motivated by fame, by shiny gold lucre, or by wanting to make a difference on our planet—or all of the above.

Maybe your plan is to win the lottery of screenwriting and have Tom Hanks produce your first script. Most of us who write want to be remembered in some way—to leave our mark. Regardless of how small or how grand your goals, try to be realistic. What's feasibly within your power?

For example, if you're out to wow Mr. Hanks himself, your bar of excellence has to be equal to the caliber of his past film work. Whatever windfall of admiration you may want from writing the script, your personal reason should be set apart from the imagined accolades of your family/friends, members of your writing group, agents/managers, and producers. You need to identify what's really under your skin and forcing you to write this script, because this is your emotional fuel.

Dating Your Character

EXERCISE #6: LOOK IN THE MIRROR

- What are you looking forward to in the process of writing?
- What do you need to accomplish to feel satisfied?
- What will make you happy?

You'll know you're on the right track if some of your responses:

- Embarrass you
- Make you want to retch
- Make the hair on the back of your neck stand on end
- Clarify your vision
- Surprise you in some way

Exercise 6

> **Reality Check**
>
> At your imagined six-figure spec sale, are you erupting in manic glee like some solvent sniffer? It's easy to hide behind a vague dream. If you rely solely on your sense of destiny, you might get lazy, bored, or frustrated. You have to do the grunt work necessary to craft a buzzed-about script, especially in today's demanding marketplace.
>
> Following through with the homework in this book will allow you to be microscopically specific with your character. You'll be able to generate greater emotion through a greater understanding of human nature. Put in the time so that your character will be more likely to elicit specific emotional reactions from your audience, and most importantly, be unforgettable.

The following exercise is different from earlier ones—it puts your emotional pay-off into more concrete terms. If you are clear and honest with yourself about what you expect to get out of the process, you'll more likely stick to the schedule you set. And, maybe, it won't become a chore, because at the point you feel uninspired or stuck, you'll know, just by the act of carving out time for yourself, you're on the road to your desired goal. Knowing *what* you are committed to—your outcome—is just as important as knowing your story. Too many great ideas lay on the roadside for lack of the disciplined motivation to bring them to fruition.

Dating Your Character

CRAFTING YOUR PERSONAL LOGLINE

According to story lore, the famous author John Steinbeck *(The Grapes of Wrath)* would always write out a sentence about what he felt his story was really about, and tape it to his typewriter, to keep him on track—and energized.

Everyone refers to standard loglines, but we encourage writers to also have something called a "personal logline." It's similar to the **logline*** for a script, but geared towards helping you clarify your objective with the script. At this stage of the game, crafting your personal logline will help you spend an hour, or more, of your day writing. What is going to put your butt in the chair—and keep it there?

- Are you looking forward to reserving an hour of the day for yourself, while hiding out from your kids and your dirty dishes?
- Are you interested in taking your daydreams to the next level and sharing your creativity with an audience?
- Are you aware that you'd like to use the screenplay to atone for choices you've made in the past, which you now wish you could undo?
- Are you investigating a family legacy that feels timely for a global audience?

Logline

* <u>Standard</u> **Logline**—the one or two sentence summary of your film's plot, theme, protagonist, and genre. Sometimes the most terrifying twenty-five words you'll ever have to write, because you are reducing your 100 plus-page script to a couple of sentences so someone will want to read it. *DYC* discusses this kind of sales logline in Step Eight.

* <u>*DYC* Personal Logline</u>—the one or two sentence practical summary of why you're willing to spend a couple (or more) hours of every day writing *this particular story*. Just like a good professional logline has character, plot, and theme spelled out, your personal logline has two parts to it; *what* you're realistically agreeing to for your schedule and *why* you're writing this story *now* at this stage of your life.

EXERCISE #7: PERSONAL LOGLINE

Fill in the blanks...

    I want to write this script because:

_____

_____

    I'm willing to write for _____ minutes a day _____ days a week.

Exercise 7

DYC Example:

One of the authors, Devo, shares her answers.

The very first screenplay I wrote was a teen dramedy called "High and Mighty." There must be something rich (and bold) there because it continues to get optioned, but hasn't actually been made, yet.

Standard Logline: Four kids, a weekend, and a game that gets out of hand.

Personal Logline: (Why) "Steinbeckian Statement:" I want to reveal the hidden world of a group of outcast teens who come to terms with growing up and the betrayal of truth that being an adult means. Adults compromise to the point where they lose their original selves. Every time I think about it, I still feel the angst, the confusion, and I'm compelled to dive back in there with my characters.

(What) Commitment: I am willing to do research and outline my story idea for three hours a day, five days a week for the first month. I will sit at my desk or at a coffee shop and write four to six hours a day, six days a week for the second month.

This is the basic bargain I strike with myself. Sometimes, I'll clock more time if I'm on a roll or under deadline. Some days I may write twenty pages, other days I may write three. But my average works out to about five pages a day over the two to four months it takes me to write a first draft.

Another of us, Elizabeth, is going to be outlining an original script, doing the exercises alongside you, while contributing to the writing of this book. Her response follows the exercise below.

> **EXERCISE #8: BE YOUR OWN BARBARA WALTERS**
>
> What do you want people to take away from your script? What is the emotion you want the audience to feel when the lights fade up in the movie theater? And if you can, what is the big problem your character will face, and why is it important for *you* to write about it?

Exercise 8

> **Example from Elizabeth:**
> Why this story? I'm interested in people who can survive in inhospitable locales. I'm interested in places forgotten by time, still largely undeveloped and primal.
>
> What to take away? I want people to be horrified by the loss of plants with the untold potential to heal or cure illness and

> disease.
>
> What is my passionate connection? I want my character to have to resort to physical violence in order to create change. I want to write this story because I have a lot of latent anger that I think it's best to safely vent onto the page.

YOU ARE DONE WITH STEP ONE.

So how are you going to bump into your ideal character, and where is that going to happen?

GO TO STEP TWO—THE MEET CUTE, where you will design the perfect location, genre, and circumstances you need to keep moving forward in your script.

If you are the producer and/or director co-creating the project with your writer, you need to find a way to express your vision from the very beginning to help your writer incorporate your thoughts. While you may want to control the process, part of the successful outcome of any collaborative endeavor is allowing creative juices to flow. We will directly address you at other spots in the book, so as to clue you in when it's best to share your passion and check in with the writer without stifling him....

THE MEET CUTE "THE SET-UP"—STEP TWO

THE "MEET CUTE" was a term coined by legendary writer/director Billy Wilder and has come to mean the charming and surprising circumstances of how two characters meet for the first time. We have borrowed this phrase for our *DYC* template and used it to describe the second phase of your developing relationship, where you first meet or are introduced to the character who will most likely become your protagonist of choice.

You probably have high hopes for writing an exciting original script and a memorable character. We're pretty sure there are cinematic characters who have stuck with you and influenced your thinking. You may consciously, or unconsciously, gravitate to these characters while you're writing. Copyright law suggests that you don't wholesale steal, but that you draw from these characters for inspiration.

Iconic characters spawn imitations that have since become standard stereotypes. For instance, Neil Simon's play *The Odd Couple* spun off the very phrase that describes two total opposites thrown together and in constant conflict, based on the antics of lead characters Felix Unger and Oscar Madison. The phrase has even morphed and become a verb, "odd coupling," to reference what is now a common writing mechanism. So, it may be helpful to think about these character touchstones before going any further. After all, we are creative creatures with a legacy of mythological and archetypical characters.

EXERCISE #9: ICONIC CHARACTERS

Make a quick list of your favorite movies. *15 movies* max...

Exercise 9

EXERCISE #9-b: ICONIC CHARACTERS

Which of these movies do you watch over and over because of the character(s)? Are there any shared similarities among the characters in these movies? Are there any reoccurring locations/types of locations in these films?

Exercise 9-b

> **Where will you meet your character?**

It's smart to go macro to get micro. Just like a portrait artist, you'll want to think about the landscape in the background in relation to what's happening in the foreground. The size of the subject in that framework, her social status, value system, and true personality are informed by the architecture of the entire panorama. As managers and producers, we're leading you to create 3-D characters because these are the screenplays we're interested in championing. Ultimately, details are precious. But if you jump to the details too quickly, i.e., come to easy conclusions, you defeat the depth-potential of your character.

Circling above your character like a falcon will give you the necessary overview to build her world—and from that create your deep connection to it, and to her. So if you think your character comes from a big city, your questioning doesn't end there. Just like your character, each city has its own personality.

Let's look at Los Angeles, California, a mega-city everyone thinks they already know. Which makes sense, because it's the most-photographed city in media history. In addition to world-famous celebrities hidden behind their green, well-tended estates, there are millions of strivers, immigrants, undocumented workers, and wannabes who call L.A. home. But often within a few city blocks, there exists a particular personality and secret vibe, because L.A. is diverse, divided into *de facto* pockets of minority cultures.

As each major metropolis is composed of many smaller identities, so is our *DYC* notion of selfhood. There are different sides to your character. Her incongruities and inconsistencies make her more believable and human. It's this attention to organic, layered detail that sets the *DYC* approach apart.

But how does thinking about a vast city help you get closer to your character? Well, any landscape may lead you to vital information about her. When you explore her terrain, you'll take the time to establish what makes her city or town unique, and further still figure out her place in the mix. Her experience of place contributes considerably to the formation of her mindset.

FILM EXAMPLE

Jodie Foster's character, Clarice Starling, in *Silence of the Lambs* left her small rural town to pursue her dream of a high-powered law enforcement job. Clarice grew, learned, and lived before we ever came to encounter her at the start of the movie. She had already adapted to survive, suppressing her natural instincts, feelings of vulnerability, and everything else she associated with the sheep farm that scarred her and shamed her.

Over the course of those childhood, adolescent, and young adult years, she valued intelligence and pure logic. She developed a tough skin and managed to assume a bland, J.C. Penney-styled veneer of professionalism. But her mentor/nemesis Hannibal Lecter will later expose her humble background to unnerve her and push her in their first meeting.

Until she can stop pretending about who she is, she cannot access and trust her instincts, which are vital in life-or-death situations. And, in the end, it's this that will allow her to triumph over the serial killer she's been hunting.

Be open and curious about how your character's formative years can tell you about who she is now. You're expanding the scope of your imagination; you're homing in, not defining. At this stage, we don't want you to fast-forward into the character-building process. It's enough to just have an active interest in the true nature of your character.

Allow the map of your character's world to first form in your mind. Scan the entire area. Scrutinize it. As you zoom in on parts of it, pay attention to what interests you. But don't put an X that marks that spot, yet.

> ### EXERCISE #10: NATIVE SON
>
> Get a map of any big city, small town, or foreign principality where you have a hunch your character could have grown up.
>
> Write about what you know, what you've heard, what you've seen about this area.
>
> Now go further, Google it.
>
> - What's the topography of the land?
> - What are its major industries?
> - What's the general character of the people who live there?

> **Note:** If you're working on a sci-fi space script, then what place on Earth is most like what the character's home planet could be?
>
> Don't race through this. **TAKE A MOMENT.** Sit quietly with the notion of your character...

Exercise 10

Ideally, you allowed your thoughts about her hometown/current city to drift for a while. This was less an exercise in figuring out what you know, but more an encouragement to let loose and experiment with your ideas. Hopefully you whipped around and looked into any of the various images that you came upon. You're gathering data, some of it will resonate, and some of it will fall away.

All of this work is stored in a kind of "character databank." From our experience, you're generating a creative mulch of people, places, things, and images that are retained and easily accessible during the development process. They just seem to pop in when a creative awakening is most needed.

EXERCISE #10-b: NATIVE SON

Now, having spent quality time pondering the possibilities of your character's origin:

- Where do you think your character lives when the story begins?
- Is there any conflict from having lived in these two places that makes the story richer?

Example from Devo:

I was working on a mystery with a scientist at the helm. She would be going to D.C. to deal with lobbyists. I assumed she might have spent her childhood in a big city, like Milwaukee, because I believed she had to have big city polish to survive in a slick big-business atmosphere.

But then I later found my initial pull to use a "big city" as her origin wasn't as strong a choice as that of a "university town," a

> protective environment. The fact that the scientist was from a protected university town, and did not have a real understanding of social conventions and politics, gave the character additional conflict, added counterpoint to the plot, and made it much more delicious to write. (The fish-out-of-water scenario works every time.)

Exercise 10-b

THE GEOGRAPHY OF GENRE

Regardless of pedigree or ambition, whether drama, action thriller, comedy, or heist caper, 99.9% of movies are genre movies. There are very few genre-less filmmakers, who completely confound these universally accepted story types. A recent example is Terrence Malick's film *The Tree of Life*.

What is genre? Based on the tone and other essential elements of the story, genre is ultimately how a story is told. It is the geography, textured landscape, and human network that the character is going to live inside of.

Choosing your genre is an invitation for the right character to step into the world you're creating. Even the broadest outline of your character is defined by the category, style, or type of storytelling you will be using. Beyond merely identifying the script's category, knowing your genre really means addressing all of the built-in audience expectations that are inherent in it. While you will not be carving out specifics for your character, the specifics of genre inform the kind of journey your character will take. It's a bit like knowing you're writing a waltz or a funeral dirge; you don't have the notes yet, but you have the tempo.

Most *crime dramas* start out with a crime. Or, as in many TV shows like *CSI*, the discovery of a crime. Feature films usually have characters wrestling with shades of right and wrong, and that's what people who buy a ticket want to see. No clear good guys or bad guys, just guys adapting as best they can to the rules of their world. Perhaps the only thing distinguishing the good from the bad is the number of people hurt as collateral damage…

In the first couple of decades of cinema, before the advent of film noir, there was less complexity in what constituted a hero and a villain. Everything was black and white. Their motives, their actions, even the clothes they wore. Today, there are more shades of gray as genres have aged and blended.

A subset of the crime movie genre is the *heist movie*, which holds even more specific expectations for its viewers. There's sure to be a motley crew trying to pull off the caper. The audience can rely on hearing how difficult the heist is during the planning stage: the specs of the building, the strength of the force guarding the target, the tightness of the time constraints, and the other characters deliberately trying to foil the scheme. There is automatic rooting interest, because the heroes are usually underdogs and the odds against them are huge. And, sometimes there's a symbolic reward greater than the score itself, as in Spike Lee's *The Inside Man*.

> **Note:** In order to make some of our points, we may make references to the outcomes of certain movies and novels. If you haven't had the pleasure of experiencing them, this may spoil them for you. But, we'll give you this warning symbol, so that you can skip over this part until you've checked out the citation for yourself.

The thieves' true motive in targeting this particular Manhattan bank is to punish the founder who profited from the pilfering of Holocaust victims' estates.

If you don't include your genre's key elements, you risk dissatisfying and alienating the writer's eventual customer—your audience. And from a marketing perspective, we'd venture to say you risk confusing your script's eventual representatives and backers. When you pen a script, you're making a kind of social contract. Though you can (and should) experiment with withholding one of these familiar reassurances to surprise your audience, it's best to follow most of the character and plot tropes in your genre.

Sometimes mixing genres works, but make sure you're hitting the expected conventions. An oldie-but-goodie is *Romancing the Stone,* an action romantic-comedy that managed to balance a female romantic novelist's need for heartwarming moments from her "real life" leading man with scenes of adventuresome flash and derring-do.

> **Sidebar:**
> This was a breakthrough film on a couple of fronts: it was one of the first mixed-genre films and it was a successful action film written by a woman. The story of how the writer sold her script was also one of the first miraculous, rags-to-riches script sales that have now become Hollywood lore. In a Meet Cute of its own, the script met its eventual star, Michael Douglas, already an Oscar-winning producer, who was lunching at a restaurant when the screenwriter/waitress Diane Thomas pushed her script in front of him and kept supplying him with drinks so he'd stay and finish it. The rest is film history…

GENRE TRAP—SIMPLE PROTAGONIST

So, what if you're having trouble delivering on the premise of your genre? If you're approaching our *DYC* system in a rewrite, you may feel your first draft is a bit plot-heavy. The **Meet Cute Phase** helps ensure that you've not been artificially injecting twists into your plot, or when you begin your writing in earnest that you do not force your characters to undergo an interior change, which feels inauthentic.

Knowing what your character has set out to achieve is somewhat defined by the genre she inhabits. Often genre expectations provide a kind of short-hand that can provide you with a rough outline of her internal journey and keep your script lively. In this Meet Cute Phase, if you're struggling to demonstrate how your character weathers ups and downs, we can help you work backward from a plot-centric approach. If you feel you know where your plot's going, as the character tackles obstacles, you can tie in specific interior problems along the way. We'll address this shortly.

But, it's important to point out we're going to continue to imagine some of the character's background environment without focusing on the foreground—the character, just yet. So let's play some "what if" games. These initial *DYC* stages are all about opening up the possibilities of your story. In order to hit upon undiscovered facets of your character, consider all the potential insight that a <u>secondary</u> character can reveal about the protagonist.

GENRE EXPECTATIONS AND SECONDARY CHARACTERS

After all, you don't really know your character's name, what she looks like, or anything about her apart from your list of basic character "needs." You're starting to let the gravity of your <u>needs</u> (not wants) direct you, as you fall freeform into the landscape of your character. Listening to what feels right and what feels wrong. Like Clarice Starling, you're honing your instincts, but as a writer.

As every professional screenwriter knows, there's action and reaction, the moment by moment progression of your story. At this point, when you're looking at your character, there's nothing for your character to react to except your ideas about who she is. That's why it may be beneficial to create a secondary character to help you hone your ideas about your main character. Almost like an algebraic equation that links one subject with another in definite terms.

In many genre movies, this secondary character emotionally affects the lead character profoundly. As you examine the type of person your character might have an understanding with, keep in mind that this buddy character often mirrors the protagonist's struggles, inner life, and opinions through his reactions.

If your protagonist may have trouble relating to strangers, this BFF, who knows the dirt on her, can draw out her more personal side. So, instead of meeting your character head-on, perhaps you can meet her through this secondary character. In life, doesn't that sometimes happen? You meet someone who will become important to you through someone else...?

As you explore the friendship between the protagonist and the "affiliate character," realize the nature of the alliance will impact the arc of your story. After all, this secondary character will either help the protagonist reach her dream or hinder it.

You may decide you don't need this secondary character for the purposes of your story, but feel free to use him to get close to your protagonist. This character can allow you into the mind of your character as you go forward in time, as the Spock character in *Star Trek* (2009) found it possible to talk to his future self to help guide him to a decision.

The kind of affiliate character who may tease out an alternate view of the protagonist is somewhat predicated by the genre. Say, for your heist movie, you have a sense that your character is a scrawny hooligan who has to repair a close relationship with a family member. Maybe there's a history of competitiveness between them. But while there's that friction, there's nobody else he'd trust implicitly.

You're wondering how he's going to accomplish healing the rift in their relationship while busy scoping out the bank and carrying out all the other necessary efforts to pull the job off. Well, realize that making inroads on the plot development can bring about progress in their relationship. Your character may become more confident and reap many other psychological, emotional, social, and material rewards.

Below is an example that shows how you can begin to extrapolate character knowledge from the protagonist seeing through his external objective. In this example, we're looking at how the creation of "a twin sister" can give us valuable information. If the sister, who probably brings a different skill set, can help him battle past some of these tests of character, it will propel your plot forward. The sister doesn't have to be on board and an active member of the heist crew.

The purpose for this exercise is to reveal what caused the strain in their relationship. This will reveal some of the flaws of our main character, which we may not have seen in any other kind of situation. (It's like a magic trick, character "sleight of hand.") Another character complicates things, because that person has a different agenda, values, and history. Another element, another person, always adds more urgency and forces the protagonist to make difficult choices. You need that other perspective to clarify your protagonist's position, like you can't have gossip about two people at the center of a juicy story, without a third person repeating what happened.

For the purposes of the exercise, the following are some suggested conditions the thug might have to endure and actions he might have to take in the course of the robbery.

- He has to learn passable Russian to be accepted into a rich criminal circle.
- His very fair skin, bordering on albinoism, means he can only go out at night.
- During day-time activities, he must wear huge amounts of zinc sunscreen and special SPF-blocking clothes.
- He has to climb a narrow 80-ft wall without ropes or handholds.
- He has to climb this wall and enter a system of vents in under four minutes.

EXERCISE #11: THE SEE-SAW

What particular actions can these characters take on the road to achieving these goals, while reaching a new understanding in their relationship?

DYC Example:

What if "Alphonse" asks his city-college professor sister to help him cross off the first item on his to-do list? She may not know Russian, either, but as a scholar, she has more of the patience required to learn a foreign language. And, though she may not believe her flaky brother will stick to their scheduled "classes," when she sees how hard he's trying, she shapes the material to cater to his learning style.

For the second item, whether the sister suffers from the

same delicate skin pigmentation or not, she's probably aware of the precautions the protagonist has to take. If in the course of their casual encounters, she inquires and presses her brother on how well he's taking care of himself, they may share a deeper and more personal dialogue.

The third item may be provided by the locale where the sister works. Maybe a school gym that is underused by the students. And since the protagonist is spending more time in the near vicinity, he may be more likely to drop in on his sister, outside of their unofficial tutorials.

How does where "Alphonse" practices tell us more about who he is?

So, try it for yourself...

How do *you* think the *fourth* and *fifth items* on his list can bring them closer together (maybe even literally)?

Exercise 11

GENRE AND CONFLICT

How can this help you create a more satisfying connectedness to your character—for you, and for your audience? Your audience may enjoy vicariously the character trying to pull off a heist, but they're going to relate more easily to the protagonist's personal problems. These conflicts create a rich drama that provides a human scale to the possibly epic scope of the plot. There are different types of conflict: conflict with the larger world, conflict with others, and the especially rich internal conflict within the individual. We're now going to focus on how you can create conflict that will ignite a deeper understanding of *your* character.

EXERCISE #12: LADDER OF CONFLICT

Given your genre, what *five obstacles* prevent your hero from completing a "must-do" task?

- Choose two problems that another character can help mitigate.
- Does the protagonist show gratitude or not?
- How?
- What are you revealing to your audience about your character by this interaction?

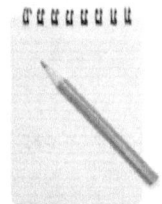

Exercise 12

EXERCISE #12-b: LADDER OF CONFLICT

How could your affiliate character (i.e., the sister in our example) "betray or hurt" the protagonist?

Write *six scenarios* where your affiliate character might, out of a sense of:

- Self preservation
- Jealousy
- Love
- Revenge

Exercise 12-b

It's rare that a protagonist would put herself out there, even tentatively, for a loved one who's already hurt her before. Yet to do so out of necessity, overwhelming love, or a delayed, calculated retribution could be a fertile, complicating layer. What would that say about her?

WHO SHOULD TELL YOUR STORY?

You're discovering that digging deeper into the requirements of your genre can help you open up the story you want to tell. Well, using concrete goals is also a great entry to finding the optimal character to tell your story. It's critical that you not lock in character traits but loosely determine *the kind of personality* you want to spend time with. In our experience, before you choose your character, you can do some reverse-engineering using the plot conventions of your genre. (It's a little like starting out with a character type and completely going against one or two attributes usually found under that umbrella of personality traits.)

Working with writers over the course of several of their drafts, we've sometimes seen them come to the realization that they've chosen the wrong lead character. It's a bummer when you find this out late in the process. Our hope is that by putting your character through the paces, you'll avoid this problem when using the *DYC* system. You'll make sure you have the right genre and ideal, multi-dimensional character. But you can't do that all at once. Right now, you have to figure out who you want to "date."

If you're thinking of designing a *Lara Croft* alpha female, but would never want to be around such a domineering physical force in real life, then what quieter or more soulful trait would make carving out time with this character worthwhile for you? To write about a special person who transcends cliché and speaks to the world we're living in now, <u>you</u>, first and foremost, have to be engaged…

EXERCISE #13: THE PERSONALS

Write a catchy ad that would pique the curiosity of your character. What would your character find attractive? And where would she most likely see this ad? Use this exercise to practice treating your character as someone with free will.

Note: this doesn't have to be a romantic ad.

Example from Elizabeth:
To run in the NY Times Personals:
WANTED—Travel Buddy

- Need someone dynamic, fearless, physically fit, and willing to travel at a moment's notice.
- Good conversation and a generous heart definite pluses.
- Fluency in Portuguese added bonus.
- If interested, stop by the info desk on the second floor at the Natural History Museum and speak to Charlie.

Exercise 13

The way you've written your ad is also a window into your genre. It should have encouraged you to concentrate on your character's métier and natural habitat. This is where she would most likely be found and what she could be doing. Your character's not a deer we're stalking, but it's beneficial to note how she interacts with the world when she doesn't believe she's being watched.

In acting, this is called a "private moment," where a character lets down her guard and shows the audience an honest moment. They are some of the richest opportunities on stage and on screen.

You're being a little like a wildlife camera that awakens and records when sparked by movement. You're just observing, not offering judgment or conclusions. Pay special attention to how your character enters a room, ruffles feathers, or goes unheeded. That's key to organically viewing her effect on the rest of the world.

At this point, it's doubtful you'll be writing down snatches of dialogue. But if she happens to share a gem, keep a notepad handy. If a character does speak to you, we encourage you to reverse-engineer from these specifics on your own.

> **EXERCISE #14: BIRD OF PREY**
> What are her usual haunts? Who does she work with? Hang with? How does she conduct herself?

Exercise 14

Throughout the Meet Cute Phase, you're just making notes…

Dating Your Character

We all take snapshots throughout our lives. We take them literally, but mostly we take them in our imagination. We love observing people and their strange, little ways. But, often we don't look back. We don't take a photographer's viewfinder and truly study the rows of pictures we've captured in our contact sheets.

Thumb through some of the mental images you've been gathering over the past two chapters. Having gotten a little comfortable with her city of origin and the landscape of the story, wander around and test the options of what your character may do for a living.

You probably have a sense if she's blue collar, white collar, or no collar (freelance). Thinking about your character's job is usually an important factor in gauging her skills and level of responsibility. It can often be a key to your character, and how, if at all, this could play out in your story.

In an interview at a Writers Guild screening, writer/director Alex Kurtzman discussed how integral it was to figure out what the protagonist in his movie, *People Like Us,* did for a living. For months, the writer/director tossed around a dozen job choices for his main character, Sam, but said that none had been serving his theme. When he finally came upon a "goods broker," a professional barterer, it immediately unlocked the manipulative nature of the character's relationships and the reason he couldn't find love.

EXERCISE #15: WORKPLACE RECON

Let yourself putter around the imagined environment of your character's workplace.

- What does it feel like?
- What's the first thing you see?
- Does she do a lot of her work outdoors?
- What kind of work is she doing?
- Does she work in a group setting?
- What do you notice about her co-workers?
- How do they seem to feel about her?
- What is the primarily tool she uses to communicate with other people? Computer? i-pad? Notepad? Prepaid phone?

Dating Your Character

Exercise 15

EXERCISE #15-b: WORKPLACE RECON

Now digest what you've just discerned. Is this in keeping with the basic requirements of access, knowledge, authority, and resources that you need your character to have in order to service your plot? If not, go back and invest more time to incorporate some of these essential components.

Exercise 15-b

There's an added benefit to scoping out the workplace environment. At the script's end, clients, friends, associates, the boss, and support staff's actions can reflect how a character's changed. Many of the exercises we assign in this book are meant to aid in the character's transformation.

TV EXAMPLE

Over the season of a TV series and in most movies, there's a recognizable element of transformation. And the job is usually one rung on that journey. It shows how a character's values have changed. In *The Good Wife,* Julianna Margulies' character goes from being a housewife to a high-powered lawyer, who eventually starts her own firm. Her cases force her to go to great personal lengths, contorting her sense of justice to serve both her client's interest and her own moral code. Though, she's sometimes scoffingly referred to as "Saint Alicia" by friends and family, she realizes that being "good," in a world filled with flawed people, sometimes means forgiving the people who have hurt you, while allowing yourself the occasional sin. This struggle makes what could be a judgmental and alienating character relatable.

Reality Check

Actors have told us they frequently gauge the character's arc by studying the <u>first ten</u> and the <u>last ten</u> pages of a script to see how vibrant and visceral that change is. So, make sure your character changes and that we see demonstrable proof over time. But, if it's a tragedy, then the change is ultimately an impossible goal for the character to pull off…

Note: A *tragedy* features a storyline where the protagonist is scarred by multiple disappointments. The character does not achieve what she wants.

Or, if she does, it costs her life or the life of someone she loves. We also see the deaths of several other lead characters. In addition to the failure to upend the status quo, your story must have these other markers of a tragedy.

The classic Francis Ford Coppola saga, *The Godfather*, features a young Al Pacino as "Michael," who, despite his moral values and college education, keeps getting drawn back in to the criminal world of his father, played by Marlon Brando. Time and again, and at great risk to his young family from his marriage to his non-Italian wife, "Kay," Michael perseveres in furthering his father's business interests and wreaking revenge on his father's enemies. While he manages to avoid being federally indicted or killed, he eventually loses friends and allies, and must personally murder his own brother.

In the same vein, beware of calling your script *cinema verite*, which might also be a way of excusing mediocrity… The "Mumblecore" phase, championed by Andrew Bujalski and the Duplass brothers that swept the South by Southwest Film Festival in the mid-2000s, featured action-lite, emotion-lite philosophical forays into young adulthood. But, even these progressive DIY

> indie films had a protagonist with some kind of goal who underwent a minor epiphany, for all their coffee bar pop-culture riffs and naturalistic dialogue. And you'll notice the Duplass brothers' 2015 HBO series, *Togetherness*, has more concrete dilemmas.

To keep the screenplay fresh and a better read for potential talent, it's vital that you allow her to differ from you and surprise you! You're basically trying to invite your character to show up, based on the few facts that you know about her, i.e., sneaky, shifty, sexy, etc.

So, at this stage of building a relationship, you need to approach your character gingerly. Devo's husband, TV writer Scott Rubenstein, has long talked about using the "bar metaphor." At a bar, the person you plop down next to has heard it all before. You have a very short window to come up with something that's going to interest her. You need to be intriguing, so you can attract the most intriguing character for your story.

Scott says, "When I was in college, I wasn't very popular, and I asked a woman to dance. To get her to continue to dance with me, I figured I had to use intrigue. So, during the pleasantries, when she asked me my name, towards the end of the song I offered up the cryptic 'My name's 13.' So she had to start the next song with me to hear an explanation."

Dating Your Character

For *DYC*, we're going to refashion this as the last preliminary step before you actually meet your character. Using improv on paper can help unlock some details that will in turn inform your character choice. We're designing it as an exercise with an affiliate character to get some intel on the protagonist beforehand. Either you or the affiliate character can be the mysterious one who makes us want to know more.

EXERCISE #16: BAR METAPHOR

Scan the room. Who is your eye drawn to?

GENRE:

_____

TYPE OF BAR:

_____

AFFILIATE CHARACTER DESCRIPTION:

_____

_____

Improv a quick exchange with the affiliate character...

Example from Elizabeth:

Let's say I'm working on a sci-fi thriller. I'm attracted to something about the blond woman that just went into the WC. So I strike up a conversation with the person she was sitting next to at the bar.

(The bar is in outer space.)

Me: I noticed your friend had to leave suddenly.

The Friend looks me over, sees I'm not a creep, and shrugs.

The Friend: She was thirsty. Downed a few. Do the math.

Me: So, what's good here? Heard the apple marstini is made out of burner fluid.

I adjust the stool under me, noticing it has spindly, organic legs.

I nearly topple over, but steady myself.

The Friend: We did okay with the ultraviolet and lime.

She takes another swig of the thick, brackish concoction, a fermented, aerated "drink."

Me: But doesn't that take you down?

I look to the bathroom, but the blonde still hasn't come out yet.

So I have time to be a little more pushy.

Me: It makes it hard to conceal your thoughts, too.

The Friend: After a rough day, it feels nice to let down your guard.

She brushes her metallic bangs away and reveals a fresh, deep cut.

Me: A rough day for me? Too many messages to decode. Too many personal stories to keep in mind.

I wave over the bartender and order a slender vial of ultraviolet.

Me: You two seem tight. You didn't give the Zambiks the time of day...

But in trying to get too close too soon...

The Friend clamps her jaw shut and the taut lines around her mouth glow a menacing red.

Me: Well, I was thinking of a career change. I was just wondering what it's like to be an Astralclimber. You need to have a high math proficiency, right?

The Friend: And, you want to know if you're the type?

Me: We don't even see many of you down here. So you're all shrouded in secrecy.

The Friend: The training we go through is expensive, so becoming a candidate is a rare privilege. When my friend comes back she'll test you, if you want.

The Friend rises. All eight feet of her. She looms over me and smirks.

The Friend: Before you even open your mouth, she'll know if you're worthy...

# Exercise 16

EXERCISE #16-b: WHAT YOU FOUND OUT BY YOUR IMPROVIZED CONVERSATION:

_____

_____

Example from Elizabeth:

What I learned and kinda liked: They're highly trained and intelligent members of some kind of warrior class. The blonde is specially trained or gifted in reading strangers. Perhaps she's at an even more elite level than the friend.

I also admit that I kind of embellished who "I" am. I wasn't sure if The Friend would talk to me, a writer, or if there are even writers on this planet. But I felt it wasn't as much of a stretch to peg myself as having a job keeping track of "messages." It also may have partially explained my overall curiosity about the blond and about the "Astralclimber" program, because I doubt I came off as being a realistic "candidate."

> As an aside, we're never completely honest when first meeting someone, are we? Isn't there some exaggeration in how we present ourselves?

Exercise 16-b

We've been encouraging you to imagine your character and not actually interact with her, because we believe in starting slow. You want to be sure this is the one you're going to spend the next three months with. What we've been doing is starting to get a sense of the character's world. You've already kind of scoped out what she does and where she chills. So where do you think you'd be able to catch her off guard? But also where she would be most receptive to stopping a moment and chatting? Bear in mind, we often become numb to ourselves about what makes us interesting that might make us interesting to others.

How forceful do you have to be to get her attention? Is she an extrovert or an introvert? Is she bound to be regaling the people around her, forming a little crowd? Or will you be able to get a little one-on-one time with her? Did she make an ass of herself at the office Holiday party? Absorb any clues to her temperament.

The "Meet Cute" is an unexpected collision of two strangers who manage to form a spark of connection—not always pleasant—in the most unlikely of situations: while rescuing a lost dog, getting treatment at an ER, at a funeral, etc. But for our book, this occasion has been staged by one of the parties, you. The Meet Cute is a material step, because it involves seeing your character in a situation where she is out of her comfort zone. It also provides a nod to genre, because in choosing how to discombobulate her, you'll probably keep the nature of your story in mind.

> **EXERCISE #17: MEET CUTE**
>
> Jot down *ten unconventional scenes* where she may be overwhelmed, in danger, feeling looser than usual, more adventurous, more trusting...
>
> Now write *one scene* where you, as the writer, chat up the character and get her to meet up with you later. Remember those awkward first moments...
>
> - How does she react to the situation itself? How does she react to you?
> - What sort of contrast is there between you and the other people there? Is it favorable for you or not?
> - How hard is it for you to get her attention? Is she magnetized to you or indifferent?

Dating Your Character

> - What do you say? How do you spark some connection?
> - Are you surprisingly helpful to her? Do you have a personal expertise which makes what you have to say credible and provocative?
> - How could what you say entertain her or pull her in?
> - Are you even the instigator? Does the character seek you out for some reason?

Exercise 17

Are you on your way to meeting her on your first proper "date?" Did she write her number on a napkin? Did she whip out a crisp business card?

What's interesting about the *DYC* approach is that the tenor of your dating arc doesn't necessarily have to follow the tone of your chosen genre or even adhere to the stages of that kind of relationship. If the character you're outlining doesn't strictly lend herself to the dating metaphor, there are still many avenues to explore your bond. Loyalty, empathy, and the ability to truly listen and appreciate a point of view—different from your own—aren't exclusive to romantic relationships. Respect and honest, casual conversation is a universal goal in the best of relationships. In each succeeding chapter we will be addressing all types of writer-character relationships in our exercises. The steps that link you to your character will be playfully seductive, only on occasion…

Some writers have a knack for hearing the character, but for most of us, this intimacy is something that is earned. We recommend spending time with your character outside of what she might normally do or the kinds of activities you think your story needs. It's when your character's free to do what she wants, NOT what she has to do, that you start to develop a familiarity with her. She may also be less wary and more open to your questions and interest during her down time. You'll also be able to pick up on different sides to her when she's with the people she's close to.

A connection can be based on your observations and shared experiences. A healthy affinity is often rooted in two people with complementary and not completely overlapping similarities. It would be difficult to find a special spark that's rooted in the physical, as in a tangible relationship. But a connection is just an internal draw, an unsaid admiration, and a desire for more closeness. An initial connection with your character could even be largely nonverbal, if she's kind of shy or withholding.

Our method is more than a quirky way of thinking about your character: We hope you're inspired as you go through these exercises, and even make up your own, until you no longer view your character as a writing tool, but an individual with needs, desires, habits, flaws, and dreams that continue to exist outside the narrow confines of the script. As in Marc Forster's *Stranger than*

Fiction, with Emma Thompson and Will Ferrell, the character has a life outside of what the novelist is conscious of and continues to evolve on his own. The same conceit charged the 2012 film *Ruby Sparks* with Paul Dano and Zoe Kazan, which Kazan also wrote. While it may take an imaginative leap to get you on board, the steady work that you do will help make the point that your character's life is as conflicted and multi-faceted as yours.

Go ahead and acknowledge the instinctive work you've been doing. As you continue, it may at times feel like a fascination bordering on an obsession. But you'll not only be a witness, you'll also be within the experience. Honor whatever you come up with in these early stages. Bumping into your character can invite curiosity and interaction free from any agenda. Since this chapter is focusing on character and genre, we will concentrate on more methods to deliver on the promises from working in your genre.

GENRE TRAP—SIMPLE PLOT

Let's consider an additional common genre foible. To spice up dramas with action content and more specific visuals, again, look to your character. A mystery, a thriller, a romance, and every other type of film you can name require a clear progression of plot. Even adult fare has to have meaningful plot twists that build on one another. Audiences want to feel that they've been on a ride. Maybe, even in some small part, that they've been changed. But, passionate protestations of love, thorny parent-child exchanges, and angry rants can't provide that satisfying experience on their own.

Use and magnify one central internal struggle to craft an impressive outward feat that also serves as a metaphor for the character's interior life. Since you're at the beginning of your writing exploration, we recommend thinking about a headache or pressing issue that you also have, so that you start from a place where you have a natural sense of investment.

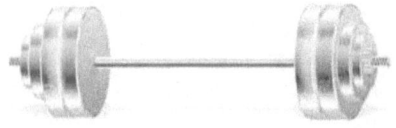

EXERCISE #18: WEIGHT-BEARING

List unexpected ways that a personal bothersome obstacle of <u>yours</u> could bleed into areas of the <u>character's</u> life and pose a public problem.

Example from Elizabeth:

I have an acknowledged issue with procrastination.

What if my **character** had the same general lackadaisical attitude to deadlines:

- Unpaid bills?
- Newspapers stacking up going unread?
- Missing family birthdays?

How could this flaw complicate areas of <u>**his**</u> life on a more serious note?

- Not submitting the paperwork necessary to qualify for a grant?
- Missing an important court filing?

How could **his** bad habit have life or death consequences?

- The character, some sort of naturalist/explorer, could decide to take in the natural beauty of his surroundings and arrive two weeks late to meet up with other eco-tourists at their base camp?
- Turning in ecological reports late could lead to skewed data, which, if in an emergency, could lead to rapid endorsement of an unsafe environmental protocol?

And how could **his** behavior have escaped censure up to this point?

- Because of good intentions like: thoroughness, having a winning way about him?
- An advisor is a close, personal friend?
- He's never worked in a department with emergency timelines?
- His work situation has always had the easy-going informality of a small enterprise run by an individual or a nonprofit?

Though all these scenarios appear random, some could feasibly intersect within the main sphere of the story.

Exercise 18

PLANNING AND PREPARATION

No matter how happy-go-lucky you are, you can't completely trust to chance and good fortune as you walk through life. As your experience probably proves, success is largely the result of planning and preparation. The same kind of forward-thinking is vital in screenwriting. While it's important to capture instinctive character choices and lightning-in-a-bottle moments of genius, most of the work involves mapping out where you want to go before you arrive. It takes time and ingenuity to show these telling slivers of a character's private life.

It's the human element that makes all the other elements believable and worthwhile. Movies are interactive in that they rely on audiences to fill in the blanks and actively empathize; that's what gives them their power. But, for there to be a symbiosis between the film and the audience, there has to be an organic pacing to the character development. We need to see the character's strategy, perseverance, and gumption, if the obstacles in her world, in her relationships, and within her are daunting.

Trust that, the more you write, the more information you gather, you will be pointed in the right direction for your plot development. As you center on your character and her ultimate goal, rally around each new fact that presents itself, question that arises, and dilemma that unfolds.

Sometimes when working on a thriller or a mystery, it can feel as if you've gotten caught up in a net mid-swim. You've lost focus, while trying to keep so many plot lines in mind: the threads of betrayal, confessions, and secret revelations. Try simplifying the process for yourself. You might concentrate on what you want to reveal about the suspects and how you want those secrets found out.

SAMPLE GENRE WORK-UP—MYSTERY

- Who is the best person to reveal a key secret?
- How do the clues build to shape the direction and misdirection within the story?

While we're going to focus on the difficulties that can come up in writing mysteries, the basic principle of employing character work to produce a more elaborate plot applies to every genre. It's important to note that mysteries, a genre known for hairpin narrative turns, rely heavily on the human interaction of the suspects. Devising a clever mystery is not just about depicting a murder scene and then rolling out facts and clues that lead to the solution of the crime. It's essential to investigate the motivations, petty and primal, that compel these characters to plot and scheme.

Agatha Christie's classic *Murder on the Orient Express* features a train-full of suspects with only a glancing connection to the murdered man. A snowdrift allows master detective Hercule Poirot the time to suss out the motivations behind the crime. It is through parsing the true identities and backgrounds of the suspects that Poirot is able to determine who's guilty. Because the personalities of the characters are so distinct, as we follow Poirot's masterful deduction, we're able to remember their slip ups and tells. After all is revealed, the character insight transcends the artifice that kept all the passengers trapped on the train.

Mysteries for TV are also noticeably light on action as well as the protagonist's character development. But these mysteries do offer something more substantial than the intrusive, voyeuristic conversations that occur within the investigation. They offer moments of real emotional connection: kind sympathy, heartbreak, and catharsis that may occur out of the protagonist's presence. And, it's hard to sculpt these scenes unless you are intimately familiar with your characters' urges, fears, and pasts.

So, while you must keep your eye on the prize and arrange the clues that will lead to a credible end to the puzzle, understanding how to coyly reveal character insight is what keeps the engine of the story purring. Whodunit is less important than Whydunit.

However, in addition to juggling the human dynamics of the

mystery, PBS series such as *Zen*, *Wallander*, and *Rosemary and Thyme*, feature a supporting storyline, where we come to know a bit more about the protagonist(s).* These series have loyal fans who alternately appreciate the glamorous, introspective, and charming cadence of these mysteries and savor the lead detective's trademark style and POV.

> * Even ensembles such as the drug thriller *Traffic* and the heist movie *Ocean's 11* have one character with slightly more screen time and more to risk than the other characters. The same can be said with two-handers like *Butch Cassidy and the Sundance Kid.* Butch is secondary to Sundance because, even though the love triangle with the schoolteacher, played by Katharine Ross, is rather friendly and open-minded, he doesn't have the carnal relationship with her.

Let's look at how carefully mining from your character's personal life can add luster to the story.

EXERCISE #19: PUBLIC/PRIVATE DETECTIVE

List *five instances* where personal problems could intrude on the detective's investigation.

1. _____

2. _____

3. _____

4. _____

5. _____

Exercise 19

EXERCISE #19-b: PUBLIC/PRIVATE DETECTIVE

Why do these problems bedevil him? What's at stake? How do these predicaments lead the detective to become more or less engaged in the investigation? And what is the result?

> ***DYC* Example:**
>
> If the detective is mourning his dead wife...
>
> How does he come to grips?
>
> He's professional at work, but still suffering horribly. This pain bleeds into his investigative duties by altering his view of women. That jeopardizes his ability to impartially evaluate female suspects. He may even show a latent hostility to them, because he's angry that his own wife was taken from him.

Exercise 19-b

The above is an illustration of how looking at the protagonist's personal experience may provide an intriguing tangent that enriches the story. One question can often invite even more questions. Don't be afraid of the onslaught of questions. Prioritize them. Answer them one at a time. Devo will often write each question on a piece of paper, and then hide this pile under a sheet of paper, so as not to feel distracted. It's a way of recording and following up on these questions, without being held hostage. Use these questions as meditations to create a deeper connection with your character. This should help you search for conflict within the flurry of your responses.

In feature film mysteries and thrillers, there is frequently a character arc where the detective has to learn to embrace a certain type of action in order to find or eliminate the murderer. It rests on a mistake in the protagonist's thinking that leads her or him astray. In *Inception*, Leonardo DiCaprio's character's guilt over his involvement in the death of his wife prevents him from having the focus and subconscious purity to maneuver in a manufactured alternate reality. Provide the path that will show the audience that the character's not just in pursuit of the facts, but is having to call upon his most private resources to outwit the perpetrator. This will allow you to take advantage of the desire for change that is hardwired in audiences. Life involves change, surprise, and curiosity, and so should the work you are evolving.

Mysteries are grand excavations of a specific place and a particular handful of people. But all kinds of movies provide the grounds for character excavation. Just as it's similarly frustrating to have a script without cogent logic, you don't want a character who bounces around from mess to mess without any underlying flawed logic, what we call a "tumbleweed type." You will be wrestling with multi-layered stories in whatever your chosen genre, and while you don't have to tie them all up in a rosy red bow, the various threads all meet at some point in a satisfying series of set-ups and pay-offs. That's why it's important to keep both your plot goals and character goals in mind.

We don't want to get ahead of ourselves. But, if we haven't

understood what the character's demons are all along, we won't care when she's facing them down, which can deflate the power of the Climax emotionally and intellectually. You aren't likely to craft a character who comes across as real and whose problems are real unless there is a framework that enables this exploration. The second half of this book is dedicated to baring your character's interior world, because conflict stems from deeply rooted beliefs and behavior. For now, let this taste of improvised introspection during the Meet Cute Phase reassure you. You will come closer to the intricacies of her true nature more fully as you continue the process.

WRONG CHARACTER, RIGHT GENRE?

Some of you may still be contending with genre quandaries. After all, can you imagine Humphrey Bogart from *The African Queen* as a hapless character stuck in a romantic comedy like *Sleepless in Seattle*? Or what if you now believe your character doesn't have the room to evolve within the constraints of the plot you're considering?

If your plot requires the hero to grow bolder at the end, to sacrifice himself, then the movie needs someone who starts out naïve and unskilled, or maybe is selfish and a bit of an ass. But, if you're more interested in writing about a character with a stronger personal agenda, then you may have to entirely rethink his suitability for your genre.

A Western, for instance, can tolerate a non-stereotypical

protagonist, maybe someone bright, but physically imposing. Maybe even someone who's against violence and refuses to align with a band of outlaws, but is intent on taking down on a murderous posse. So far, so good. In darker Westerns, the character usually gnaws on the actions that have resulted in his current predicament.

GENRE AND INHERENT PACING

If you want your character to spend real screen time dealing with private issues, then you have to make sure the pacing requirements of the genre allow that on his ultimately hardscrabble road to redemption. If you want <u>this</u> character in <u>this</u> genre to also teach his father to read, how will you accomplish that? Will you be satisfied by showing this metaphorically? Perhaps by relying on a couple of bookending scenes to chart the course of their relationship? Or will you actually want us to see the father's struggle, the range of books they cover together, and the lessons in those books that they take to heart?

FILM EXAMPLE

In James Mangold's 2007 remake *3:10 to Yuma*, earnest and long-suffering Dan Evans, as played by Christian Bale, always seems to disappoint and alienate his adolescent son, William. Their tense relationship simmers in the background. William sees his father's pitiful difficulty in keeping the family homestead going. With each successive setback, he vows to become the complete opposite of his father, who accepts come what may stoically. It is the son's propensity for brazen displays of manhood and violence that make the lifestyle of charismatic stagecoach robber, Russell Crowe's character, dangerously seductive.

The additional pressures that Dan feels because of William are largely unspoken, because Dan doesn't take any intermediate action to prove to William that his way is justified or acknowledge any of the regrets from the decisions he's taken. In the Climax, Dan compels himself to go on an all-but-guaranteed suicidal mission to escort Russell Crowe's Ben Wade through the town, where the gang's all ready to shoot it out and extract their leader. Dan has chosen to do this not only to earn the payment that will save his home, but to demonstrate his courage to his son. But we haven't seen if this final act will be nearly enough to convince him to follow in his father's footsteps and work the land.

It is because the film hasn't explored Dan's flaws throughout that his sacrifice feels like he's putting on a desperate show, rather than committing a noble and rational act the audience can understand and empathize with. As we've argued, this example fell slightly short in delivering a resonant Climax. *3:10* is a Western that ranges widely in tone, mixing the insouciance of Ben's escapades with the more introspective narrative of Dan's reversals. Its purpose is rather bipolar, split between the devil-may-care get-rich schemes of a band of rapscallions and the hard-scrabbled reality of a rancher hemmed in by greedy land barons.

It's important to recognize the limitations of your tone and genre at the outset. This will conscript you into allocating time to explore all the dynamics that you can set up to pay off in an emotionally persuasive ending. Genres that are more open for character relationship arcs include sci-fi thrillers, family dramas, coming-of-age dramas/comedies, fish-out-of-water comedies, and action comedies. More complex characters can thrive in these environments, where that figure is constantly being delineated and thrown up against the world.

Check out the following genre checklist:

GENRE CHECKLIST

Action—Thriller—Sci-Fi—Western—Mystery—Drama—Mob Drama—Family Drama—Teen Drama—Coming-of-Age Drama—Comedy—Coming-of-Age Comedy—Fish-Out-of-Water Comedy—Romantic Comedy—Action Comedy—Satire—Political Satire

TONE

Beyond some of the plot circumstance and character types that make up these genres, there are tonal associations as well. What is tone? Tone is the general emotional and narrative overlay that colors the majority of the script. For example, a thriller has a palpable sense of menace coursing throughout. A rom-com features a light touch in its treatment of romance.

It's essential to maintain the overall mood, but scripts can certainly have moments of genre dissonance. In fact, scripts greatly benefit from these small and unexpected tonal change-ups, where a scene that is a lot lighter and funnier can punctuate a more serious and brooding piece or vice versa.

FILM EXAMPLE

In Joel and Ethan Coen's *Miller's Crossing*, there is a scene in an alley where a young boy finds the body of a dead man. But the tone of the scene is markedly different from the tense, noir feel of most of the previous scenes. The boy isn't scared; he's fascinated by what he's found. The state of the body is decidedly undignified: the dead man's toupee is missing. Besides the inherent humor of the scene, it is a subtle, frightening reminder that murder affects even the young and the innocent. Notice that this breather in the taut, fast pace of the drama isn't without menace. It also lets us know that there's no way out from the oncoming storm of bloody retribution; because we're not just dealing with a sliver of the underworld, the fallout affects everybody.

To see if you've nabbed the tonal parameters for the genres in the previous list, match some of them with the descriptions below:

EXERCISE #20: GENRE CHECKLIST—TONE

- A fairly straightforward story with clearly understood forces of good guys and bad guys where there are plot points requiring physical force or violence.
- A story taking place in a historical era defined by rugged individualism in the face of an untamed natural landscape and hostile groups.
- A story featuring realistic characters wrestling with deep internal problems.
- A thoughtful story featuring the unraveling of a puzzle in an atmosphere of general unease.
- A bloody and gory story that sets up multiple moments for the audience to anticipate pain and brutality.
- A story that deals with the characters' problems in a light-hearted fashion.
- A story that extrapolates technological advances or theories to forge an alternate reality that mirrors our own and a political or philosophical statement.

Dating Your Character

Exercise 20

Once you're nearly certain that you've chosen the correct genre, there's still one more test. Think about who's most likely to be affected by your story and drawn to your genre. The audience for one of the *Fast and the Furious* films is obviously different than that for a film like *Jane Eyre*, adapted from the classic Charlotte Bronte novel.

FILM EXAMPLE

Jane Eyre is what is called an "evergreen" film in the movie business.

The plot is well constructed and the protagonist so three-dimensional that you can revisit the story and put a fresh spin on it for today's market.

There are several traits that are recognizably present in any reimagining of the character of Jane Eyre, yet she isn't quite a cinematic icon.

ANSWER KEY: MOB DRAMA, WESTERN, DRAMA, MYSTERY, HORROR, COMEDY, SCI-FI

She is a resilient, stubborn young woman from a poor background, who grew up in an orphanage due to the unkindness of her distant relations. But Jane exists in the totality of the story. She alone isn't a touchstone, because there is no Jane Eyre without Mr. Edward Rochester. And when Mr. Rochester (the divine Michael Fassbender) appears to love someone else, it's even more crushing to see her suffer in Cary Fukunaga's 2011 film version.

Mia Wasikowska gives the governess a modern sensibility with a greater awareness of her self-worth and individuality as a young woman. She is blisteringly honest with herself and her sad predicament. She's a woman who completely inhabits her mind. Having retooled the character to attract the more empowered woman of today was likely an artistic as well as commercial consideration.

DEMOGRAPHICS

How is it best to convey your message to your target demographic? You may need to recalculate how much you're going to rely on action versus sophisticated dialogue, or broadness versus subtlety. If your story has a political bent, you may want to address the generally more patient and thoughtful people who favor dramas. But you may feel a softer target would be young people, who are dissatisfied with the current state of affairs. If that's the case, younger demographics tend to show up for movies with a lot of action, so work on synthesizing your characters' moral quandaries into physical trials of a more exciting and athletic nature.

Below is a quick sheet of genres, along with their key audiences.

GENRE CHECKLIST—DEMOGRAPHICS

- <u>Dramas</u>, which by their nature are introspective, most often appeal to college-educated folks.
- <u>Actioners</u> favor a young male demographic and do well in foreign markets, because the language of action is simple.
- <u>Thrillers</u> are crosses between action-heavy films and dramas and therefore have a wider appeal.
- <u>Westerns</u> generally appeal to males, but older males, since there are frequently long stretches, where nothing happens while rough and weathered men reflect on their life's regrets.
- <u>Science fiction</u> can cross over age and gender, depending on the seriousness of the theme, violence quotient, style of execution, and character development.

- <u>Comedies</u> are usually hybrids: romantic comedies, action comedies, lowbrow comedies, and highbrow comedies that can bring in a combination of people from each niche.
- <u>Horror</u> films tend to appeal to young people mainly interested in a reason for grabbing each other. And, therefore, appeals to three of the <u>four quadrants</u>: young men and women.

The "<u>four quadrants</u>" is a marketing tool used to evaluate a film's natural reach:

YOUNG	OLD
MALE	FEMALE

Note: Keep in mind, though, that regardless of your intended audience, if your characters "feel real" and have something to say about the world we're living in, other people will give your film a "see" because of word-of-mouth. Authenticity generally helps sell more tickets.

Audiences all over the world embraced Danny Boyle's zanily energetic 1996 film *Trainspotting*. In spite of thick Scottish brogues, electronic music that wasn't popular Stateside, and some gut-wrenching scenes of withdrawal, the small film's mad

> bender went on to recoup six times its budget, including P and A.* The film's depiction of the urban drug culture of Edinburgh is filled with gritty details of poverty, but in such an improbably upbeat way that it feels like a rave, a cautionary tale, and a dystopian travelogue.
>
> * "P and A," prints and advertising, of movies with a budget of at least a million dollars routinely comprises an additional thirty percent of a film's total outlay to garner initial interest and to make it available to theatres.

Writing at a professional level means not only writing for your own pleasure, but delivering a marketable screenplay. At every step of the writing process, we feel it's best to keep your audience in mind, because in most cases that forces you to challenge yourself. Though, we admit, not all writers like to cater to the audience while they're creating. But, just as we believe conversing with your character will lead to a deeper understanding of her, interacting with the audience in your imagination as you outline your script and craft your scenes helps to put you in their place. Whatever you write creates a reaction. But, you have to know if they're frightened, delighted, and/or aroused. Or, heaven forbid, bored, lost, and disappointed. In upcoming chapters, by tapping into the perspective of your audience, you'll learn to probe the specificity and richness of your characters' actions.

YOU ARE DONE WITH STEP TWO.

As the Meet Cute concludes, you're starting to know "who" you need for your story, versus an artificial list of accomplishments and physical traits that you may have thought you needed.

You are armed with several must-haves:

- Your story's relevance to your future audience.
- Your character's personal disposition, basic skills, and available resources necessary for her to achieve her external goal.

You have also amassed fact sheets that have enabled you to:

- Determine the tone of your story and your genre.

Timeline: If you've allowed yourself to concentrate on your daily screenwriting session for *an hour* or thereabouts, then we estimate it will have taken you *one to two weeks* to think about the exercises in Chapter 1 and Chapter 2.

- You will have gained an understanding of your own personal investment.

- You will have teased out your theme so that it piques your likely audience's interest.
- You will have gotten started on what comprises the attitude of your protagonist.
- You will have roughly sketched the arc in her relationship with an affiliate character.
- You will have a sense of what kind of location might best serve your character's growth.

You are so primed for the next phase in developing the writer-character relationship:

STEP THREE—THE FIRST DATE.

THE FIRST DATE "THE INCITING INCIDENT"—STEP THREE

YOU'VE DONE SOME soul-searching about why you're interested in telling this story, and you've picked up on influential details in your character's environment. You've even exchanged a few words with your potential protagonist. Now, the adventure of real dating begins…

Thus far, you haven't written a page of your actual script. You're probably feeling protective of your future screenplay, worried it's not growing and developing as fast as it should be. Don't be one of those overachieving parents who worry that their two-year-old isn't talking yet. To jolt him into language, they coax him to play with his plastic alphabet letters. They download *Baby Einstein* classical music tracks to train his brain to listen for patterns and to assimilate complex rhythms. But privately, he's been quietly observing and absorbing this information all along. Then, one day, it all comes together and he begins speaking in full sentences.

You're working in the world of imagination. Some of you will be progressing steadily, others will be creating internally and only after sitting with your material, suddenly arrive with pages and pages of ideas at once. It's okay, if you're a little nerve-wracked and worried. You're bound to be, but you've just got to dive in. For this to be a worthwhile experience, you'll have to allow yourself to take the *DYC* conceit seriously enough.

Dating Your Character

And, what *is* the conceit, besides the fact that you're forming a "real" relationship with you character? A secondary part of the equation is that you're willing to grow as a writer, because you don't have all the answers. That you, yourself, may even change, as you learn to understand your character. So, don't let ego get in the way of good writing...

For those of you who still have reservations, it's not about creating a secret fantasy love life. It's about practicing getting close to your character. So that she seems more real, because you've breathed life into her. If you feel squeamish with the playfulness of some of the exercises, then focus on their stated intention. Don't let the particulars of this stage—the First Date—or any stage—freak you out. Remember, you're probably not going to be doing anything that you haven't done before in your life. The *DYC* process trades and expands on that accumulated knowledge, putting your human essence to work for you.

What is the "human essence?" It's what makes the story universal and relatable. It's why we care about your character. The vacillation between certainty and doubt that makes your character a fully-realized 3-D person: her need to dream, her tendency to stay in denial, her temptation to give into fear.

When Marilyn read the screenplay adaptation of Josefina Lopez's *Real Women Have Curves*, she saw how quickly the writer was able to emotionally engage her on several levels. The story was about the struggle for identity, what it means to be independent, and the vitality of female friendship. And, that's what drew Marilyn to the project.

You're now aware of the concept of seeing the character as separate from yourself. In real life, just as you can't control everything in your relationships, these exercises will prevent you from imposing yourself too heavily on the narrative in your writing life. This book helps you defy clichéd writing, which often is about making easy assumptions. All along you're going to be asking yourself how you can be open to everything your character has to offer: her feelings, opinions, and values.

Eventually, through the tasks we set you, you'll get used to releasing the steering wheel and coasting as your character tells you what to do. Somewhere around the midpoint of this book you'll be able to let go and have your character's ideas come to you, rather than seeking them out. There's an underlying power to be tasted in that reckless freedom.

In the Austin Film Festival series *On Story,* the writer of *Thelma & Louise,* Callie Khouri, confided that "I honestly (and unfortunately) believe, that [at] some point, some other thing has to be summoned that comes from outside you... When you're writing at a higher level than you feel like you would inhabit, there's something else at work there."

By practicing all the back and forth of communication—texting, writing, calling—you'll begin to trust in the *DYC* technique and your character. In this chapter, you'll learn how to let the character set the pace of your interactions. You'll initiate some of the conversation, while at other times relying on her to follow through, all in the hope of finding common ground and accommodating each other. You'll interact with her when she's cooperative and when she's frustratingly unavailable.

At this point, you've been operating at the most general level, working from the outside in. It's as if, in camera language, you've started with an establishing shot of your character and her environment. In doing so, you've identified the possible rules of that world to see how she functions in it. Right now, let's take a moment to review the restrictions, clues, and character needs from Chapter 1: THE PREP and Chapter 2: THE MEET CUTE.

EXERCISE #21: REVIEW AT A GLANCE

On a sheet of paper, write down a vertical list of the character's non-negotiable traits from Chapter 1. Put at least *three inches* of space between each trait. Now, write *three lines* to the right of each trait, showing how those are supported and defined by the environmental limitations in Chapter 2.

DYC Example:

Perhaps you've been tinkering with the idea of your character as a medical professional of some kind with a penchant for luxury objects out of her reach.

Medical Knowledge
Works the graveyard shift
Administers care out in the field
Can prescribe medication

Rich Tastes
Loves fast cars
Loves being pampered at a spa
Loves bespoke tailoring

Daring Streak
Drives on empty till the last possible moment when she needs gas
Shows up for a big meeting unprepared, confident she can wing it
She takes on assignments she's not quite capable of, but thinks she can grow into

Exercise 21

Now, that you've refreshed this info in your cache, let's put you back in that "dating" frame of mind by analyzing what you learned from the Meet Cute.

> **EXERCISE #22: TAKING INVENTORY OF THE MEET CUTE**
> - What did you think her first impressions of you were?
> - Why did you think she agreed to see you again?
> - If she tried to get out of a second meet-up, how did you engineer it so she'd change her mind?

Exercise 22

> **EXERCISE #22-b: TAKING INVENTORY OF THE MEET CUTE**
>
> How are you able to <u>contact</u> each other? Did she:
>
> _____ give you her email?
>
> _____ give you her cell number?
>
> _____ give you her home number?
>
> _____ tell you to drop by where she normally hangs out?
>
> _____ refuse to give you any information at all?

Exercise 22-b

Clarifying the details and specifications of your character are what will sharpen your writing. But, it's vital to think about all the minutiae of where the First Date will take place. Then, there'll be a better chance she'll actually show up. So, given your early sense of her, where would she feel most comfortable?

Dating Your Character

SETTING THE SCENE

> ### EXERCISE #23: LOCATION SCOUTING
> You're trying to get a feel for her inclinations. So, think instinctively about her likes and dislikes…
>
> *Circle* one answer for each pair:
> 1. Public   **OR**   Private   3. Budget   **OR**   Expensive
> 2. Informal   **OR**   Formal   4. Familiar   **OR**   Anonymous
>
> - Come up with a few venues that most fit the character's preferences.

Exercise 23

As you know, there are so many elements that go into planning a successful meeting. But, those elements are perhaps even more crucial when arranging a first date. Presumably, you want your protagonist to look forward to your date with some level of enthusiasm. So, you'll need to think about what you'll be doing, where it'll take place, and when it'll happen…ahead of time. After all, you're both taking time out of your busy lives to meet up.

(Unless, depending on when your story takes place—or the character's financial or medical condition—you're conforming to the norms of another era and squiring her to the venue. A lady in the 1940's had to be picked up at her parents' house.)

What kind of a date do you want? A fun, informal get-together? Something that she can easily slip into as a part of her day? It's important to take the time to run through all these factors to foster the kind of connection you want to make. After all, the first time you saw her and she saw you, you were thrown together. She may have been out of her element, and the two of you were generally confused…trying to fix something, avoid something, or get over something, etc., in the Meet Cute.

Dating Your Character

> **EXERCISE #24: COMFORT ZONE**
>
> What kind of place will put her at ease? Is it close to:
>
> _____ her best friend's? (Maybe, she'll want to do an instant post-mortem with her...?)
>
> _____ where she lives? (Maybe, she's already planning on cutting it short and safely exiting?)
>
> _____ where she works? (Maybe, she'll be more willing to talk to you about work...?)

Exercise 24

Regardless of who initiates the meeting, a scene is being set. A scene is a recipe for social interaction and all the players have to be thought about. The setting of a scene can function in many different forms:

- It can be just where the action will take place.
- It can cause that action.
- It can comment upon or undermine that action as another layer of the theme*.

- There are actions that are motivated by unconscious thought, which writers refer to as subtext**. They may seem random or unexceptional, but they're the result of a hidden compulsion. Unlocking the meaning underneath is one of the many character puzzles that the script will attempt to reconcile.

* We will discuss what the theme is, its place in your story, and start to smoothly integrate it at the end of this chapter.

** Subtext will be more directly addressed in Chapter 6, but you'll get a taste of it on page 128.

FILM EXAMPLE

In Spike Lee's *Do the Right Thing*, the neighborhood is as much a character as Mookie (Lee), Pino (John Turturro), or Sal (Danny Aiello). A slice of life view of community can reinforce mainstream stereotypes, or upend them. And in Lee's movie, it does both. We see the active side of Bedford-Stuy and how normal, enterprising, and family-oriented the area is. The thriving, positive vibe initially makes ridiculous Mookie's hyper-vigilant sense of political equity. Then, it belies the smooth words and easy camaraderie of pizza joint owner Sal without Pino, his thin-skinned son, saying a word. We feel the heat of the kitchen. The sweat pouring down Turturro's angry, frazzled face. When Jade comes in for a slice,

Sal's parental affection for the young woman he's seen grow up oozes into a kind of puppy love, which embarrasses and disgusts Pino. All these elements that contribute to the conflagration that occurs at the end of the movie are as much spoken as unspoken.

Clearly, the setting is more than its address. It's more than the weather, the time of day, and whether it's an interior or exterior scene. Most vitally, it's the people, who lend it its atmosphere. It's the character's personal history, if any, with the place and the people to be found there.

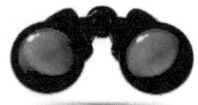

EXERCISE #25: PEOPLE WATCHING

- What kind of folks is she most apt to run across?
- How well does she, in fact, know these people?
- Does she have a relationship to this place?

Exercise 25

> **Example from Elizabeth:**
>
> (Re: my world-traveling, South American priest)
>
> Local townspeople. People who he ministers to. But not the volunteers he sees every day at the church.
>
> He probably knows the proprietor. I think it could prove interesting if they have a private friendship because he had been able to get the proprietor out of a scrape in the past.
>
> Naturally, this allows my character to get special treatment: maybe the best table in the place, or the option to sit in a little anteroom a bit removed from everyone else.

We're leading up to that first real experience we've been talking about, where you're going to be fostering a connectedness with your protagonist. But what does that *feel* like?

Well, contrary to what you might have thought, writing's not just a sedentary and cerebral exercise. It's a form of pre-acting. According to the great-great-grandfather of writing teachers, Aristotle, in his *Poetics,* said that for all of us, acting stems out of natural curiosity.

Dating Your Character

As the writer, you're responsible for running through your scenes and playing them out beat by beat to inhabit them: to see how the drama flows, what it sounds like when the lines are said. If your words really live and breathe, you can look forward to there being a discernible, added element in your script's overall effect, when read aloud.

Take care to set the mood for the scene. It's nothing like taking a snapshot of a place and then transcribing it. If you're not really familiar with set dressing, perhaps you ought to take a trip to the type of venue you've been mulling over. Maybe, your imagination isn't providing the overheard background chatter that could invigorate your scene. It's important to listen for and pay attention to all these elements.

EXERCISE #26: FIRST DATE FIELD TRIP

Go to *three venues* of the same type, just absorb your immediate impressions. Be prepared to spend *half an hour* at each. You don't need to take notes while you're there.

Note: You don't have to do all this on the same day.

After you've soaked in the atmosphere of *one venue*, consider the following:

- Is this place part of a well-known chain or an independent outfit?
- How hard is this place to find? (Is that part of its charm?)
- Who does this place cater to? (Students, hipsters, mid-level professionals, retirees?)
- What emotional connotation is the lighting trying to set? (Romantic, blithely efficient, family-friendly coziness, etc.?)
- What is the demeanor of the regulars—both workers and customers?

What are its plusses and minuses? (Is it in a sketchy place?)

Exercise 26

Dating Your Character

> ### EXERCISE 26-b: FIRST DATE FIELD TRIP
> Now try and contrast all *three places* from one another. Even if they're striving for the same clientele how are they different? Using only *one* of your *five senses*, focus on the ways particular items help brand the "experience" that each offers.

Exercise 26-b

You may have to take your research duties further, depending on how demanding your date might be. If you recognize limitations in yourself, don't wait to be caught out. Remedy the situation. Like doing some fact-checking before a job interview, so that you sound aware of what's going on. After all, if you somehow bonded over a shared interest in cultivating orchids, you may want to bone up on your showiest phalaenopsis trivia.

You don't want to look out of place or feel like you don't know what you're doing. So if she wants to eat sushi and you fumble with your chopsticks, a little practice might be worth it. Exploring the trendiest sushi places in your city may give you a more sophisticated appreciation of the cuisine. Picking up a table book of Japanese art will allow you to knowingly name-drop in the conversation. You never know what funny or incisive little moment might arise from considering how these real world details can ground your work later.

Sometimes, dates grow out of a casual acquaintance or friendship where there is already a certain level of comfort. Other times, going on a first date is a leap of faith. (With *DYC*, we're here for you. We're that friend over at the bar waiting for a signal if things get weird or awkward.)

Think about what you hope to achieve from the First Date. You want her to have enough curiosity about you to meet up again. You want the interest you have in her to be validated. You also want to feel that there's some sincerity in your conversation and that she's not playing you.

Keep in mind that on a first date, most people say what they think the other person wants to hear. Even when the truth is embellished or omissions are made, though, these are helpful clues. While you're looking for information, any kind of feedback is helpful. Even, if the date's a total disaster!

What could happen?

- She walks out on you?
- She ignores you and talks to someone else?
- She tries to *kill* you? (Pretty awful, huh?)

But, all of these incidents can provide valuable insights. And luckily for you, if she does draw blood, you'll recover as quickly as your imagination lets you.

Dating Your Character

Get comfortable with the fact that you can't guarantee the outcome. That's one of the lessons here. The date's *not* all up to you. If it goes wrong, you aren't wholly responsible. It's merely a set time to confront your character and see what she puts out there. There will be no "wrong way," just one less alley to go down.

Plus, remember, you've probably *never* been more prepared and open to possibility. After all, you already have some familiarity with your character's basic background info, along with likes and dislikes. You've written down successful mood-creating elements, so you can incorporate those details in your date venue.

So, how much input will she want to have? Will she be *annoyed* if you take it upon yourself to arrange everything? Or will she be charmed by your care and attention…?

> **Note:** If a "first date" as such isn't a proper fit for you and your character, then simply carve out a special time for you both to meet up. All the ingredients of place specifics activity and attention to her comfort still apply.

EXERCISE #27: DATE PLANNER

You make the arrangements:

- How easy is it to pin her down?
- Is it hard to get her to commit to a time?
- When you call, does it always go to voicemail?
- Do you text, but get no immediate response?
- Is she cooperative?
- Does she send you a pic of what she's doing, as a friendly afterthought?
- Does she connect with *you*, before you get in touch with her?
- Does she recall who you are straight away?

Exercise 27

EXERCISE 27-b: DATE PLANNER

She makes the arrangements:

- Is she controlling?
- Does she pepper you with texts on parking tips, menu

recommendations, etc.?

- Does she text you when you're five minutes late?
- Is she flaky?
- Does she try to weasel out of it at the last minute?
- Does she arrive with someone else and "forget" she was to meet you there?

What do her choices tell you about her?

What do they imply about her basic value system?

Exercise 27-b

FILM EXAMPLE

In *The Shawshank Redemption,* an important prearranged meeting between Andy (Tim Robbins) and Red (Morgan Freeman) is set. We know Andy really well by this point. Though even on its own, the way Andy extends an open invitation to his former prison-mate Red provides insight into the kind of man Andy is. Andy's considerate to the extreme, using clues in a postcard he sends to his friend. It leads to funds he's hidden, so Red can actually travel to the secret beach rendezvous in Mexico. All these little details really do matter. If Red accepts Andy's dare, he'll be able to jumpstart his life when he finally gets out. This proposition isn't any empty promise. They add up to a real chance at a new life.

In the *DYC* realm, all the hypothetical writing you do is about testing yourself and your assumptions, as well as grounding your knowledge of your character in specificity. (You could get turned down by your character. Something could come up at the last minute—if she's a cop or a doctor, for instance.) So, you have to make an effort to beguile her and draw her out. In thinking about what would appeal to her, you'll start to discern her tastes and tendencies. After hammering out the date deets with her, at the minimum, you've already discovered where she falls on the sliding scale of a few essential character traits. How…

- sheltered she is.
- thoughtful a planner she is.
- much she prizes routine.
- technologically savvy she is.
- spontaneous she is.
- money conscious, fashion conscious, or trend conscious she is.

Dating Your Character

If you can't say with all honesty that you've gathered this background, please go back and revisit what you've learned. Maybe you just need to do a better job of launching into exercises and sitting with them. Don't throw up your hands and say...*I don't get it*. Don't be that newbie actor who blames his own lukewarm performance on his scene partner... *It's not me.*

Take ownership for when things don't go well. It's true you can't control all outcomes, but the more you hold yourself accountable, the more likely you are to be objective and improve. We know it's difficult when you think you're working hard, but still can't stop the backsliding. At least take heart that during that backward motion, you're getting incontrovertible evidence that tells you where you are and where you need to go.

Steep yourself in the scents and crackling texture of your character's world. Don't wrap yourself in a raincoat and "wellies." Take on more of any earthy residue that sticks: feel the mud, the leaves, and the dried flowers. The more you know what she's running away from, the more you'll both know where she's running to. That physical sensitivity may repulse you (and the character), but you shouldn't discount what you're feeling and the information you're getting, even if it seems to be delaying your progress. If you knew in your gut what you wanted to write and had the patience and curiosity to explore that territory, you'd be doing that. But, if you've hit a little bump, you have to be willing to write "poorly."

Don't be prissy! Don't scrape off whatever seems like trash.

You will begin to write well again, the more words, ideas, sensations, locations, and snippets of dialogue you have down on paper. If the architecture of your story hasn't been shaped yet, at least your writing will become more informed. It will show you what you're fixated on, what you're willing to spend time getting right.

If you suspect you're going in circles, then ask yourself questions. You might be afraid of going to the next place. If you're bogged down, then take a mud bath and just relax. Being rigid or overly cerebral is really not the same as trying hard. You may need some daydreaming time to incorporate what you learned. Studies have shown that pre-visualization techniques, popular in professional sports, can help you achieve your goals.[1]

Your job is to identify the feel of a scene, which includes what each individual character is feeling. We at *DYC* believe that framing characters in conflict and constructing cool plot set-ups are secondary. Plot twists, punch-lines and witticisms are tertiary. But, these screenwriting parts all stem from how well you know your character, her world, and her concerns.

GETTING IN HER HEADSPACE AND PHYSICAL SPACE

You've been trying to be accommodating to ensure your first date is one of more to come. Yet, it might be an unsettling prospect for her. After all, it's an event that's fraught with missteps, with snap judgments that are quickly made and cannot be undone. Your protagonist's already run into you and maybe doesn't quite know why she agreed to see you again.

You might have used an air of intrigue at one moment to keep her interested. But, your run-in probably didn't last more than five minutes. So, what will she be feeling? Anxious curiosity, sweet anticipation, dread?

If so…why? Start to get comfortable with that question. You're not going to be peppering her constantly with that question, like an annoying kid, because a lot of your *DYC* work is internal and observational. It's about not settling into what you think you know. You may unearth things that feel rock solid. But you can't stop asking her for more insight, because you feel you already know. You need an ever-increasing understanding of what makes her tick.

The below is an empathy exercise. Sometimes, you're not getting information. You're just trying to get a sense for what it feels like inside her skin. This may help you identify with her. Any time you acknowledge fear, a connection happens. Even, when that connection's the smallest form of fear. Nerves.

EXERCISE #28: TAKING YOUR CHARACTER'S TEMPERATURE

Put a check on the line next to the thermometer marking which best represents the level of her anxiety/eagerness. This exercise is not based on the body's standard temperature of 98.6F. It is simply a tool focusing on the theoretical "heat" given off due to her nerves.

100 – breaking a sweat	100°	____
90 – breathing quickly	90°	____
80 – heart rate aflutter	80°	____
70 – flushed with excitement	70°	____
60 – warm and tingly	60°	____
50 – coolly indifferent	50°	____

Exercise 28

When you begin to explore your First Date, this physiological clue should inform every aspect of your first moments of interaction with the character. Previously, you've started thinking about her state of mind, but are now going beyond that to tap into her central nervous system. It's time to see your character begin to emerge as an organic being and not just a figment of your colorful imagination.

This level of attention and care is how you make scenes come alive for actors. Actors respond to the "pulse" of a scene—its rhythms, breaths, and potential for emotional and physical movement. You cannot go ahead and write for someone like that, unless you're attuned to your body and life force. In a sense, we're adopting the kind of mindfulness of yoga, where movements are fluid, actions are studied, and thought is slowed to the point of restful consciousness. A point where personal focus is merged with an intuitive heedfulness of the outside world.

THE PRE-DATE PREP

You're in the process of going micro into your understanding of her experience, so you can viscerally perceive what it's like to be her. Remind yourself that she has feelings, sensations, even a past and a present that predates your meeting her. Get used to the idea that her life doesn't just switch on when you start writing…she "exists" when she's not with you.

Your character will go into the date with some expectations of her own. Considering what these factors may be beforehand, will help ensure you both have a positive experience. This will help you anticipate your best course of action.

The reason is if this is an epic fail, you need to ensure that she'll at least have a pleasant time regardless of her specific encounter with you. Nothing here is a given. You don't know how she'll react to you as a person.

But people can bond through conflict, too. Everything doesn't have to be smooth sailing, especially if she comes in with a less than positive attitude. You don't have to be walked on, acquiesce to her every whim. Just be aware of how much effort you're extending. What works, what doesn't.

EXERCISE #29: MANAGING EXPECTATIONS

There are **three prongs** that probably comprise a successful date from her perspective:

- The Impersonal: Everything about the experience, except your personal imprint (is trendy, Japanese cuisine)
- The Personal: How she gets on with you.

Write down what could irritate her, before she even meets up with you. Write down her thoughts about the last two aspects of the date. (Even, if she isn't this practical or forward-thinking.)

What would elicit a positive or negative reaction?

***DYC* Example:**

The Petty:

She could be *pissed off* if:

- you're late.

- you split the bill with her.

- she can't find parking and has to walk in her fashionable and really uncomfortable Jimmy Choos.

The Impersonal:

She wants to have a good time. You're the perfect excuse to check out a new place. She's lonely and hopes you'll be the first good friend she makes in town.

The Personal:

That you listen to her? Entertain her? That she's photographed by a society columnist while there?

Exercise 29

EXERCISE #30: ESCAPE HATCH

Take at least *a paragraph* responding to the following three questions:

1. What would her reaction be if she's disappointed? (Hidden? Clearly expressed? Shared loudly and publicly?)

2. If this date doesn't go well, what are her plans to mitigate it? (Has she made an alternative plan B? Is she willing to just wing it and hope for the best? Does she tend not to think of "what ifs" and "afters?"

3. How will you know when she's working off plan B? (In action and dialogue?)

Exercise 30

Her train of thought is useful to track down, because now you're becoming privy to how she thinks. You're starting to sniff out more of the components that go into her decision-making. You're no longer just relying on observing the reactions you see and hear.

But, how do you gauge her reactions for their nuances? You first have to know what to look and listen for...

Dialogue Checklist:

Her accent.

How good a listener she is.

Her style and range of vocabulary used.

Her conversational pacing and its rhythms.

Her degree of consideration before answering.

Action Checklist:

Her habits.

Her body language.

Her level of intentness in you.

Her interaction with other people.

How do you parse her dialogue? Well, word choice is important. But, there's more to it than that.

Let's play with a little exercise to see how many ways there are to get a point across, to create an action, or to change the emotional temperature of a discussion.

The smallest calibrations can make all the difference for

Dating Your Character

audiences to start getting invested in your characters. Audiences will pick up on the clues you leave, and make assumptions, which you can choose to turn on their head. The simple exercise below should get you more comfortable inflecting nuance from the barest of statements.

EXERCISE #31: USE YOUR WORDS

Say this <u>three</u> different ways:

"I'm hungry."

DYC Example:

"So, shall we order?"

"See that woman over there? Her prime rib looks heavenly…"

"Listen, get a few facts straight. One, I'm no salad eater."

In our first response, it's less about her asking a genuine question than her politely taking control.

In the second statement, she sounds prepared to enjoy herself, angling for a dish on the more expensive side of the menu. This could possibly betray a suggestibility, too.

In the third version, she's direct, telling us that she means to have a solid course. She's certainly not interested in being overly feminine or bewitching. She's almost goading you to be turned off.

Now here's one just for you:

"It's getting late. I have to go."

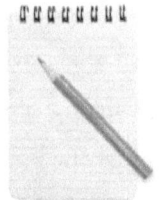

Exercise 31

Dating Your Character

This is your first proper exposure to **subtext.** This exercise allows you to discern something about the speaker from each response. Seeing past what she's saying to 1) what your character's really saying and 2) figuring out what she's prodding you to say or do. Characters, like people, rarely say exactly what they're thinking. They can be vague, evasive, deliberately misleading, or flat-out liars. Often, being cajoling or flirtatious to get what they want. As the Charles de Talleyrand quote says, "Speech was given to man to disguise his thoughts."

So, how do you get a true sense of them? Well, dissecting the spirit of your character's delivery can give you key indicators of her mood and personality type, but also her possible agenda:

- Is she commanding or subservient?
- Is she well-mannered or rude?
- Does she leave an opening for you to respond or just roll over you?

Noodle on the fact that she'll be feeling you out, too, during the date. She may deliberately try to push your buttons by insulting you coyly or leaning in and whispering to try and establish a false sense of intimacy. If your character's harder to read, it's even more crucial to start making these early calibrations.

Who do you believe is going to be more conversationally dominant? Even in an ideal setting where the conversation flows back and forth, there is likely to be someone who is slightly more prominent than the other. That preference depends on both your personal make-up and the character's.

Accommodate her manner, but also set the scene for conversational success. Make a plan so that the talk goes beyond superficial chit-chat. Think about both the subject matter itself and your style of lead-in. If you want to find out what it was like to grow up an orphan, talking about your favorite sports teams isn't much of a segue...

> **EXERCISE #32: FIRST DATE PATTER**
>
> Think about the <u>three</u> things you're most curious about. What would be the best way to broach that (or those) subject(s)?
>
> **Item #1**
> _____
>
> **Item #2**
> _____
>
> **Item #3**
> _____
>
> **Example from Elizabeth:**
> - **Item #1** How he got in his line of work?
> - **Item #2** How he met his spouse?

(You're not necessarily having an "adulterous" affair with your character. You're hoping to build any kind of relationship where you can eventually be yourselves.)

- **Item #3** Why he recently relocated?

Re: Item #1

I'll use the location of the date to my advantage. My South American priest's competing with a cadre of well-meaning activists for the faith and loyalty of the local indigenous population, who routinely gather at the only bar in a twenty-five mile radius. Maybe I'll make a disparaging remark about these interlopers...

Though he vainly tries to disguise it, I think my character's rather arrogant. Putting these first-world activists in their place will show him that I'm not another spineless, PC-spouting person. And, that cutting remark will show I know the political climate of the place.

Re: Item #2

It's probably a question he gets from his parishioners all the time, because though he's now a Catholic priest, he was once married. As a religious figure, it's part of his vocation to accept curiosity in all its forms, and in his view, even on the most personal level. But, to ease into such a private question, I may

> lead with an observation about the many tradeoffs he's probably had to make because of his devotion. His material comforts, but most importantly sacrificing the relationships from his other life.
>
> **Re: Item #3**
> I may mention the time I spent a week's vacation in his old city of Salta, Argentina. With a few choice mentions of the local gems of the area, I may ask for his tips about what to see and appreciate here, in Manaus, Brazil. But, as a modern, impatient, and self-reliant guy, I have a feeling he'll just tell me to get on Apontador, a Brazilian Yelp-type app.

Exercise 32

Leading questions can also pave the way, if you're subtle. Remember to be complimentary! You're less a hardened P.I. than someone friendly who's expressed an interest in your character. Play it cool. As you see yourself interacting in the scene, it would be really weird if you recorded her or jotted down notes. But try and pay attention to her reactions. Is she more open talking about some things and not others? Which questions make her nervous or falter? File away these clues…

If you pick up on the fact that she keeps twirling an imaginary ring on her fourth finger (or she has a tan mark)—an indication of a former marriage or a canceled engagement—that might be too tempting for you not to broach. But if you want to mention that possibly still-raw subject, you'll most likely have to confide something rather intimate, too.

Perhaps, offering to share something personal, in the same vein, will lead her to divulge some of her experience. It's unlikely she'll want to talk about something so private unless she has some great desire to unburden herself. And, only if you feel she'll be receptive to this thread of conversation. *You have to make sure you don't alienate her.*

At every step of the way, you have to be conscious of her comfort level. Obey the rhythm she's laid down. If she's not that chatty, then maybe tone down your won eagerness. You have to fill the void, but you don't want to overwhelm her. If you are bursting with curiosity about her personal life, it may be more important to think about why you're asking at this rather early stage. Surely you can afford to be a little patient. *You don't want to rush things…*

This is also true for more of an informal coffee meet-up than a date, where your character probably isn't expecting a deep or probing conversation. Anything worth knowing merits careful investigation. Let her information dribble out organically. If you accept that she's not going to be as obliging as you, you'll naturally start to value her as a three-dimensional person.

EXERCISE #33: LIE DETECTOR TEST

Why do you have to know *now?* This is not about having a one-night stand, coming together briefly, never to connect again. We need to dispel some of the fears, the roadblocks, to you sustaining a relationship with your character.

<u>Fears:</u>

Are you afraid you won't be able to draw her out over time? That she'll never open up or be interested in forming a serious relationship with you?

Correction: You don't need her to explicitly confide in you, though that kind of eventual discussion would be satisfying. You only need to be around. To be there if she needs to vent, to prod her to make the necessary changes to accomplish her goal.

That she'll grow bored with you and "talk" to someone else?

Correction: Of course she'll be talking to other people. At this point—and perhaps at no point—will you be the most important person in her life. It doesn't matter how often you see her, either. The trick is to snatch what you can and evaluate it later.

Do you think she has a limited amount of time on earth and so have to move fast?

Correction: Remember, time is fluid in the storytelling continuum. You can have coffee with her a year before the story's events will take place. You can choose to not count time spent with you as time that impedes her adventure, as if she's returning back to Earth after a long journey traveling at light-speed, basically the same age as when she left.

"Truths" you tell yourself:

Do you and your character seem to immediately hit it off? You're thinking, why go slow when there's already momentum?

Correction: You don't want what you have to fizzle out. You don't want her to think she can just snap her fingers and you'll come running. There has to be some "work" involved. And beware, if things come too easily, you're not going to develop the tools to unearth the deeper insights that you're moving towards.

While significantly based on you—your likes, your goals—your character is indeed different?

Correction: If you already closely identify with her, there may

> not be enough freedom for her to grow. After all, if you're a beginning screenwriter, chances are you're interested in writing a happy ending for her, because you have the same problems or conflicts. You have to force her to acquire the skills and go through the metamorphosis that will enable her to work out those riddles. Just know, when she's firmly in control of her story, she'll leave you behind.

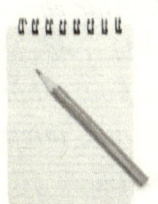

Exercise 33

She's not going to arrive at your date, poised and pristine, a receptacle begging to be filled with purpose and various charms. Think about your character's frame of mind prior to your meet up, since she's not going to be solely focused on what will happen there. Rewind the timeline a bit… Change your fixation from when and where the date's going to occur.

This is an exercise in totally shutting off your brain. Your objective is to feel out the scene. You're like sticky tape, accumulating dust motes, lint, and particles of behavioral information. You're there to pick up and collect minutiae, details that provide context. The throwaway gestures and words that people don't pay attention to, but can be most revealing…

Dating Your Character

Many development people capriciously cut a writer's work to the bone. It's far easier to work backwards from a finished script and try to retool it, than starting from scratch, from a place of potential.

Many producers and directors, who have great story instincts, have trouble figuring out how to get into their writer's headspace... let alone the character's!

This exercise should help all creatives practice the craft of story creation and character development.

It will walk you through the steps to entering the consciousness of the protagonist, so that you can be sure your future story notes keep the core integrity of the character in mind.

EXERCISE #34: FIVE MINUTES BEFORE

5 mins.

Step one: Figure out where she's coming from...

(Directly from home? From work? From running errands?)

_____

Step two: What was her agenda there?

(To sneak out without being noticed? To get a raise? To go to extreme lengths to save money?)

_____

_____

Step three: How much of that agenda does she bring to the date?

(She comes in with a foul mood, because she was caught? She's flush with extra cash and of a mind to spend! She's very confident and chatty?)

_____

Dating Your Character

Exercise 34

Example from Marilyn:

As a producer/manager, I won't be writing a story any time soon, but I imagine the kind of character I'd be interested in getting to know more about would be a young, Latina professional. Someone who works with kids. And, if I wanted to gain more of a familiarity with her, I'd want to see how she spends her nights.

I'm going to assume she's extremely busy with family commitments, friends, work… and since she's always on the move, she practically lives out of her car. So, if our "first date" were to take place at a happening bar in an ungentrified part of town, I think she's the kind of person who'd be rushing to get there, applying lipstick, combing her hair while at a red light. She's probably a little scattered, because most fun people are, in my experience.

As a teacher, she's probably drained, not only by the needs of the kids, but by the demands and politics of the job. Nowadays, being a teacher isn't just about teaching, it's about the additional pressure of making sure students aren't going hungry and are able to arrive to and from school safely. All that and the testing teachers have to prepare for.

There's such a strong charter school movement, that I gather regular teachers feel under assault. If their schools become annexed as charters, not only is it easier to be fired, but their pay and benefits usually aren't what they were. So, they're under more pressure to be accountable, while working that much harder for less pay.

I think after a long day at work, maybe staying after school to help her students, she'd be more than happy to spill the beans. I hope she'll be sociable, funny, and straight-talking. But, if not, a couple of cervezas might loosen her up.

I don't think she would complain to me specifically about the politics of her job. However, if she arrives irritated, I might figure she had to finish some kind of district paperwork or other bureaucratic interference.

How do you get into that lazy space of immediate consciousness?

Dating Your Character

Whether you're a screenwriter, novelist, or poet, you need to be in that space, where there's no pressure other than a writing prompt's timed exercise. The outset of the discovery process is different from the latter stages of writing a finished script. But, you can make use of some of *DYC*'s benefits in the context of a professional writing assignment...

Most of us go about the routine of our lives in a kind of fuzzy blur, doing the bare minimum our jobs or other responsibilities require, not truly alive to the people and natural settings we come across. In order to write an extended scene that operates in an organic sequence, you need to awaken your sense of the world. Develop that calm watchfulness as muscle memory. And, the first step may well be for you to adopt a more quiet demeanor. Do whatever you need to relax. Roll your neck around, crack your knuckles.

For those of you who have written short stories or novels, the following exercise (on p. 145) will probably feel like coming home. Because those longer forms look for small movements to see what they reveal about a place and the people there, you can take your time to craft an immersive reality that is communicated only through the written word. But, in scripts, you don't have the page count luxury of a book. Scripts thrive on the telling, minute detail.

It's kinda crazy, but only after you've invested 300 hours into researching, doing exercises, playing with certain scenes, and sculpting the script itself, will you have produced a script that can be absorbed and appreciated in two hours, if seen (three hours, if it's read—and *read*, not skimmed)! That's all you get... It's not fair, it's life.

Actors go over and over the same ground to create a character. From the get go, we're helping you give what an actor will later require of you. Right now, you're swimming in confusion, and that's fine...

Professional scripts of the highest quality manage to imbue that lived-in sense in choice, one- or two-sentence descriptions. It's a different gear of writing, one that you have to practice shifting into for a sense of authenticity that makes your story ring true. Sampling what it's like to simply take in what's around you—without judging it or making it fit a purpose. Giving a time and place as accurate and telling a portrayal as you can.

FILM EXAMPLE

In Sam Mendes's *Road to Perdition*, based on the graphic novel by Max Allan Collins and Richard Piers Rayner, there was an eerie quality to the framing and color scheme used to render the latter stages of the Prohibition era. The grays used to show us the wretched photographer/assassin-for-hire (Jude Law) seemed hazy and gauzy. The palette seemed to suggest that this scene was going to be transcendent, something slightly different from the matter-of-fact Tommy-Gun murders we'd become accustomed to.

Unlike other mob pictures, the mostly inky black fabric of the men's heavy woolen coats, the black background and dim lighting during the party celebration held at the home of John Rooney (Paul Newman), showed a *consistently* grimy texture. The motion picture is scrupulously without many sentimental family scenes or exhibitions of grand wealth from their criminal misdeeds. There aren't any of the colorful galas that appear in *The Godfather* trilogy.

Lest you lose yourself congratulating Conrad L. Hall, the cinematographer who won an Academy Award for his murky, charcoal composition of the graphic novel, keep in mind that even scripts without a rich visual medium to draw from have to imply certain tones. Writers can do that by focusing on characters' fashion, the décor of a room, or how the light streams in. These vivid touches are important clues for crucial scenes, if something thematic is being insinuated or if there is a marked difference to how we've seen characters and locations from previous scenes. It'll be as if we're imagining the future movie just by reading your script.

Throughout screenwriter David Self's script, the dialogue is very spare. So the actors relied on subtext in the description itself to understand the nature of the men they were playing. As Tom Hanks who played the lead mob enforcer, Sullivan, now on the run with his young son, Michael, said in an article in *USA Today*, "It's all about denying that anything is going on, while at the same time observing everything that is going on."[2]

In a bravura move in the final 20 minutes of *Road to Perdition*, the first draft has only six lines of dialogue. As the gory denouement plays out, there's no need for language. By this point, we already know the dramatic investment each character has. The extended killing sequence that's going to come is just and it only remains to be seen how Sullivan will pull it off. Especially with a wild card assassin on his tail.

The grim postcard quality of the last sequence itself had to be communicated on the page, so that the intended power of the ending could be felt. But, in order to unsettle the reader, a momentary lull is offered up to break the continuum of inexorable violence. This free-floating breather is expressed in the same rather crisp, soberly staccato language that characterized the bulk of the script, so that it still belongs tonally to the entirety of the work:

```
The day is clear and blue, like the first day
of Spring. Sullivan and Michael come down
through the woods and out onto a desolate,
beautiful beach on the lake front. A light
breeze blows in off the lake. Magic hour…
```

After all the miles Sullivan's put the car through, it pulls up. He and Michael are forced to appreciate the pristine remoteness of the place, the peace it offers. As they get close, they become alive to the transformative power of its beauty. The chill wind seems to brush away the pestilent horror of the last few weeks.

To prolong this soul-cleansing scene of family, redemption, and new promise, father and son walk down the beach. They have an easy exchange about the weather, baseball. Their banter has a taste of Americana, implying the hopeful future they're both trying to believe is in store for them. The sense of danger that's been with them for so long is gone.

Aunt Sarah's dog comes bounding down the beach to greet them. Sullivan is treated to his son's renewed childish lightness as he cavorts with the dog. But, the dog leaves bloody paw prints on the boy...

DYC's main focus is getting you to let the colorful little details of real life seep into your writing, as you're setting up meaningful moments of anticipation and drama. But, we don't just want you to paint with words— to fall in love with pretty turns of phrase or to rely on stunning visuals to transport your audience. It's a tool and not the ultimate end goal for your script. It's just one of the many keys to getting "must-read" coverage* status.

> **EXERCISE #35: SOAK UP YOUR SURROUNDINGS**
>
> Find a place you've never been to before. And, sit and write.
>
> Absorb your surroundings. This is a stream-of-consciousness exercise.

Exercise 35

> * Refer to page 190 for a definition of the ten fundamentals on which scripts are graded.

That free-flowing writing, that openness to whatever assaults your senses, is the kind of momentum we want you to have when you approach your first proper date with your character. You've already thought about it, prepared for it. Now, get out of the practical-minded hemisphere of your brain and let go. Give yourself permission to stop captaining the ship. Just ride the waves.

There is an art to silencing the propelling force of your story. Forget any deadlines you're on. If you're at home, turn off the TV or anything else that roots you to the here and now. Close the blinds, the windows. Add some soothing music, lighted candles. If you're at your favorite café, slip on headphones to block out any distractions from the outside world. Take a sip of your favorite tipple. Put yourself at ease…

Synchronize your heedfulness with her internal clock. You already know where your first official interaction with her is going to take place. So, now just pay attention to her and how she moves in this environment.

Try to get the conversation flowing. Feel out the rhythm of how you both interact. It's not about pumping her for as much information as she's able to spew. The design is to make the whole scene have the semblance of reality. Like the real give and take of a fumbling, well-intentioned, first date! Remember, it's not meant to be an artfully crafted scene, but a more organic, searching experiment…

EXERCISE #36: THE FIRST DATE

Push yourself to write for between *fifteen* and *twenty minutes*.

You don't need a timer. You'll know you've put in a solid effort if you end up with *four* to *five written pages* or *eight* to *nine typed pages*.

Exercise 36

So, how do you know "if it worked?" You don't ever want to just go through the motions and not get anything out of the exercise…

EXERCISE #37: SCENE EVALUATION

Please *circle* **Yes** or **No** below to help determine how real an effort you put forth and how useful this writing workout was for you.

Did the scene have:

… lulls? **Yes   No**

… awkward pauses? **Yes   No**

… exciting rushes of newness? **Yes   No**

Were you:

… surprised? (How often?) **Yes   No**

… caught off guard at any point? **Yes   No**

… mildly entertained? **Yes   No**

For the below questions, please expand your answers.

Did the experience feel forced? Like you were doing all the

work?

Did it resemble any of the first dates you've been on?

Did the tone change during the conversation?

Did "life" seem to interrupt here and there?

Did you seem as if you were reacting, rather than engineering what happened?

How did the scene unfold?

Exercise 37

Taking stock of all the verite elements in your First Date can be a painstaking process. We started with a list of prompts to get you thinking about how it went. Let's try to re-experience the scene, while looking for the telltale details of location you were practicing earlier.

TV EXAMPLE

Unlike other sleuthing shows, the lead detective in the CBS/A&E procedural *Unforgettable,* based on the short story *The Rememberer* by J. Robert Lennon, not only revisits crime scenes, pores over old clues, and analyzes the murder board summarizing the case's pertinent details, she exceeds those tried and true methods. She routinely walks through the digital recorder of her mind, panning around the crime scene or settings of prior suspect interviews to focus in on particulars that initially seemed insignificant.

She goes way beyond building a memory palace, that trick for retrieving names, places, and dates that people use to help them map out important facts that would otherwise clutter the mind, because she has total recall.

She re-experiences everything she saw—even her own

movements, where she was looking, conversational snippets she didn't realize she'd overheard—in a kind of virtual-reality reenactment.

EXERCISE #38: CARRIE WELLS MEMORY WALK-THROUGH

In going over your scene, think about the following:

When you first entered...

How were you regarded?

Did you command more attention than you're used to? Why?

What was the vibe...

Were people in a rush, or more chill? Did this place have more of a prescribed purpose or was it a hang out?

How easy was it to find her...

Where was she sitting? Did she have a visual advantage?

(Was she on a balcony? Was she on a private bench with a vantage of the entrance?)

Was she sitting with people...

Casually chatting with someone? Busy with some activity? Or was she alone?

How did she get you to notice her...

Did she seem to perk up? Did she warmly wave you over?

Did she not even bother...

Did she maintain her cool? Avert her eyes?

Did you speak first...

Did you start with small talk or were you prompted by other people in some perfunctory conversation beforehand?

What two things surprised you?

What two things played out as you expected?

Exercise 38

Dating Your Character

So far you've been taking her wants and desires at face value, trying to please her. You've tried to discern her train of thought, while looking for clues of her other priorities and hidden dissatisfaction. Besides specific things you picked up from the encounter, you've started to gauge the rhythm of the date. You've paid special attention to the opening moments. Did you notice any differences of opinion, were there any awkward bumps?

EXERCISE #39: CHARTING THE ARC OF THE SCENE

How did those *first few minutes* differ *twenty minutes* into the date?

- Were you two more comfortably settled?
- Did any goodwill dissipate?
- How did the nature of the conversation change?
- Did it turn to more weighty issues?
- Did the focus move from the two of you to a peripheral character?
- And, how did you know it was coming to an end?
- When the waiter handed you the check?
- When all conversation seemed to dry up?

Even if the later stages of the date were rather tepid and uninspiring, how did things end?

- Pleasantly?
- Awkwardly?

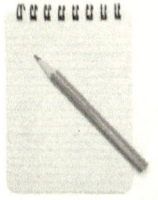

Exercise 39

EXERCISE #39-b: CHARTING THE ARC OF THE SCENE

Now that you're attuned to the turning points in the scene, write a diary entry of how you were feeling at the beginning, middle, and final stages of the date. At least a *couple of paragraphs* for each section.

Take pains to write this assignment in a dramatic fashion, i.e., each section itself should develop and change from how it was launched. If you were a little nervous but optimistic in the beginning, by the middle portion were you even more gung ho or were you disappointed by her lack of effort? Make note of any transitions and variations in emotional temperature.

Exercise 39-b

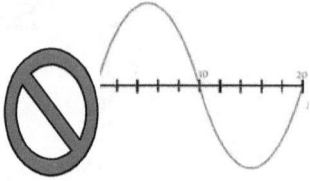

EXERCISE 39-c CHARTING THE ARC OF THE SCENE

Chart the ups and downs of your mood as you entered each section of the date. Whatever the shape of your arc, when you conclude the date, how you feel should not be a mirror image of your overall vibe when the date first unfolded.

You should not have a perfect sideways "s" shape.

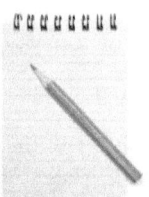

Exercise 39-c

> **EXERCISE 39-d: CHARTING THE ARC OF THE SCENE**
> At the end of the date what "conclusions" did you draw about your character? What did you "lock in" from what you learned about her? Remember she can always change your mind…But what struck you as especially relevant and true?

Exercise 39-d

> ⭐ **EXTRA CREDIT:** You may want to try repeating the First Date experiment by reversing the roles, if you were the lead. You may surprise yourself with how much the character comes to the fore to make up for your lessened participation. However, it's highly doubtful a take-charge character would appreciate you trying to run the show, so if you were to reverse the Set-up by trying to assert yourself equally, you're likely to create tension and animosity.

You've studied how to approach different types of characters in the hopes of getting them to open up. Hopefully, you've also peeked at a side of your character you may not have originally considered, because it's outside the confines of the plot. Your character may not be digging you yet, but at least you're a surprise, something new. Perhaps, you're not her type, so she's surprised by your interest. As a result, she may start to look at herself a bit differently. Perhaps, where the date took place was a welcome look at a part of town she wasn't familiar with. Whatever the degree of pleasure or freshness you were able to provide, at minimum it served as a disruption of her routine.

Assuming your first date was at least palatable, it should buy you enough goodwill for an informal follow up. An opportunity for her to show you something she's interested in; some hobby or project that she's spent time on, but doesn't necessarily consider integral to who she is. It's something that gives her satisfaction and she wants to share with you.

She may take you to a special location, somewhere she volunteers. Or a job site that's the cumulation of months of preparation. She may be the one in charge and want to exhibit the importance of her role: the manpower she's leading, the sheer size of a building that's set for a controlled demolition. This isn't a personal sharing of confidences, but it's a way to find out a little more about her skill set and what she cares about.

> **EXERCISE #40: HANGING OUT**
>
> She names the place for the meet up. Allow yourself to fade into the "b.g." (background). Try to get a real understanding of why everyone's gathered there and how she contributes to this group enterprise.
>
> - Watch her in her element doing something she likes.
> - Ask her questions.
> - If she lets you, ask questions of the other people on site, too.

Exercise 40

You're starting to unearth the foundation of the character's life. In previous exercises, you also touched upon her past in order to understand how she came to be, because for change to occur you first have to intuit the character's status quo. Change is often about revealing the neglected parts of ourselves, abrading past little hurts so they come to the surface and declare themselves.

So, how do you boil down the character's problems? By really rooting out what could unsettle her. That way you're channeling her rage or confusion rather than relaying the problem secondhand. For the following exercise, you have to try and turn off your analytical brain. You may have to put yourself in a suggestive trance to drink in the telling details that emerge in your conversation.

- Take a little nap to calm yourself or listen to atmospheric music that may slow down your thoughts and make you more receptive.
- Or if you crave more stimulation to become more aware of your surroundings, a quick sprint of aerobic activity may give you a mini adrenaline rush.

> ### EXERCISE #41: BUBBLING UP
> Write *one sentence* from your character to you. Whatever first bubbles up… Then, respond to her.
>
> There are no other parameters. Explore your character. Obey the give-and-take rhythm of the encounter.

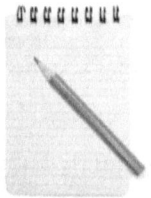

Exercise 41

Resist the urge to evaluate her initial conversation too deeply. Your character may be the type to take selfies and quite happily toss out superficial info. But, in being playful, she may also deliberately choose to lead you astray. You could make an incorrect assumption that just seems to fit the facts.

We want you to pinpoint what's on the uppermost level of her mind, because it's important to know what's occupying her. But, understand there are other burps of consciousness that will rise up as well from the cavernous reaches of her inner psyche. It would probably require a seismic shift in the character's thinking for her to admit these needs to herself, let alone to a virtual stranger—you. So, you have to continually demonstrate your usefulness and unconditional support to her to get her to connect with you.

What role should you play in your character's process of self-realization and transformation? Well, on her own, she may *not* change. So, she may not have a story without you or her affiliate character. You're not going to go on the same journey she does, but you'll help her advance by coming up with the obstacles that can prepare her for the hardships she'll have to encounter on her own.

To come up with authentic dilemmas for her, you need to totter on the precipice of change yourself. Think back to the times in your life that led you to make a drastic change or come to a tough decision. That moment of doubt, followed by determination is what we're looking for...

> **EXERCISE #42: RANDOM WEATHER PATTERN**
> Make a list of all the discussions, events, and odd occurrences that conspired to shock and motivate you to make a big-moment resolution.

Exercise 42

INCITING INCIDENT

Just like you probably were before that significant, personal declaration, your character will be resistant to looking at her life. **The Inciting Incident,** the moment when your character decides her life has to take a different path, will provide a moment of awakening that can be jarring for her. It's an unexpected development in "her story," the content and very nature of which she's probably always taken for granted. This is the first real instance in your script that makes her more aware of who she is or how people see her. It's what gets the juices of your narrative flowing.

> **EXERCISE #43: ROCKING HER WORLD**
> So, what combination of elements would be strong enough to jolt her out of her routine?
> - Come up with an alteration in one of her relationships that would unnerve her.
> - How can you frame this so that it appears to come out of the blue and totally blows her mind?

Exercise 43

In standard screenwriting structure, the Inciting Incident is the first event in your script coming between page 5 and 15 that so unnerves or excites your protagonist, it provokes a disturbance in her state of mind and rocks her emotional equilibrium. The scene appears to epitomize absolutely everything that's wrong. Before, even if she had misgivings, she didn't take them seriously.

Now, she begins to question and reevaluate her life. The Inciting Incident is much more than a setback. It causes her to call all her actions into question. There will be no quick fix; it'll take more than a minor adjustment or small correction. Her assumptions and her very philosophy have been thrown into doubt.

For you to have an involving screenplay, you must think about the major changes that she'll be forced to undergo. In order for her to achieve anything meaningful, there has to be a measurable difference from what she was to what she will become. It's in that space that the story takes place.

She'll have to construct a new foundation for herself on top of a squishy feeling of uncertainty. Whatever fresh agenda this inspires in her, she'll most likely find it frightening and invigorating. After she takes some of her first steps on her heroic journey, the plan she devised may not even seem possible. Throughout her campaign, she'll run into many more reasons to quit.

Your Inciting Incident can take multiple forms. It could be something that:

...happens suddenly.

...makes a previously compromised situation completely untenable.

...has been of concern to some of the supporting characters, who until now haven't been able to tell the protagonist.

The character's been going through life believing she's awake, functioning, and vitally alive. But, that's not really true. She's unconsciously blocked things out that don't mesh with her idea of herself and her place in the world.

Where her mini-meltdown happens isn't as crucial as where

the soul-devouring disintegration will occur during the **Act II Turning Point***. In the beginning, it's important to establish the landscape and rules of the character's universe. In Act II, you'll show how she makes an impactful seismic break to undo everything that's been retarding her progress.

> *** Note:** In the **Act II Turning Point,** also called the midnight hour, the personal crisis unfolds in a locale that represents all the character holds most dear and thought she could depend on. This generally appears 20 pages before your grand Climax. It is a momentous reckoning with a large buildup of tension and anticipation. Usually the more brash a character, the more the moment that cuts her down to size is quietly poignant. And conversely meeker characters meet their devastation in a public sphere as in the below film example.

FILM EXAMPLE

In the Academy Awards' Best Motion Picture of the Year for 2010, *The King's Speech* written by Oscar winner David Seidler, shy stutterer Bertie, King George VI, has to overcome his nerves on the most public stage imaginable. He has to give a speech that restores trust in the monarchy, which is broadcast live to the entire world. The Inciting Incident is the sudden abdication of his beloved older brother, Edward VIII, which he hears over the radio

Dating Your Character

in the family's study along with the rest of the British public.

When deciding where the Inciting Incident should materialize, consider how other people create the texture of the environment whether they're merely extras who are witnesses to her downfall or major supporting characters. Generally, at least one friend or family member is looking on, because he or she will help mark the character's growth on her journey.

Try to think of creating echoes in your script, or ripples. Moments of meaning that you can then riff on and we can experience in diverting ways. Noted screenwriter Everett Freeman, who wrote the original version of *The Secret Life of Walter Mitty*, said that "the Inciting Incident is the bell that is rung…that's rung louder later on."

Movies are a wonderful medium for revisiting the past, the present, and even the future like the *Back to the Future* franchise. You can have a scene play out one way, then if the desired result is a miss for the character she can get it right the second time. Like in *Groundhog Day*, where seeing the same scenes gently tweaked show us character Phil Connors' (Bill Murray) growing humanity as he comes to understand the problems of the people in the small town in which he's trapped.

While the sci-fi-comedy examples we cited are wholly

obsessed with the fluid nature of time, all scripts can benefit from these recurring moments, or moments of similarity turned askew.

The scene of the Inciting Incident can take place:

- publicly on a grand stage.
- among co-workers, friends, or family.
- where the character's surrounded by strangers, but isn't the center of attention.
- in a small, intimate space.
- where she's completely alone.

INCITING INCIDENT AND GENRE

FILM EXAMPLE

To take another Colin Firth period piece, 1995's *Pride and Prejudice*, confident, winsome Lizzy Bennet (Jennifer Ehle) is shocked when she overhears Darcy scoff at her supposed reputation for beauty and wit. While she doesn't resolve to change her manner or sense of her own worth, she does vocally resolve to make a permanent enemy of Darcy.

She's not been deeply hurt, but she nurses such a dislike for the man, that it cannot be all down to her pride being injured. She can easily dismiss his comments as rude and without merit. But a nerve is struck, because while his comments are uncharitable, it may be possible that in the wider world they are not far off the mark. She's led a sheltered life in the village of Meryton and has only been exposed to the judgment of her friends and neighbors, whose opinions she privately doesn't value, anyway.

Not a spiteful, cruel, or vengeful person, Lizzy immediately changes her temperament and natural inclinations in order to punish him. Or if he will not notice, then to signal to her friends her low regard of him. She is no longer content to smirk in secret. She puts her "pert opinions" on display for anyone who will notice. This is as much to avenge her wounded pride as it is to dazzle her audience with her previously maligned wit. This is the only real way she can assert her spirit and intelligence. And so, given free rein, she does, enjoying a verbal gymnastics with her unsuspecting competitor.

Your character's alternate course can find life as a compulsion or a vow and become more specific as time goes on. Unlike most Inciting Incidents, Lizzy doesn't go off in search of new friends, connections, or employment. She can't. She's a character of her historical period, who can only stray so far off the accepted path of womanly behavior. The only clear resolution she makes is to discount Darcy's opinion of her, which goads her into being more voluble and tart than usual.

The Jane Austen book was originally called *First Impressions*. The three families primarily involved—the Bennets, the Bingleys, and the Darcys—carom off each other, going in different directions based on the initial assumptions they make about each other. Even with the introduction of the new tenant of a local large estate, life goes on much as it has with neighbors dropping in on each other for afternoon teas, suppers, and dances.

The nature of their further dealings is based on the first impressions each character created. Since, only cursory conversations could hope to shed light on a person's true character beyond a couple's publicly supervised social interactions, the results were pointedly revealing for society of that time. We later find out that Lizzy's educated father was essentially bamboozled. He's now mismatched to a dull, petulant wife, because of a rushed courtship that she engineered. It's that kind of arbitrary game of chance that Lizzy's railing against when she challenges the status quo.

Lizzy's determination registers as a small deed on the Richter scale of radical goals. But, given the strictures of the time, it was a comparatively radical conclusion to snub Darcy, a man from such a great family dynasty. Your character's goal or mission doesn't have to be epic or take place on the world stage. Everything is relative, all depending on the limits of the character's universe. As the story unfolds, it will test her, taking her as far to the edge as she thinks she can go, then pushing her over...

How does the Inciting Incident propel your story? It sets your character on a new route through life. It flips what we've just gotten used to, surprising us and the character, and hews very closely to genre. For instance, if you're writing a romantic comedy, your Inciting Incident is not just seeing your character lose her job, but that she loses her job because she was indulging in a romantic daydream or visiting her match.com site. Throughout the story, problems in other parts of her life will dovetail to compound her journey, but the very first stinging slap to her face clearly stakes out the story's territory.

You must test, try, and abuse your character to mirror the everyday, and not so everyday, struggles that real people suffer through. That doesn't mean you necessarily have to go for obvious, clean fractures. *Don't* be afraid of smashing your character into little pieces. You want her to grow stronger from the experience, for the fissures to be re-calcified and annealed. (Though, pulverizing her into ash might be a bit too much…)

TV EXAMPLE

Young Bran Stark, in HBO's *Game of Thrones*, has been thrown out of a window, paralyzed, and orphaned after both his parents were elaborately murdered. He's been forced to journey to the fearsome edge of the kingdom in the hopes of figuring out the origin of his mystical power of mind control. And Bran is only ten (seven, in the books by George R. R. Martin) when most of this happens. In today's landscape, even young children can be cruelly impacted by tragedy and forced to transcend the brutality of their experience.

So, what would be the basis for a rift in your character? What in the Inciting Incident would cause her to break out of her old life and question everything she's ever known? To figure that out, you have to work out what it is that she cherishes. If you were playing poker, this is the time to put your story's cards on the table.

EXERCISE #44: BROKEN FLUSH

What is she willing to gamble on? What is she willing to hold out for, even if the odds are against her?

For each prompt, answer **Yes** or **No**.

If you answer **Yes,** set your timer for *a minute* and elaborate on your answer.

Is it something to do with her career? **Yes** **No**

A relationship? **Yes** **No**

Something more intangible... **Yes** **No**
(a philosophy, a memory...?) **Yes** **No**

Is this something you wish you could vow to do? **Yes** **No**

Does the world need a positive role model, who chooses to change the way she lives for the good of society? **Yes** **No**

To start to consider the larger implications of your story—its universal message—it's time to revisit what motivates you.

What is your story about?

_____

Why does she decide to do what she's about to do?

_____

Why does your character put herself in this position?

Exercise 44

FILM EXAMPLE

When we first meet a character on the big or small screen, there are lots of clues dropped for the audience, so they can start to form an impression. A great example Marilyn likes to use in her workshops is the 2000 historical-action flick *Gladiator* starring Russell Crowe. As the film opens, we're in a field of wheat. We hear children's laughter. A hand lovingly embraces each blade. The colors are warm and hearth-like. Soon, the colors shift into a monochromatic, cold, gray-blue as the shot widens to reveal a battlefield. We can tell just by his gestures that this warrior longs for home. Home is what he values and that's his most deeply felt goal throughout the entire film. A few minutes later, we see him in a small recess placing religious figurines, or perhaps family totems, near an altar.

You want to deftly establish your character's emotional core—what's most important to them without coming out and saying it. Think about the kind of images that can capture what your character's all about.

All of these are important clues that you can build on when introducing a character. An introduction is not a formal or laidback affair. It has to accomplish so much: provide a plot teaser, epitomize the theme of the script, and grab us with a direct portrait of the character in the type of activity he's going to be involved in throughout.

Santa Fe 7 is a script that's been optioned several times and which Devorah has been tinkering with recently, re-invigorated by the exercises in *DYC*. It's about six kids who grew up on an off-the-grid commune from 2000-2014. The commune breaks up when their leader dies from mysterious circumstances. Devorah introduces Coyote, Redfeather's son, driving a motorcycle on the edge of a cliff. He jumps his bike over a crevasse and clears it. He's riding a jerry-rigged bike, it has Native American talismans hanging from the handles. When he jumps the chasm, he lands by an abandoned car and then curses with a "Fuck you, Dad."

What reasonable assumptions can we (Marilyn, Elizabeth, and you) make? What do we learn about Coyote that is not explicitly said? He's clearly angry, and he's gutsy. He's maybe a little too prone to suicidal acts of daring. He probably doesn't come from money, since his bike is patched together, and if we've surmised correctly, the junked car was his dad's.

You have to understand, on a gut level, both your motivation and your character's in order to start crafting the series of obstacles that she will have to confront. Because, they're not just physical obstructions, but tests that challenge her and cause her to question both the way she approaches things and how she defines success. The best sequences manage to combine the personal within the showy set-pieces fans have come to expect.

Many people feel that movie theatres function as our modern day churches, because going to the movies is a catholic experience, in that it's universal. We congregate to feel that there's something bigger than we are, something more wonderful, something more awful...something *more*.

To deliver that tentative wonderment, you should never be completely in charge and assured of yourself as you formulate the story. Like a shaggy gnu goat, you need to keep checking your balance. *In fact, you should count on losing your footing at least once or twice.* As you're not the master of the story's universe, you should experience unexpected global shifts as the character embodies actions you didn't envision.

As you progress, you'll see your character's journey from different heights, looking down on the valley floor where she started and which initially formed the scope of her vision. As she ambles up hills and rocky trails, the perspective will incline to something inherently more heroic. The feeling akin to a delicious mix of vertigo and adrenaline. Much like the new *Oculus Rift VR* system is by turns disorienting and invigorating, you'll have the same alternating sense of anxiety and pleasure as you try to make sense of your new surroundings.

For you to truly shock anyone, don't you think you ought to blow your own mind along the way? Feel things out… Go down a path you didn't imagine could connect to your story in any way.

Take timid toeholds as you explore this new terrain and look around at the vantage point it offers.

Elizabeth, who's been playing around with the idea for an ethnic, primeval adventure/drama using *DYC* exercises, was surprised to learn just how rich and varied a life her priest character had before joining his seminary. His rough character and jaundiced worldview didn't make him seem like a resolute humanitarian in the making.

She has to figure out what else will give rise to the level of suppressed rage coursing underneath his acts of advocacy. She doesn't know where his fervid sense of righteousness comes from.

For anyone to sacrifice the comforts of life for religious seclusion usually implies a long-held devotion or a recent, soul-shattering tragedy. The deeper Elizabeth dug, the more she realized that it wasn't just the great loss he suffered, but a crushing numbness that started to overwhelm him.

She had thought this character would rise up to be the voice of reason, calming the chaos stirring in angry mobs. But, rather than a mediating force, he appears to want to be seen as a lightning rod, designed to attract attention, perhaps even misery; an instrument, rather than a shield, wielded in the coarse hands of a disadvantaged people. He's not someone who wants to deflect pain, but who wants to focus it. So, his activism is rooted in a preening vanity.

In the same vein of keeping yourself unsettled, we

recommend having an ongoing "conversation" in your head with your character, and your audience, as you write. This isn't so that your own voice is squelched. It's to gauge how much you're writing from the character's insular, personal perspective, while also making your story accessible.

In a sense, the *DYC* style of dating is about making choices that push you out of your comfort zone. We don't want you to write from a place of stodgy safety. Our ethos is all about practicing satisfying someone other than yourself, so you get used to being in someone else's headspace.

One way to push yourself is to refrain from identifying too closely with an audience you know very well…your friends and family. Often, the people who love you will have the most difficulty being truthful. They're part of your own personal fan club and they probably feel you can do no wrong. But for anyone's comments to be truly helpful to you, their feedback has to be honest.

You may not realize it, but meanness and unthinking flattery can be equally detrimental. Each approach in its own way has your reaction as the end goal rather than objectively trying to take the measure of the script. Neither serves to tell you how the script is really registering with your audience. This will only postpone the inevitable discovery of how your script will be received by most people.

THE CRITIC

While it's a challenge to imagine soliciting the opinion of a person who finds fault easily, if you look at any critic's motives, you'll probably conclude that he's not out to get you. "The Critic" genuinely wants to find himself involved in your story. But because of a series of let-downs, with films failing to deliver on initially interesting premises, he's hesitant to give you his full attention. You'll have to *earn* it. Coming up against that kind of attitude will dare you to produce your very best...

"The Critic" isn't someone to be afraid of or avoid. He's simply someone who doesn't just accept what's thrown at him. He's highly verbal, opinionated, and has a secure reliance on his own taste and judgment. Hopefully, he has reason to be, if his cultural knowledge is also grounded in some historical context. His outlook could be especially useful, if he has a rich literacy in both cinema and fiction.

So, to satisfy "The Critic" and the likely demographic for your movie, you're going to have to make yourself an expert in all aspects of the story: the protagonist, the antagonist, some of the supporting characters, dueling POVs, and the environment.

Dating Your Character

> **Note:** to your FUTURE self…
>
> When you're satisfied with the first draft of your script—after it's registered with the Writers Guild and Library of Congress—try and seek out "The Critic". His questions and insight can tell you if your story's missing some emotional beats.
>
>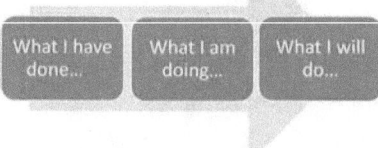

You're on your way, if you're good with what you've learned in this chapter:

- You've become acquainted with the various factors in establishing a scene's vibe.
- You've written a natural and free-flowing scene to develop a nose for what feels real and what feels forced.
- You've practiced scenarios that have allowed you to interact with your character, embracing her spontaneity, moods.
- You've gotten a sense of her normal routine—people she can be relaxed with, places where she hangs out.
- You've listened to her and are now privy to what preoccupies and motivates her.

- You've sussed out what she's willing to upend her life to achieve.

You are ready to jump into the next phase in developing the writer-character relationship:

STEP FOUR—SERIOUS DATING.

Dating Your Character

SERIOUS DATING "ACT I TURNING POINT"—
STEP FOUR

UP TO THIS juncture, we've been gauging your character's comfort level. *DYC* has been helping you accommodate her in trying to engineer a successful First Date. For those of you who have had a rewarding experience with your character, you can skip the following detour. Continue on to page 189. However, if your connection to your character is still a tad weak, here are some other versions of First Dates that'll help you create that spark.

Not everyone's the same. Not everyone wants to play it safe. Your character may crave newness and risk. After all, you could be dealing with someone who's spoiled or particularly demanding. Raise the bar to entice her.

For the speed demon or adrenaline junkie, arrange to do something that she hasn't done before but is up for...

- Hot air ballooning?
- Bobsledding?

- Target practice at a gun range?
- Bungee jumping inside Villarrica Volcano in Chile?

You can go anywhere in her story (or your imagination). Remind yourself that the way to her heart is through your creativity, passion, and curiosity about her. If, for instance, the activity doesn't lend itself to conversation, because you're screaming at each other in a wind tunnel, then plan to spend quality time on the long drive up or include a meal tagged on afterward.

With such an exacting partner, you'll need to have a mental list of *two* or *three key topics*. Not specific questions. You don't want her to find you pushy.

EXERCISE #45: ADVENTURE (REBOOT) DATE

If you can share curiosity about something she genuinely loves, you may hit one of her relationship sweet spots. Plus, she may relish the opportunity to correct you or enlighten you. Write your list of two or three key topics:

_____

_____

_____

Your Adventure (Reboot) Date will be comprised of three parts: initial contact, the activity, and the follow-up analysis of your chat…

For the <u>initial contact</u>, write *freely* for *five minutes*. Jot down everything that comes to you. What is the kind of approach she'd appreciate and respond to? Later, you can pick apart and study what seems most meaningful.

Exercise 45

EXERCISE #45:b: ADVENTURE (REBOOT) DATE

For the <u>activity</u>, plan the broad brushstrokes. Who will handle the registration, etc.? Are you part of a small group or are you alone?

How do you control the situation so she focuses on you?

Then write the scene as a *scene*. Use mostly dialogue with a brief description of your location. What do you wish you could say but don't? Remember, dialogue can take different shapes. Consider any awkward silences. Maybe, there will be speedy "shares" where you have moments of talking over each other. Did she seem to have an obvious agenda with you? Essentially, get comfortable with *her* rhythm and flow. No judgment, good or bad—just a heightened degree of awareness.

Exercise 45-b

EXERCISE #45-c: ADVENTURE (REBOOT) DATE

Now write about the <u>chat</u>. Tap into the moment; this is a *prose* exploration. What conclusions do you draw from her silences, her gestures, and her more vague responses?

You can use some of your natural editing instincts to monitor your gut; this isn't free association. If something irritates you or confuses you, that can be a red flag—a good red flag. Don't discard that information.

In the past, *DYC* has asked you to just let it rip. Here, though, we want you to pare down any random or tangential thoughts that inevitably crowd your mind during your improvisational scribbling.

This is an important intermediary step between free association and "real writing." You've practiced letting go, now it's time to exercise some control.

Exercise 45-c

If you need to step up your game for a spoiled, fashionista type, do something you know would appeal to her, but exceeds anything she's ever experienced. (You're living in your imagination, so your wallet is bottomless. You've got juice, too.) Fly her to Fashion Week in Paris, for instance. Or, to the Galapagos Islands, on an eco-tour, to help a vulnerable population of giant tortoises hatch. Something to shake up her world-weary ennui.

This is a great opportunity to stretch yourself to expand the scope of the world you and your character share…

> **EXERCISE #46: GLAMOUR DATE**
>
> Pick one of the below:
>
> - Close down a celebrity chef's restaurant for a private soiree for just the two of you.
> - Use your sports connections, or artistic or political mojo, to get a behind-the-scenes tour or some other kind of special access at a major event: the Olympics, the Oscars, a Presidential Inauguration.
> - Ask her to pick an envelope from *three* that you hold in your hand. Each with its own destination and activity…
>
> Write the scene.

Exercise 46

Living and creating without boundaries is a way of pushing yourself and your character to extremes. About the only constraint in the previous exercises would be the time period or the era of your story.

FILM EXAMPLE

While we're still in this detour mode, exploring how to shore up your First Date connectivity, we'll leave fantasyland behind and examine another of Russell Crowe's memorable roles. It'll be constructive to trace his character's arc in 1997's Academy Award-winning *L.A. Confidential*, a great hardboiled ode to film noir set in Hollywood in 1953.

In order for you to craft meaningful challenges for your protagonist, you'll need to familiarize yourself with what motivates her and how this motivation develops—and even changes—over the course of the story. Let's sketch out how character Bud White's intention wavers as he encounters more and more obstacles.

Bud White is a bulldog of a cop. The kind of guy who punches first thinks second. He's respected within the LAPD and for some reason has the ear of the Chief of Police. When a local cop hangout is shot up, Bud begins to doubt the party line that explains away the multiple homicides. Bud's going to have to doubt his own racist explanation for the murders in order to pursue the truth. He also has to overcome his jealousy of a new, college-educated detective Lt. Exley (Guy Pearce), whose kiss-ass attitude and political savvy riles him. Eventually, he has to partner with Exley, despite his disgust with this young hotshot.

The deeper Bud digs, he has to question the loyalty with which he's always served his LAPD masters. When he realizes he's become unwittingly involved in a department-wide cover-up, he has to accept the fact that he's essentially a hired thug with a badge. He'd always taken it for granted that, though he got his hands bloody, it was for a good cause.

After the conspiracy kills one of Bud's closest friends on the force (Kevin Spacey), he cuts himself off from most of his cop ties and tries to make amends. He does all this—bucking the department brass, risking his career, and, putting his life in danger—to flush out the crime syndicate that controls his department.

He has to resist the temptation to beat information out of suspects to play the long game. He has to actually become more contemplative and consider the political dimensions of the murders.

As we experience his core values modulating over time, we identify with him even more and emotionally invest in him. He could choose to leverage his gains into a more comfortable career up the law enforcement ladder, but is uncompromising about what he knows is right—the reason he became a cop in the first place.

On some level, your wants and desires will be shaping your character's. In the last exercise of the previous chapter, we questioned what's important to *you*, because it'd be foolhardy to disregard your own feelings. If you're sensitive to this subliminal influence, you won't be waylaid by nagging doubts that you've artificially engineered any elements.

Actors acknowledge what they bring to their work, tapping into themselves as a way to enrich their characters. Meryl Streep says, "Acting is not about being someone different. It's finding the similarity in what is apparently different, then finding myself in there."[3]

Understanding the unique fusion between artist and character—especially what makes you and your character tick—adds texture to any genre of story. Even a blow 'em up action picture benefits from the emotional logic embedded in its explosions.

Regardless of genre, scripts are judged based on several elements that encompass plot and character. It would be savvy to become conversant in the lingo and expectations of standard script coverage. Though the elite agencies and studios in town hire script readers in the Story Analyst Guild, at smaller companies, script coverage is an assignment usually given to interns. (They also write two-page summaries, so that, at a glance, agents, managers, or producers can cite basic facts and pretend they've read it.) Whoever reads it, exec or intern, the pages containing the analysis are most often referred to as "**coverage**."

Coverage: The ten fundamentals on which scripts are graded:

- **Action**—the use of stunts in extended chase or fight sequences for big-budget set pieces to showcase **SPFX** (within studio movies or international co-productions); the ability to captivate readers with epic, emblematic visuals tied to the character's objective.

- **Character Development**—the progression of a character's problem or goal, implied by the amount of internal and external change that the protagonist undergoes in order to achieve it.

- **Dialogue**—the effective rendering of naturalistic, incisive discussions that steep the audience in the world of the character; features successful uses of subtext and gradual reveals to make sense of characters' hidden motivations.

- **Marketability**—the wideness of appeal, i.e., anticipated audience interest, for the script's genre and premise.

- **Pacing**—the tension, rhythm, momentum, and clip at which the story moves, evolves, and shape-shifts.
- **Plot**—the shape of the story; its twists and turns that take the reader by surprise, but deliver on set-ups and pay-offs with ever increasing investment in the outcome; the adherence to genre and ability to deliver upon its inherent expectations.
- **Theme**—the philosophical message or POV that the character epitomizes, which is in conflict with the status quo of the world of the story.
- **Tone**—the consistent, stylistic rendering of narrative voice and character insight, regardless of plot deviation.
- **Uniqueness**—a commodity prized not for its quantity, but for its choice moments of flavoring in an otherwise familiar story environment and plot point sequence. (Think of a tub of plain vanilla ice cream perked up by a swirling band of caramel or raspberry jam.)
- **Viability of Star Attachment**—the likelihood that an A-list star would want to sign on to your script, giving the project more credibility.

In order to craft a story engine that hums, you'll have to test drive it to make sure every piston is firing. You'll need to have your course down from every angle to know its sharp curves and switchbacks. You'll have to anticipate every question that can be asked of you by your development team—the producers, actors, director—and have ready, well-thought-out answers. That's why you've got to run through all the plot's possibilities, sure of why you made specific choices and not others. For you to really "own" your script to this degree, you have to have faith in your character so she has authority over the direction of the story.

At this stage of our *DYC* system, to help you deliver on that vital, in-depth character knowledge, you've begun to develop an "emotional intimacy" that's becoming almost palpable. On the way to your **First Act Turning Point***, you've kept the questions coming to engage her and understand the kind of thing she would do in a certain situation.

---

*Note: In standard screenwriting structure, the **First Act Turning Point** is a further development of the quandary introduced in the Inciting Incident. It's when the protagonist decides to risk it and attack her main problem head on. Sometimes, in such a surprising fashion that it makes it seem like you're almost in a different story.

In *DYC,* this **Serious Dating Phase** locks the link between your character and her plot. The trajectory she'll cast is starting to take form; you have a sense of your character's goal, her "need" underneath, and a sense that something daring has to happen now that will fuel the rest of the story.

She wants something and realizes there may be sacrifices along the way. During it all you are HERE to HEAR what she has to say. She's shared some of her goals and/or secrets. You've taken steps with her into her past—hearing about events that shaped her and how those might be similar or dissimilar from your own. Collecting details from her past helped you gain awareness. You've noted her expectations for the present. But your character is very much meeting you in the ever-present now. Her job is just to show up. And, by the way, that's yours, too.

The ultimate goal is to create an ongoing and unbreakable bond with your character as you write. You'll have more confidence regarding the deeper well of ideas motivating her. This bond will help you combat boredom, smash writer's block, and confront clichés that crop up.

Just like in any relationship, there's work involved and a time investment. You've decided to let her store a few items at your place, because it's just easier that way. After all, there may be some late-night or early-morning talks. You may even give her a spare key, but that may not be such a wise arrangement.

Dating Your Character

> **EXERCISE #47: MAKING SPACE FOR HER "SHIT"**
>
> - If she will get a key, who initiated that?
> - If she introduced the idea, were you able to deftly decline, if you didn't feel comfortable giving her that much freedom?
> - What did she bring with her?
> - Were there any things that surprised you?

Exercise 47

> **EXERCISE #47-b: MAKING SPACE FOR HER "SHIT"**
>
> Now render those surprising items in even more detail.
> - What is something you can tentatively draw from looking at the items she chooses to bring?
>
> **_DYC_ Example:**
> She schlepped her journal, a stuffed animal, frozen chocolate chip cookie batter, and her *Field Guide to Birds of the Desert Southwest*.

> But not just any "stuffed animal." A dirty, ragged Snoopy with a tag still hanging that says it was from the Orange County Fair. Given its age and condition, this isn't something a former boyfriend won for her; this is an ancient Snoopy from her childhood. Maybe something she won with the quarter her father gave her to play skee-ball. Clearly a sentimental choice, but maybe she's uncomfortable having Snoopy visible at her place. At yours, he's just comfortably tucked in a drawer, in case of an emotional emergency.
>
> Her bringing her journal is puzzling. A journal is usually a private, ongoing conversation with yourself. Some of the questions that surfaced for us are: Does she want to tease us into taking a peek? Is she so trusting that she'd never believe we'd succumb to that temptation?
>
> Does she think she's hidden it so well in her little drawer that we aren't even aware it's there among her other things?

Exercise 47-b

However odd to you, these items make her think of home or reinforce her courage for the adventure she's about to take with you. Some of them may be quite necessary, like pills. But what's familiar to her may be completely unfamiliar to you. She could be from another country or planet.

Think about the genre in which you and your character are co-creating. Did she play into it? Was there something funny (*comedy*); was there something scary (*horror*); was there something romantic and funny (*rom-com*); was it full of innuendo and dripping with depth (*drama*)? If not, then include one item that seems to speak to your genre but also fits with what you know of your character so far.

> **EXERCISE #48: GENRE-SPECIFIC HIDDEN CLUES**
>
> Add an item that she brings, or perhaps reshape or refashion one of those previous possessions, so that it reflects your story's genre. Besides being a clue into her personality, can this item serve a function in the plot?

Exercise 48

Be mindful of how the objects your character chooses to plant in your pad can be used as your story progresses to clarify her character and help us notice her changes. Most professionals realize that the subconscious handling of objects can be utilized as a mirror for the state of mind of a character. The skateboard in *Back to the Future* runs through all three movies in the franchise. It's a vehicle for Marty McFly (Michael J. Fox) to sail through life without really being responsible. While occasionally getting him into trouble, it allows him to be clever and solve story problems.

Sometimes these objects are part of larger activities that serve to move the story forward. One might even be a **"MacGuffin,"** something that seems loaded with meaning and importance, propelling characters into action, but is an artificial reason to change the direction of the plot. In director John Huston's classic *The Maltese Falcon* starring Humphrey Bogart, based on the Dashiell Hammett novel, the plot centers on a golden, bejeweled falcon that has been disguised in a layer of black paint.

Usually, whatever arbitrary significance is invested in the token is never questioned in the course of the screenplay or is developed further. It's the accepted raison d'être for all the characters in its orbit. Once in a while, this prized object merits the attention of the characters on its trail and becomes more than a found object, but generally its function is revealed at the end without much fanfare. It rarely has a revelatory power of its own but purely is a mechanism for the story to get going.

Dating Your Character

In Devorah's script *Santa Fe 7*, the teen mystery thriller mentioned in Chapter Three, when the main character Karisma discovers a box of personal effects belonging to a murder victim who had an aura of invincibility, it leads her on a path of discovery that uncovers the true nature of those totemic objects.

As you think about the seriousness of her moving some of her "shit" into your place, you're literally co-mingling your realities. You're becoming more of her story, and she's becoming more of your story. The narrative's not just emerging from your head; it exists in a limbo where you're *there* together. She's wet clay and has an essence, an emotional core, and life…

Together you are forcing her hand to help you craft her story, inspired by your understanding of the details and what they mean to her. Undoubtedly you will surprise each other, but only if you're willing to surrender what you think you know about your character—for what she can become. Can you let go enough?

Borrowing from our actor and director bag of tricks, there is an exercise known as a "Trust Walk." Actors blindfold one of the cast or one of the students in the class, and that person is guided through a space. It grounds the actor's or character's awareness in space, location, and sensation. You can practice this with another writer or a friend to discover how surprisingly powerful it can be. Make sure you are in a relatively safe location and that your partner stays close to protect you from falling over or bumping into walls.

EXERCISE #49: TRUST WALK

For *DYC*, we will do this in an imaginary space. Let's pretend this is the first time you're going to get to "see" her apartment. You'll have to touch things to learn what they are. Reach out and imagine your way through the realm of touch, the textures you might feel. Sometimes it's important to go to a new environment and isolate a sense if you want to go deeper and make a visceral connection.

Exercise 49

Dating Your Character

> ### EXERCISE #49-b: TRUST WALK
>
> - Now open your eyes.
> - Is her pad messy or neat?
> - Did the objects you touched accurately represent her overall aesthetic?
> - Where would you say she spends most of her time when she's home? *How can you tell?*

Exercise 49-b

Her place has probably conveyed a couple of things to you. But even if your desire for more closeness is shared, it also involves careful consideration about the best approach to take.

How would she wish to form a meaningful romantic relationship with another character in her world? Loosely inspired by the popular non-fiction book *The Five Love Languages*, by Gary Chapman, let's look at how your character expresses and receives love.

> **EXERCISE #50: DYC LOVE LANGUAGE QUIZ**
>
> Ask *her* to fill out this easy questionnaire on a scale of one to ten. One (1) being "hardly at all," ten (10) being "that's me completely:"
>
> 1. Hearing words of affirmation make me feel more loving. _____
> 2. Seeing you sacrifice for me, or others, loosens my heartstrings. _____
> 3. Receiving thoughtful gifts is the primary way into my heart. _____
> 4. Spending quality time will create those moments of sincerity that I need to bond. _____
> 5. Being touched physically, or imagining that, reminds me of my desire to get close to you. _____

Exercise 50

As you probably gathered, a person or character's love language is a clue to how she likes to give and receive love. But, don't mistake any of her answers from above with an indication of her "values." When she's being honest, these are just the chords that, when struck, will most likely fashion the right kind of melody.

FILM EXAMPLE

In the classic 80's film *Romancing the Stone*, a reclusive writer falls in love with a swashbuckling, self-absorbed, amateur treasure hunter. After finding out her sister has been kidnapped, prissy Joan Wilder (Kathleen Turner) finds herself in the jungle. She's forced to depend on sometime, exotic-bird smuggler Jack Colton (Michael Douglas). She has no one else to help her and initially resists him. He claims he can't stand having to be her personal protector.

Simple guy that Jack is, what ignites his interest comes down to continual physical proximity to her—and maybe the promise of solving the riddles in the treasure map he learns she possesses. When all the ramifications of her predicament dawn on Joan, she loses some of her feminine armor: she breaks a heel and her neat chignon becomes a mud-spattered, bird's nest. The first moment where he actually starts to "enjoy" her company is after they both slip and slide down a muddy bank. He lands face first into her lap, cracks a devilish smile, tickled by her shattered sense of propriety.

We expect Joan to prefer the kind of man's man she gushes over in her romance fiction. And Jack's vision of her as a sexless, uptight tourist changes when she lets go enough to revel in the wacky adventure she's been forced to embark on. He responds to her "wilder," rough-and-tumble side.

But in the end, it's not Jack's daring feats that win her over. She gives him her heart when she believes he's finally acting in her kidnapped sister's best interest and not his own. He could never write her a love letter or whisper sweet-nothings, even though her idea of romance has been shaped by this kind of chivalric etiquette.

Why is it important to tie personal desire to plot? Understanding the "love language" of two very different characters is a way to see how they can authentically come together in a way that appeals to both of them... *And* it's also a place to look for conflict when love languages don't line up!

You're trying out new moves, trying to make sure your message of interest and growing attachment is received in the best way possible. Your character may be taking some real risks and sharing her feelings with you. Hopefully, she's also starting to make connections with other characters in the story that will help her get some traction toward her goal.

As we go forward, it's helpful for you to write down not only what you know about her, but to be absolutely clear about the problem she is trying to solve. Her problem will be the fulcrum of your story—and your relationship. The First Act Turning Point traditionally is a time where the story and the character make some major shift.

You care about her and the outcome of her goal. And because of that, you're going to be throwing obstacles her way...to force her to deal with the very things she's afraid of. Together you'll help her get stronger and brainstorm solutions so she gets where she needs to go.

Just like a physical trainer helping an athlete, you're working with her to develop the emotional, spiritual, physical, and maybe even mental prowess she'll need. The First Act Turning Point is when she'll make the decision to radically change the course of her life. But she won't have to immediately trash behavior that's seen as weak: she can make more acceptable, moderate shifts. In fact, it would probably be impossible for her to race to the finish line; otherwise she would have had an *aha* moment earlier and done so already.

As you collect your thoughts about your evolving story, you'll see that, in this earlier part of your script's development, your character's working with what she has. And like an arrow that has a direction but hasn't found its mark, she's on a trajectory, taking small steps on the road to that final, grand gesture where she throws her cares to the wind and gambles for a better future.

EXERCISE #51: PRESSURE POINT

Devise a scenario where *one* of your character's *weaknesses* will likely ruin any chance of her accomplishing her goal. If slight modifications are made, can your character be successful, while still not completely overcoming that penchant or behavior?

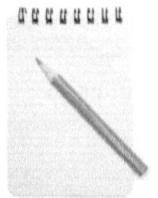

Exercise 51

FILM EXAMPLE

Take the example of the lead character in *Erin Brockovich* (Julia Roberts). She needs credibility in the legal field that she works in, but her personal fashion sense is expressed in low-cut tops and tight skirts. This wardrobe is incongruous for her workplace and undermines her initially, until she's able to use her flashy style and sass to win over wary potential claimants.

She's certainly proud of the way she looks, even if her sexiness is over-the-top. But underneath is an anger coursing through her stubborn resolve. In a perverse twist of the American dream, she's a woman who is convinced she can have it all. She's a fierce single mother, doing what she can to raise her children and be a role model for them. Balancing job, her man, and family, all on a blue-collar salary. She doesn't want to compartmentalize her life. She's very upfront with guys, letting her handsome neighbor George in on all her important deets and digits: her finances, how many divorces she's been through, the number of kids she has.

This is a woman with issues. Erin merely needs the proper channel for her tenacity and anger to achieve the kind of financial stability, peer respect, and sense of accomplishment that she believes she's always deserved. She feels life has done her wrong and that she's capable of so much more, if given the chance. That self-righteous bitterness means she's constantly two steps away from a flare-up.

Erin has a shorter fuse than most characters. Others, when they're riled, may not even choose anger as their go-to emotional explosion, until much later in the script. Erin doesn't flinch or make any accommodations when the pressures mount. She continues to do as she likes, prancing around in clothing that makes her feel good about herself, asserting herself when the high-powered firm that takes over the claimants' case tries to brush her aside. She's so on-the-ball and driven, fighting the good fight, that she manages to have a major impact on the utility industry. She has to reckon with demons and reversals, but on every level—from her superficial idiosyncrasies to her core—she remains as feisty, committed to her cause, and strong as she ever was.

While this was an Academy-nominated script, the only criticism that comes up is about screenwriter Susannah Grant's daring choice to center a rather episodic screenplay on this character—*something* happens, *the next something* happens, but not always as a direct result of Erin. Though, since the script was based on an actual person, it's hard to quibble when documenting a real example of heroism in the face of heavy odds.

Within the difficult moments that stack up and besiege your character, there will be one big "trigger" that catapults her into a new direction. This trigger is something that offers your character a choice, where she can decide to go on much as she has, regardless of the consequences, or accept that there must be a different way. For the writer, the opportunity for creativity isn't in presenting options to her, but in starting to expose the hidden problems that are the reasons for her past failures. Being aware of what can rock your character's inner equilibrium is key to co-creating the situations that will test her.

Like people, characters can have myriad flaws that hold them back. But you can get more dramatic mileage from a flaw that has really deep, personal roots. If your character is unable to confront her behavior, anything that exacerbates this particular vulnerability can be a clue to her past; how she dealt with being embarrassed, disappointed, or hurt, probably formed a familiar rut or scar over this "trauma."

Dating Your Character

The character could have had one particularly painful standalone episode. Or, a series of similar incidents that damaged and could have even "broken" her. Before we get ahead of ourselves, one of the many examples of psychological or traumatic underpinnings that inform characters, let's stay with your character a bit longer.

> **EXERCISE #52: EMOTIONAL TNT**
>
> Think about the most important disappointments your character could have suffered.
>
> Who else was present in these situations?
>
> Was the same key person involved?
>
> Did these scenarios fall into some basic type of situation?
>
> - A physical challenge?
> - A moment where all eyes were on her?
> - A choice to stay true to herself or go with the herd?

Exercise 52

If there is a "type" of scenario in her back-story, then consider framing her future challenges in the same way. Inevitably, it's satisfying for a reader or audience to anticipate how such a repetitive motif will play out. Besides, you already know this is vulnerable territory for her. No other kind of situation seems to encapsulate the factors that make her go weak in the knees. Even if you have to revisit your ideas for your plot, look to see how you can incorporate some of the elements of her personal "kryptonite" to heighten her unease. You want to dare your character to fail.

This is her chance to transcend her past mistakes, not skirt around them!

Make sure that each subsequent challenge is magnified in dramatic stakes. If your audience has seen a similar set-up, you'll create anticipation for future revisitations. They'll try to guess how the conflicts can be amped up, how the scenes will play out. For an audience, trials of this kind will be more meaningful having been experienced previously from different angles.

If you've found that your character has had setbacks that don't fit one mold, consider if there's an emotional link, the same fearful thought, or perhaps an outside force that contributed heavily to her poor outcomes. What we're looking for, but not imposing, is a pattern.

In dramatic structure, there is a natural pleasant sense of satiety in a sequence of "threes." This is a golden rule in sitcoms: for jokes that may need to fall three on a page, or on the microcosm level of a joke, the rhythm is a list of three, the third being the surprise or payoff. Also, within the macro structure of a show, you'll often have a development of a one-liner or sight gag by continuing it in three spots throughout the episode.

Most people like to feel that there's some "story wisdom" embedded in what they're watching. Not that there's necessarily a moral judgment, though there probably is to a varying degree in the overall theme or character's POV. But people are hardwired to prefer stories that have some kind of filter sorting the messiness of life. So there are meaningful bits of experience we can learn from, emulate, and be inspired by.

FILM EXAMPLE

Sometimes you'll expose those roots to the audience, other times they'll only see the effect on the current life of the character. In the film *Blue Jasmine*, by Woody Allen, a wealthy socialite through marriage (Cate Blanchett) takes a big fall from grace when her husband is arrested for a white-collar crime. We do not witness the origin of her ensuing bizarre conduct. We only know the current trigger—her loss of social status and income. Her fragmented stream of constant commentary, her lack of interest in rebuilding a relationship with her sister, her tendency toward solitude, her secretiveness, and her later unconsciousness about her disheveled appearance could be termed schizoid behavior.[4]

She's always had a habit of looking away from the ugly details of life, but now her whole life *is* ugly—there's no refuge in a beautiful estate and she has zero finances to support her former lifestyle. Before the couple's downfall, she had only a shaky hold on the workings of the rarefied world she'd married into. These days, she's completely lost any tenuous association she had to the real world. All she can do is zone out, having "conversations" with people—monologues, essentially, eavesdropped on by bystanders unwillingly brought into her orbit. Even her memories take on a haunting disconnection. She revises scenes in her head, editing out any unpleasantness.

While your character's downward spiral doesn't have to be that severe, any kind of self-defeating or irrational practice could lead to an understanding of her inner frailty.

Every human, fictional or real, has had some sort of trauma in their past. But how does that shock play out in the story? How does it hold her back or propel her forward? In our opinion, the "soul juice" stemming from a character's "wound" is the push-pull of all great scripts—and each memorable character. Its very existence will continue to make her uncomfortable, even in relatively benign situations.

The "wound" is that subterranean time bomb that, with the right pressure—over the timetable of your story—will cause your character to implode. It'll take some time to truly know what lies beneath all her behavioral machinations—to put your hand on her pulse and know what makes her tick.

TRAUMA > WOUND > GOAL > BEHAVIOR

On the next page is our "*DYC* Character Liability Claim Check," which is a general visual tool designed to help you identify your character's wound. It's a contract that was inspired by a parking lot claim check.

CHARACTER LIABILITY CLAIM CHECK

0357911

This contract is between writer and character and limits writer's liability - READ IT:

Writer assumes no liability for everything designed for the above Character and Character assumes all liability for previous damage incurred by Character; provided, however, Writer acknowledges that specific pre-story damages (aka back-story wounds, family legacies, DNA, etc.) can and will inform Character's trip throughout the story (and any sequels, if relevant).

Failure of Character to advise Writer of all previous damage associated with and to their title prior to commencement of screenplay, novel, book, teleplay, etc., will result in further Character exploration during the writing process. Additionally, if Character does not pony up to its total flaw(s), foibles, or idiosyncrasies before completion of screenplay, then and only then, can Writer make claim that they must choose a different character trait or flaw before taking screenplay to market. Also, Writer reserves the right to modify, amend, deepen or even drastically change damages if said damages do not serve the story and vise versa in the development of a memorable and authentic character, or are in some way deemed to impede script's marketability.

Possession of this Claim Check conclusively constitutes evidence of taking ownership of Character as of _____ date. _____ Your initials. _____ Spit.

Copyright 2011 - Jen & Carla-Rubenstein. The Ra pl Sakes® Educational Technologies a division of Active Interventions, Inc. 8250 Brookes Ave - 204, LA, CA 90048 www.thescriptworks.com

DAMAGE

AGE
1-5
6-10
10-20
20-30
30-40
40+

"X" INDICATES EXISTING DAMAGE

EXERCISE #53: CHARACTER LIABILITY CLAIM CHECK

Read the contract part. After you've studied it, sign it and date it. On the other side of the chart are a car and a human figure.

- Where does your character sit in the car during this part of the writing process?
- Is your character in the driver's seat? The passenger seat? In the back?

The age-range numbers on the right are to help you figure out what year the character suffered her most significant wound.

- Put an "x" by the range of numbers when this occurred.
- Put an "x" on the parts of the body where any physical injury was suffered.
- If the character witnessed or heard any violence, circle the eyes or ears.

Speculate on what might have happened to her…

Exercise 53

This exercise can generate metaphors as you write your action and narrative prose, too. If a character almost drowned at the hands of a sibling, for instance, then water metaphors might be used throughout the script. In Ang Lee's *The Ice Storm*, the weather reflects the sexual repression and denial of the upper-class 1970s Connecticut community.

Hopefully, at this point, your character's the driver (an active protagonist) and not a passenger. (If your character can't or won't drive, you can review the chart metaphorically so that it respects the logic of your character.) If she's still a passenger, she'll have to find a way where she's more active in advancing her story. If your character isn't prepared to lead the charge, then you've got to at least stick her on the front lines!

> **EXERCISE #54: ACTIVATE YOUR PROTAGONIST...**
>
> Pluck out *three actions* from your outline or script. If she's pushed to take this action, rework it so that it's *her* idea: she's the one rallying the troops, or she's the one volunteering for dangerous duty.

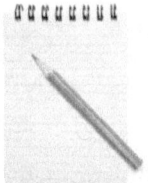

Exercise 54

> ### EXERCISE #54-b: ACTIVATE YOUR PROTAGONIST…
>
> Now come up with *three* additional *actions* that seem "too big" for her to take on.
>
> - How do you downsize them slightly so she might give them a stab?
> - What has to happen to compel her to go outside her comfort zone?
> - Who does she need by her side?
> - Does this outreach for help activate a relationship development?

Exercise 54-b

Some of you may not have it in you to "hurt" your character or to imagine her going through a hurtful situation. So, for those of you kind-hearted souls, we're going to school you in "bringing da pain." Putting your character through her mental, emotional, and physical paces is going to be necessary to keep your audience invested. The more she believably stretches to reach her goal, the more the audience will be with her.

When you think about how to define your character's trauma,

you can start by doing some reverse engineering that looks at the echoes created in her everyday behavior. This unresolved pain has continued to compromise her future opportunities, whether she's realized it or not. This is a way of seeing what she was like prior to this horrible experience (or series of experiences) and how she coped, if at all. It will be the tether to her life before the main action of the story occurs.

EXERCISE #55: HOW BAD IS…<u>BAD</u>?

Which of the following humiliations can be considered so traumatic, causing such long-lasting reverberations, that they are arguably the flash point for all a hypothetical character's future dysfunctional behavior?

1. Failing an algebra final…?
2. Attempting an axel and falling down on the ice in front of the guy she's crushing on…?
3. Lying to her mother about why she's sneaking in late, hiding the fact that she's just come back from a trip to a Planned Parenthood clinic three states away…?
4. Jeopardizing her legal career by smuggling contraband to an incarcerated client…?
5. Cheating on her boyfriend with the cute bartender around the corner, who shares the camera pics at work to prove it…?

> 6. Stealing a couple of frozen *Lean Cuisines*, stuffing them down her sweatshirt, escaping from the security guard who sees her do it, then having them crash onto the asphalt as she runs across the street…?
> 7. Seeing her sister abused by her boyfriend…?

Exercise 55

Snippets of extreme emotional or physical violence, however brief, are naturally at the root of most traumatic origins. But the more complicated and specific-laden the scenario, the more your character is likely to find the pain lingering. Looking like a klutz, after trying to impress, is bound to sting for a couple of days. If the severity of the bruise from the fall spans across her thigh and continues to ripen into a purplish blue, there's a greater probability that she'll mull over this relatively minor mishap.

ANSWER KEY: 1. No, 2. No, 3. Yes, 4. No, Need more info about fallout, 5. Possibly, 6. Yes, 7. Yes

On top of that, if this accident causes her to miss out on a ballet performance, because her tights can't disguise the ugliness of the bruise, then the loss she may feel will go beyond the initial hit to her pride. Focus on the different levels of her suffering and how long the after effects persist. If you feel that moment truly has tragic ramifications, then follow the trail of tears.

> **EXERCISE #56: COURT REPORTER**
> If your character will only admit to bland examples of past misfortune, consider telling her how *you* imagine a certain scene went down: Every excruciating detail, from her high hopes at the outset, to the horrified gazes of the other people who witnessed her bungling or injury.

Exercise 56

Chances are she'll sheepishly admit that she didn't tell you the whole story and the reason that this singular episode stuck with her. But, cocooning herself from this particular kind of pain is now intrinsic to who she is. She thinks she's protecting herself, but she's really cutting herself off from life.

Dating Your Character

A flaw is something that narrows the protagonist's vision, so that she's not even aware of a more successful action that she could take. This flaw takes up more time and space than an immediate cause and effect. It's a miscalculation that, for some reason, gets repeated over and over 'til it's no longer just a routine error. But it also closes her off to other experiences, POVs, and the ability to embrace her potential.

We'll talk about the depth of the forces behind your character's wound a bit more in Chapter 6, and how these play out over Act I and II, leading to your Midpoint.

As you launch into the Second Act, you're at the bottom of the big climb, knowing her goal may or may not be met. You're beginning to share the same physical field with her, perhaps hearing her voice. You're creating a relational attachment which is the ultimate and necessary ingredient to lead you to the truthful choices that your character would make.

But what is she leaving behind in order to pursue this dream with you? What sacrifices will she offer—or does she intend to endure—to get where she claims she wants to go?

Say your character is on an adventure that will require tunneling through volcanic rock to unearth an entombed treasure.

- Does it mean asking for a few unpaid weeks off from work?
- How will she raise the funds to launch her effort?

- Does she first need to dig up the map itself?
- Will she need to get it translated?

> **EXERCISE #57: THE PRICE OF ADMISSION**
>
> Write down *one challenge* that your character views as positive. Something she thinks she'll enjoy doing, rather than something that's frightening.
>
> Now think about how she could be disappointed by the challenge. Is it the expected sensation of being triumphant that she doesn't get to experience? Is she first put through the wringer, though ultimately successful?

Exercise 57

EXERCISE #57-b: THE PRICE OF ADMISSION

What does your character realize she has to part with to go past this hurdle?

- Does she understand that she'll have to make this sacrifice at the outset?
- Is it in the middle of the scenario that she comes up with a compromise to eke her way through?
- Is she waylaid at the end, having believed she got through things smoothly enough, only to realize that was never what this scene was about? That she was really being played by the antagonist or an affiliate character?

Exercise 57-b

EXERCISE #57-c: THE PRICE OF ADMISSION

What can't she grab, as she jumps into the air? What are the tips of her fingers only just grazing? What happens if she does have to lose something or make a trade-off, but still falls short and doesn't get what she wants? As it relates to this particular challenge, be as specific as you can.

Exercise 57-c

DYC Example:

In the previous section, the character wanted to go on a treasure hunt. She needs to solve a special cipher to decode the map, which is located in a remote place—undersea...

In order to raise funds for the trip, she applies for a university grant, but realizes her thesis advisor, who has grown to hate her, is on the board. When she approaches a wealthy alum at a university gala and manages to make a pitch for her archeological survey, is she later bitterly disappointed when she realizes he's having a secret affair with her thesis advisor?

When she finally gets together the cash to go on her deep-sea diving expedition, does the underwater sonar not pinpoint the exact location of the cipher? Does she have to rely on her instincts to explore a twenty-five square foot underwater cave miles away? As she plumbs a crevasse, does she get scratched by a coral reef? Does that scratch get infected?

After all this...does she *still* not translate the hidden language of the map?

When the beam of her flashlight hits the titanium cylinder holding the cipher, is the paper it's on too corroded to be legible?

In some ways, you know a tad more about the story than she does. Ultimately, you have the vague map of the journey she needs to take. She may inform you about the who, what, when, where, and how, but in terms of the arc, you have a bit more perspective. If she knew how hard it was going to be—it's possible she would never take the journey.

If she's too wimpy or weak to confront her boss for a promotion, you know she'll soon need to develop those confrontation muscles. You'll have to push your character into places she's resisting. You may even have to offer words of support to reassure her.

With the following exercise, try to isolate the fears that are holding her back. First, she may provide you with numbingly feeble answers, so "DDD" to expose the raw nerve that's encased in them.

EXERCISE #58: AFRAID, ME... REALLY?

Set a timer for *five minutes* and write spontaneously, using the following prompt from your character's point of view:

"I'm a little afraid I'll _____ if I pursue my dream/goal/desire of: _____."

Exercise 58

> **EXERCISE #58-b: AFRAID, ME...REALLY?**
> If the unthinkable was to happen, what would that be?
> - Being fired?
> - Being dumped?
> - Being killed?
>
> How can she try to operate proactively, while balancing the precautions she has to take to avoid one of these results?

Exercise 58-b

Characters are meant to be round, full-bodied, red-blooded humans (usually). No character, no matter how hardy and brave, can possibly face setback after setback and not want to check out for a while. So, you've got to be aware of how far you can push your character. After a big reveal, or arduous stretch of action, she'll need some time and space to mend. You might want to back off and let her relax, before throwing her out into the world again.

If you also allow *yourself* a day or two away from your work, you may return to it with vigor and a new flow of ideas. When doing this intensive character study, it's got to have the organic heartbeat of a real unfolding relationship. If you push too hard, you'll exhaust your own imagination and her goodwill.

In your progress so far, you've identified some of your character's weaknesses and have been assiduously exploring and exploiting them. These flaws may seem to stack the odds against her eventually conquering her goals. And over time, they're bound to annoy you…and the rest of her community. But it's best to be careful about labeling eccentric behavior, though problematic, as a "flaw." Your character's bound to have quirks that are just…odd. Some may even be mildly distasteful. They may have developed in response to other people in her environment. Are these traits or tendencies part of who she is innately or do they reflect her current condition? (She's preggers and crazy for peanut butter and pickles?)

EXERCISE #59: COMPATIBLE NEUROSES

- Have these off-the-wall drives impacted her negatively?
- If she's aware that she puts people off when she does certain things, then why does she continue?
- If it's not helping her get what she wants, is it a ripple from the past crippling her future chance of success? (Assuming it's less out of a desire to be contrarian than an expression of a true preference.)

Exercise 59

EXERCISE #59-b: COMPATIBLE NEUROSES
Take a look at the more questionable actions she's taken and come up with a rationale that can at least partially excuse them.

Exercise 59b

EXERCISE #59-c: COMPATIBLE NEUROSES
Now make a list of your own odd or less sociably acceptable behavior.

Exercise 59-c

> **EXERCISE #59-d: COMPATIBLE NEUROSES**
> Take a look at both of the lists.
> - Is there a connection or any overlap?
> - Do you find something compelling that is the very opposite from what you would do?
> - Is it something you even intensely dislike, but pulls you toward her like a tractor-beam?

Exercise 59-d

This dynamic of opposites creates a kind of duality—or an engine between you and your character. Now that you've identified her most "strangely" compelling trait, write it down on a piece of paper at the top. Fold the paper in half, then in half again, until that trait is hidden. Get the folded paper as small as you can. Then put it away for a day for two. Perhaps put it in your wallet; but wherever you put it, consider it "baking" in your imagination.

We may never see this potentially embarrassing trait in your script. But you knowing about it should give you the comfort to see her as an imperfect, unique creature, capable of the little surprises and inconsistencies that make us all too human.

Independent films, in particular, thrive on characters' foibles that are usually overlooked. They're postage-stamp portraits whose very small scale allows for a more intimate and natural voyeurism than most mainstream films offer. Because this type of film doesn't rely on escapism to sell tickets, their characters have to be so much more nuanced, relatable, and indelible.

FILM EXAMPLE

Films made outside the United States domestic market also lean on carefully rendered characters. While most of you may not know the Academy Award-winning Japanese film *Departures*, it's a delightful study of a sensitive, suddenly-unemployed cellist who takes another job to please his wife. But there is a stigma associated with the other job that he can't tell her. He's helping families cope as a sort of funeral parlor "therapist." His passionate dedication surprises him, confounding his wife and the community when they find out.

It's important that you know about your character in her more private moments. She may profess grand desires, but when she's alone with her thoughts, what does she really *need*? In her darkest hour, she's going to call on this singular hunger as a reserve of strength.

At this juncture in the story, however, what's her emotional state? Ask yourself what can happen in your proposed scenes to get us closer to her boiling point? What can you do to set up tension and conflict between her true inner needs and her socially-approved outward desires?

Creating conflict and the opportunity for dramatics isn't enough. Your audience has to understand, even feel, as the character does, all along the curves of the story, so when she finally has enough, so do they. Her breakdown into rage, or some other extreme emotion, has to be recognized as stemming from some known place. It can't come from nowhere. It's got to erupt from an established pressure point.

But most characters don't walk around cataloging all the annoyances or enervating slights they want to avenge. They fume or perseverate, trying to take in stride whatever befalls them…until they *don't*. Until they make a break with their past apologetic waffling or seeming indifference.

So, how do you quickly get us in their head space so that we're prepared for the new agenda that the Inciting Incident sets in motion? Well, you don't necessarily have to have a conversation with your character. Just listen to her inner thoughts, tart asides, and self-critical comments. Sort of like her ongoing internal soundtrack, muted by headphones. Imagine your character at her workplace and adapt the following prompts…

EXERCISE #60: MIRROR, MIRROR

Using the POV of your character, *check one:*

1. Watching herself in a mirror in the bathroom at work, she's thinking: "I'm…"

   ____ … a babe.

   ____ … a slave.

   ____ … a total fraud.

   ____ … an alien being who doesn't fit anywhere.

2. Next to a spilt cup of coffee at her workstation, she's thinking: "This is concrete evidence of…"

   ____ … my incompetence.

   ____ … my utter brilliance.

   ____ … my scattered creativity.

   ____ … my draining workaholism.

3. Pinned to a bulletin board in her workspace is a picture of South America and a travel brochure. It suggests: "Someday I will…"

   ____ … rule the world.

> _____ ... discover my roots.
>
> _____ ... go to this beautiful country.
>
> _____ ... volunteer in relief efforts for indigenous peoples.
>
> 4. In her email outbox is a project she's just sent. She looks at it and thinks:
>
> _____ ... What an embarrassment...
>
> _____ ... What a waste of my time, *yet again*...
>
> _____ ... What a masterpiece – I'm totally getting a raise!
>
> _____ ... I forgot to check the grammar! Damn! Is it "you're" or "your?"

Exercise 60

With or without your character's help, you're starting to see what's going on with her at a deeper level. You're getting familiar with her quirks, flaws, and the idiosyncrasies that can delay her progress, but also are a fundamental part of who she is. Maybe you even have an inkling how one of her flaws could be turned around and used as an asset—with some careful reframing or restraint. You're starting to tune into her wavelength and how she sees herself. (But there's only so far you can go without her active cooperation.)

No matter how damaged or self-loathing your character may be, this particular stage in her evolution is all about the trigger point; finding the right situation, person, place, or object that can help aggravate the wound so that she'll start to imagine the possibilities of her goal. She may be feeling frightened, excited, annoyed, or any number of emotions, now that she's made this commitment with you to "attack this story." But at present, she does believe it's a worthy goal. While she may not be convinced she has what it takes, she's willing to give it a try. And, you want her to take this incredible journey…

YOU ARE DONE WITH STEP FOUR.

CHAPTER FIVE—MOVING IN TOGETHER will show you tricks of the trade to coax your character into taking you further into her confidence. You'll also clarify her true motivations, outline the limits of what she thinks she can achieve, and be taught how to get her to transcend those self-imposed boundaries.

MOVING IN TOGTHER "THE MIDPOINT"—STEP FIVE

UP TO NOW, you've successfully spent time easing into your character's life. You've noted specific influences in the people, places, and things that have forged her. You've learned to see both the obvious aspects of her shenanigans as well as sensing the more hidden sides of her personality. You've begun to circle around the traumas that shape her behavior, i.e., her core wound: an original injury to her psyche that informs some of that behavior. You've begun to see some of her protective armor: how she fashions her responses to keep from having to deal with any situation that causes her anxiety, even though you know her tactics impede her goal.

If you were a lawyer, *DYC* steps one through four would be part of the "discovery process." In traditional terminology, you've started filling in her back-story, which is everything that has occurred in her life prior to the point in time that the adventure takes place: childhood on up to the previous minute of the very first scene.

To review from prior *DYC* chapters, you know certain tangibles and intangibles about your main character, in addition to her three non-negotiable traits:

THE PREP PHASE

- A sense of her general attitude...
- A choice detail, what actors call "a gift," that lends insight into who she is...
- A sensory experience from the character's POV...
- The kind of character that best suits your story...

THE MEET CUTE

- Her job...
- Her general hangouts...
- Her kind of personality...
- The backdrop of her childhood...
- How her childhood determined or affected her decision to move to her current location...
- Details informing her lifestyle choices and habitat...
- The discovery of a supporting (but not necessarily supportive) character...
- How this ancillary character helps and/or hinders her in ways that bond them...
- Why this (or another affiliate character) could be persuaded to hurt her...
- Five obstacles to an ultimate must-do task necessary to her goal...

- Ten scenes that would take her out of her comfort zone and trigger transformation...
- An inner flaw that has significant consequences on her achieving her goal...

THE FIRST DATE

- The rhythm of her daily life...(hectic or lackadaisical)
- Her manner and social presence...(people pleaser or rugged individualist)
- How she speaks and expresses herself...(voluble or close-mouthed)
- The level of risk she can tolerate without too much trouble...(resolute or retiring)
- How detail-oriented she is...(sweats the small stuff or a feckless daydreamer)
- If she's more of a planner...(anally prepared or impulsive)
- A loose idea about her relationship to money...(spendthrift or scrooge)
- How honest she is in sharing dissatisfaction...(brusquely opinionated or feigning contentment)
- How self-regulating she is...(control freak or chill)
- How flaky she is...(dependable or irresponsible)
- How available she is...(free-spirited or heavily scheduled)

- What ticks her off…(feathers ruffled easily or generally indifferent)

And…you should also know:

- What's really important to her…(or negligible)
- What sets her off on her new journey…(or postpones it!)

SERIOUS DATING

- How to construct a glamorous or daring date to shake a demanding character's tongue loose…
- What items make her feel comfortable…
- Finding out what her pad is like…
- What her love language is…
- A look at her weaknesses…
- Her most poignant disappointments…
- A possible pattern in these disappointments…
- When she suffered a trauma…
- How to make her more active and daring…
- How to shrink obstacles that seem too big…
- What has to happen to compel her to be audacious…
- Who would galvanize your character to attempt the impossible…
- How her new boldness might change her relationship with this figure who inspires her…

- How to distinguish her bad moments from truly epic fails that will continue to haunt her...
- How it's possible to view challenges as positive possibilities...
- How she experiences her first reversals...
- How she deals with making surprising sacrifices...
- What happens when she gets so close, but doesn't make it...
- What she's afraid of...
- What the worst possible thing could be...
- What any of her neuroses are...
- If there's any overlap with her neuroses and yours...
- What her most strangely compelling trait is...
- Whether she's secretly insecure...
- Whether she accepts blame...
- What one of her dreams is...
- How she regards her work performance...

Are things simmering to a gentle boil yet?

Whatever the temperature at the moment, we don't want you to ditch your main squeeze. Sometimes the same bad habits that previously waylaid your writing are often surprisingly similar to

Dating Your Character

what may have dogged your romantic relationships in real life. We feel it's wise at this point to take inventory and "pull from" both your imagination and your romantic-relationship experiences.

To vanquish your ghosts, you first have to resurrect them…

EXERCISE #61: MAPPING PERSONALITY PITFALLS

Take a moment to elaborate on any of the below writing snafus that you may have encountered. What did they feel like? What were you thinking as you suffered through them?

Writer's block:

_____
_____

Procrastination: (Did you miss a deadline or self-imposed target date?)

_____
_____

Inauthentic characters: (Did you know this or did feedback make you aware?)

_____
_____

> Flat, uninspired, clichéd dialogue: (Did you suspect this or was it read aloud?)
> ___
> ___

Exercise 61

If you run into this kind of setback again, reassure yourself that it's not a permanent condition. The reason for this paralysis is that you've stopped connecting to your work, the character, her circumstances, or the stakes implied within a decision hanging in the balance.

One trick is to *talk* yourself back into productivity…

> **Writer's Block: NIFTY TRICK**
>
> Talking is a great way to get out of your head. It simplifies what you want to say in your script, how you want to say it, and why this way of looking at something hasn't been done before.
>
> Meet up with a writing friend. Share the reasons you've embarked on this particular story. We're pretty sure this person's good taste and approval will encourage you, while his helpful questions will force you to:
>
> - Defend the concept
> - Fight for the novelty of your story's essence
> - Reveal your passion for your protagonist and her struggle
>
> Remember, you're *not* trying to pitch this person. You're just talking up what inspires you, in the process sharing a vital element that perhaps has gotten lost.

Burn out is inevitable for most creators, especially in the accelerated timeframe of production deadlines. Lulls in the process are to be expected. Remembering *why* we love a project is key. As the story goes, writer John Steinbeck (*Grapes of Wrath*) would write out his reasons for embarking on a story and then tape this paper onto his typewriter as a sort of inspirational map.

The first step to fostering connection is becoming aware. In your personal life, taking as much blame as you should, think about why certain relationships fell apart. Touch down on the event, even if it's only some small specific that you recall. Sit with it. Allow it to just present itself. Be honest...

This kind of fearless honesty, this connection to yourself—tapping into that part of you that can share what your character's going through—is one huge aspect of what we feel keeps your story alive.

You'll need to morph and build on the genuine experience of the human heart—yours. Even if you're a psychologist, social worker, or teacher steeped in human dynamics transitioning to writing, this particular work is rarely easy.

> **EXERCISE #62: ROMANTIC ROADBLOCKS**
>
> - Did you have too many expectations?
> - Were you unable to block out others' attentions to you?
> - How invested were you in her/him? Did you prioritize friends, family, work, hobbies... *over* her/him?
> - Did you have difficulty being honest with her/him? If you pulled back...why?

Exercise 62

What's important for you to realize is 1) what makes you tick as a writer and 2) what can potentially shut you down. Having acknowledged mistakes you may have made in the past, we feel you're less likely to use them as crutches or bail out on your character. In fact, you're more likely to "post bail" for your character when she gets into trouble. It's best to be candid when rating your relationship with your character, so if need be, you can repair it.

EXERCISE #63: THE RELATIONSHIP RAINBOW

Where does your relationship to your character fall in the overall spectrum?

GOOD...TO...OKAY...

You two genuinely enjoy your conversations.

You look forward to finding out more about her.

You want to move things along, but she's more hesitant.

She sometimes puts up a fight, but usually compromises and cooperates.

OKAY...TO...NOT SO GOOD...

You haven't learned any more about her than your initial meetings.

You haven't gotten past the public face she presents to the world.

She's making it harder and harder for you to get together.

She's trying to break it off.

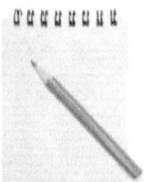

Exercise 63

Dating Your Character

Maybe her willingness to participate isn't the issue. But you can still expect to have reservations about your character. What if you're finding she's not as interesting as you once thought? Maybe, as you've gotten to know her, she's let you down. You might even be bored.

Maybe she refuses to let you into the darker, more interesting recesses of her back-story. You may need to bring more of your own vulnerability to the table.

EXERCISE #63-b: THE RELATIONSHIP RAINBOW

Spend some time reflecting on how your first official date and subsequent talks went.

- When did you start to become confused or disappointed?
- How did that specifically manifest itself?

Conflict is something you want to nurture not shy away from. Once you pick up on a "sour note," or sense something percolating underneath her exterior, then you need to step up your inquiry:

- Do you wish you were getting something else from your character? (Does this behavior suit the story, though?)
- Are you wrestling with her contradictions? (Don't *you* have a few?)
- What conflict with her are you sensing that you can use in your story?

Exercise 63-b

Dating Your Character

As long as what you initially learned about her is still true—those core couple of characteristics—then everything else is shading and contouring, adding to and layering depth and surprise as your story unfolds. Together you're shaping subtext as things are left unsaid, but expressed in her actions or in silences implied in the "white space" of your page.

Be open to her inner contradictions. In this next phase, our focus will be on the war between two opposing ideas. Many actors gravitate to the emotional footing of a character by noting the forward movement of her clear action with her corresponding backsliding to her status quo. Each instance can eventually point to an underlying truth, an irony that reconciles the two opposing views or actions in conflict within her.

How is what you're feeling an authentic reflection of your character? How do you know if the mishmash of affection, concern, and anger that you're feeling toward your character is "good," "bad," or even useful? After all, we've been encouraging you to challenge your equilibrium. As a signpost, the most quantifiable answer we can offer is the sheer number of questions that have arisen as you've continued with the process. At this stage, you always want to arrive at more questions than "answers."

When Marilyn and Elizabeth were working with one of their clients on his YA Western book, they encouraged this new writer to accumulate as much research as he could on his three main characters, before settling into a groove. This technique posed important questions and opened up so many storytelling avenues that might have been overlooked had the writer progressed in a more straight ahead, linear fashion.

In *The Last Ride of Caleb O'Toole*, three kids travel across the United States before the Civil War to escape a cholera outbreak. One of the characters had little to do, beyond act as a lightning rod for danger. But when the writer suggested she master a special skill (nursing), she became a true equal on the journey, helping the little band to withstand the perils they met. The fuller development of the character's spirit and emotional range was supported by her increased activity, rooted in the writer's research.

Though, we admit that sometimes research can be a trap. Especially, if it teams up with procrastination. However, your character will be in good shape if she has a specific goal. A doable, actionable goal. A goal that seems impossible, but has a clear destination, if not a path. With enough ingenuity, commitment, and research, your character—if she really wants this—will find a way. How you choose to hold up your character will also become apparent and manageable, too.

As long as you're still benefiting from your engagement in the discovery process, then trust in this course of refinement. It may also force you to rethink or reshape those things that may now seem obsolete based on what you've dug up.

But here is a short list of some purely self-destructive behavior that needs to be called out.

The "BAD" List:

- Anything that keeps you from writing is **bad**. Anything that causes you to doubt yourself is **bad**.*
- Doubt, in the form of procrastination, stubbornness, or isolation, is **really bad…**
- Laziness and smug contentment is **bad**.
- Not constantly being curious about the character and the world of the story is **bad**.

*While doubting is the key to certain religions, it's bad if you've flipped that magnifying lens on yourself so that it becomes obsessive. If you can no longer operate, out of fear, confusion, or loss of appetite, then your self-criticism is not helping you stay true to your purpose but is wiping out any chance of you ever continuing on your course. Art is intended to ignite insight—into life—yours and your characters.

How you feel is crucial to making inroads into your character's background and essential personality. You need to be enjoying the journey, cherishing every little new discovery. If it hasn't been fun, you could be censoring the playful improvisation of the exercises. Just like any craft, there are bound to be moments of exhilaration and then moments where there are lulls.

Perhaps you've chosen a particularly obstinate protagonist and to get her to be forthcoming is feeling like too much work. If you're disenchanted, how much of the blame can be laid at her feet? Perhaps there is some unclaimed benefit to her resistance…

- Have you been rudely awakened in some sense?
- Are you judging your character?
- Are you discounting the information she's sharing with you?

You now know—as if that's a huge revelation—that your literary beloved isn't perfect.

- But how has your view of her changed?
- Does she seem to be heading in a vastly different direction from the one you imagined?
- Is it still at least within the rough bounds of the outline you imagined?
- Has she shocked you into retooling your original premise?

As long as you trust that her instincts are on target, so what if she's taking you to places you've never been or didn't anticipate going? She *should* know more than you. After all, it's *her* story…

It's okay if you can't always definitively say what she's feeling. But at this point, you should be wired into her neurons.

Dating Your Character

- Are you able to guess what she's thinking, even before she speaks?
- Are you able to identify what's being left unsaid with what's really going on with her?
- Are you acquainted with her general rhythms to make the most of your time together?

The rhythm or internal music of your character is somewhat intangible, like the voice or style of some writers. It's something you'll begin to pick up on to inform your choices. Dialogue is an integral place where your character's specific DNA shows up.

As a method of exercising control, some writers pad their characters' language with adjectives or constrict it within precise phrasing that doesn't sound like everyday speech. It's more important to capture the spontaneity and memetic nature of dialogue. It's less a complex science than one of simple observation. Below is a straightforward partnering exercise that's a lively way to practice being in the moment.

> **EXERCISE #64: DRUMBEAT**
>
> Enlist the help of a friend or a fellow writer. You start things off by slapping the table with both hands and shouting out the *first word* that comes to mind. Your partner responds with the *first word*, *phrase*, or *sentence* that pops into his mind.
>
> **<u>Note</u>: Your partner won't be pretending to be your character.**
>
> Don't let more than a *couple of seconds* pass between replies. Just get used to the ping-pong action back and forth between you. Pay attention to the pacing, humor, and change of emotion as you two face off.

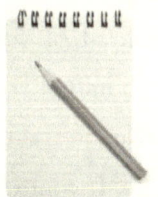

Exercise 64

If you're in tune with your character, then odds are your relationship is going well, and you'll want to keep progressing. If you're having difficulties, then you need to decide if it's because you're not communicating or if it's because you two just can't seem to mesh.

Your character's bound to have flaws and inner deviations that flummox you. Regardless of where you currently are in your relationship, she'll likely give you plenty of reason to wish you could sever ties at some point. But if you persevere, you'll reap rich rewards, you'll sort through her inconsistencies, and render a 3-D character worth getting to know.

How do you know if it's beneficial for you to continue? You may need to coldly assess who your character really is. You don't want to get farther off track with a character that's going to be irredeemable, unless you're tackling an especially ambitious and tragic story. As long as there are enough positives to warrant investing your time in her and her story, plow on.

On the other hand, you may be struggling with a different problem, something that you've been hesitant to consider. What if your character still seems *too* good to be true…?

Being blindingly enamored of your character is as much a problem as despising her. It means you're not seeing her clearly. You're not looking at the unpleasant personality traits that are getting in the way of her goal. If your character actually is relatively transparent and honest, she may need a sprinkling of dirt to make her more opaque. She has to have enough of a mystique to command 90+ minutes onscreen or keep the small-screen audience tuning in.

We've got to feel it's worth it to stick around and learn more about her. Why is the full length of the film needed to establish, then reiterate, the **archetype** she conforms to? An archetype is a general compilation of traits that roughly form a commonly-recurring character in literature, film, art, and life: the high school jock who's a meathead, the socially awkward accountant, the hooker with a heart of gold. We suggest all writers examine archetypes to understand the root dynamics of their character. We recommend using Carolyn Myss' set of *Archetype Cards* to start thinking about the composite traits commonly associated within types of characters. But you'll notice we don't recommend starting out your process with these cards, because they can limit your focus too quickly.

Archetypes can be a reasonable way to check that you've more than started to round out your protagonist. These readily recognizable personae represent the bare minimum level of character development, because they only fulfill on a standard grouping of traits. This isn't where your character creation should end. If you've been following the writing prompts in this book, you should realize how important contradiction and nuance in your character is. For her to effectively embody a certain type of person in the current culture, she has to have the same ridges, whorls, and hooks in her fingerprints that we do. We should be able to see and identify the same level of complexity in her.

If you feel you haven't broken through the surface of your character, the following example and ensuing exercise will highlight reservations you don't realize you hold. It will tempt you to probe more deeply.

FILM EXAMPLE

In *Leave Her to Heaven,* a really bizarre 20th Century Fox movie of the 1940s, superficially lovable Ellen, played by Gene Tierney of *Laura* classic-film fame, horrifies her family by the lengths she will go to retain her husband's attention. This film was Fox's biggest moneymaker of the decade and earned Tierney an Oscar nomination, partly because of the dual-edged strength and intensity that Tierney showed in inhabiting a beguilingly feminine woman who is also capable of icy calculation.

Ellen makes herself a flawless paragon of womanhood, keeping herself young, free…and conspicuously without child, for as long as she can. Her beleaguered husband, played by Cornel Wilde, has to decide if he has the strength to acknowledge his lovely wife's increasingly sinister actions.

> **EXERCISE #65: TAKE HER, OR LEAVE HER TO HEAVEN**
>
> Write down everything about your character that:
>
> - Moves you...
> - Relates to you...
> - Fascinates you...
> - Disgusts you...
> - Makes you nervous...
> - Makes you want to know more about how she came to be that way...

Exercise 65

These questions may have led to more specific instances that are bothering you. But can you get past whatever overall judgment you may have reached? Have you retained the initial fire that drew you to her in the first place? Can you carry on?

The specific causes for friction can be resolved. But if you've settled into a stale routine and become content, then you have a larger problem. Contentment is bad because it stops you from demanding more. *DYC* is all about honoring a serious questioning process, where you question your assumptions. It calls for you to operate from a place of doubt, pushing for deeper reasons for any puzzling behavior that continues to crop up.

If this is the case, it may be time to do a reset. If it isn't feasible for you to build on, and embellish, the core of your character, then you owe it to your story and your future success to dump her.

You won't be beginning from square one. Surely there are aspects you gleaned that can be recycled or repurposed. When you go back to the drawing board, you're reliving some of the steps you took and reexamining many of the same features of the landscape. You don't have to toss out the hard-won insights you're learned.

Another client of Marilyn and Elizabeth's came to the painful realization that the madcap story he wanted to tell was best explored through a less cynical worldview. And of course, that changed everything… The dialogue had to be refracted through the now younger character's sensibility and vernacular. It also drastically limited her finances, which helped generate more obstacles for the plot. While at the time it was a bother to have to refashion his TV pilot, he admitted that once he committed, he gained momentum and the writing became much more engaging.

If you must backtrack, do two more exercises below, as well as the note, which concludes it on page 264. It may jumpstart your voyage of rediscovery…

If you decide to put in the effort to make your relationship work, let's reconcile the problems you may have encountered. How do the traits that create tension between the two of you complicate the list of non-negotiables for your character? By further defining what irritates you, you're daring yourself to accept or jettison these traits. If, after you first compare them to the core list, you find they're not necessary, you may allow yourself to get rid of them.

EXERCISE #66: LIST OF PET PEEVES

List all the *traits* that drive you up the wall. Limit yourself to <u>ten</u>... For each, describe the earliest event where you were exposed to this. And perhaps imagine future events where you might be exposed to this behavior.

Exercise 66

EXERCISE #66-b: LIST OF PET PEEVES

- Was this comment or action directed to you?
- Someone else?
- What context gave rise to this outburst?

DYC Example:

Let's say your character's core non-negotiable trait is that she fears violence of any kind. An authentic psychic, she's incredibly proud, having grown up in a family that cherished her gifts and recognized them at an early age. Instead of accepting her gifts gracefully, she became snooty and irascible. She relays long lost secrets to her clients, who reward her monetarily, but her entitled attitude's made her rather withholding—she holds herself above all others. And in the area of love, no one is ever trustworthy enough.

Are these flaws in direct opposition to her essential self?

No, but her predilections complicate things for her, especially her penchant for disrupting the ambiance of places with her diva-like demands, a behavior that could give rise to violence.

But maybe she's freer than most in her readings, because she has good boundaries and instinctively knows just how far to push her clients with disagreeable information. Perhaps another hidden benefit of her gift allows her to foretell the near future. It would be nice if she were easier to get along with, but that's just who she is.

A list of her more aggravating qualities could be:

- She has to have the last word.
- She feels she's always right and gets annoyed with those who challenge her.
- She's very finicky and not afraid to voice her displeasure—especially to wait-staff and other people who don't really have the means to argue back.
- She has to be the center of attention.

Perhaps after you expressed your curiosity, the psychic felt comfortable enough to invite you to accompany her as "her assistant."

Maybe, on the way to a special reading at a star client's house, you and the psychic got lost and arrived late. So the psychic showed up on the woman's doorstep in a foul mood. Having to deal with the pampered woman's snarky attitude proved too much to bear.

While trying to manage this difficult client, her strong sense of self was further exacerbated during the session. Instead of placating the client's needs, the psychic deliberately riled her. She sensed the woman just wanted closure for the death of a loved one. But instead of giving her that, she chose to guilt the woman for her unkind treatment of the deceased, chastising her with his words from the other side. The psychic did this, not only to be cruel, but because she felt that an injustice had to be righted. Directing her venom at this woman was a bonus.

You may have been uncomfortable during this possibly distasteful scene. But it doesn't look like the psychic was even aware of you, once she got started. And she definitely didn't feel any compunction about causing a disturbance in front of you. Maybe, subconsciously, she wanted to condition you into accepting that she's the kind of woman who's always in charge, and that part of her core purpose is justice—to right wrongs.

Note: If you're past retrieving anything salvageable from your relationship, then come up with a list of the exact opposite behavior that would be more palatable to you.

Exercise 66-b

Stay loyal to your character, the person who's turned up in all her infuriating glory. Choosing to figure out the basis for her annoying habits and deceptions may channel any deeper trauma that could have formed her. These unexplained edges of her may add flavor in jarring, surprising, and satisfying ways as you mount your story.

All of your interactions with her mostly take place in a "creative cloud"; a limbo world of theory and possibility. Nothing here has to appear in her story. Nothing here is permanent. It's a place with its own reality and rules. It would be best that it closely resemble *her* reality.

EXERCISE #66-c: LIST OF PET PEEVES

After reviewing your list of peeves, start extrapolating:

- What kinds of circumstances seem to bring out her "mean" streak?
- How many of these proposed situations have you thought of for your script?
- How will these personal defects get her in trouble with other characters?
- Is there a comic foil or an antagonist who will be able to pick up on her weaknesses?
- Will he mirror them back to her in a positive way or exploit them as part of her undoing?

Exercise 66-c

Don't be afraid to let your character suffer because of her impulses...

EXERCISE #66-d: LIST OF PET PEEVES

What consequences will she face because of her behavior?

- What are the worst possible outcomes you can devise?
- How many character-based obstacles can you construct that impact her goals?
- How can you build out these scenarios so that she can learn and grow from her mistakes?
- How does she start to realize there's another way to conduct her life?
- Do other characters point this out?
- Does she see someone else act in an alternative way and benefit?

Exercise 66-d

Sometimes exaggerating or amplifying palatable traits can be arranged so that even positive traits can hamstring her progress. In the right circumstances, "kindness" can be a dangerous and debilitating trait. And one person's "kindness" is another person's "credulous gullibility."

In the example above, some of the more benign-seeming character excesses include the psychic's confidence in her ability to read people. That could compromise her with an all-important client if she overestimates the limits to which she can push this client. Maybe, having chosen to discount valuable, professional advice, she trusts her gut about the gravity of the complaints the client makes and is blindsided by a lawsuit. We're mining the possibilities of her flaw to up the stakes and add interest.

How can the psychic operate and bring in new clientele if people sense she's put off by them? How does she have the patience to consult the spirit world if she feels like cutting her customers (and perhaps the ghosts themselves) down to size?

Try to break down your character's bothersome behavior into bite-size specifics that you can address. For the psychic, if her goal is to find a true, just, and fair love, doubtless she'll have to become a more tolerant and affectionate person. Her internal, external goals, as well as minor goals, can all feed into each other and show us her advancement or recidivism in turn. If she makes small improvements, she can also address any antagonism she may have caused in the audience.

MAKING YOUR CHARACTER LIKABLE

In thinking about your audience and considering their overall reaction to your character, we don't ever want you to pervert the *DYC* process and make your results superficially attractive or too PC. Applying concealer and foundation can discreetly enhance natural beauty and charm, but you don't have to airbrush away the grittier texture of your character.

Even if there's a chance your character will be able to accomplish her goal without addressing her attitudinal issues, focusing on what can get under *your* skin and cause irritation are great clues to what's overwhelming her, too. Bacteria-laden secrets can burrow there. They're partially the result of inflammation from stress, showing what's systemically wrong. Later in this chapter, we'll help you lance the actions and decisions that could be contributing to this congestion. Remember "disease" is really "dis-ease," whether you're talking physical or emotional pathologies.

Be selective when including the array of these all-too-human flaws. In your developing script, if we don't yet have much of a reason to root for the character, then, at a minimum, we have to see how she's learning to manipulate her environment to her advantage. If we're unsure about our empathy for her, we enjoy the havoc she wreaks, because she's a corrosive agent of change and the status quo needs this corrective jolt. Often a despicable character is the root of change for others: *Six Degrees of Separation* explores a con artist's impact on a rich family's denial.

FILM EXAMPLE

In 2006's BAFTA-winning *Notes on a Scandal,* the narrator/lead Barbara, played by Judi Dench, is rather odious. She's a covetous lesbian who despises those who have what she obviously doesn't: youth, beauty, and hope. But her cackling reflections amuse us. The fact that our guide into the dysfunction of a public school is such a bitter, condescending gnome could be intolerably uncomfortable for a few theatergoers. While the crackling wit of her misanthropic cynicism is entertaining enough to forgive her more glaring shortcomings, the swift introduction of a distractingly attractive affiliate character (Cate Blanchett) puts less pressure on Barbara to singlehandedly carry the movie.

Further, it must be said that writer Patrick Marber's rule-breaking film (based on a book by Zoe Heller) is also remarkable, because it's an example of a "protagonist" being the villain. It isn't until later that we realize Barbara's not just a caustic antihero, but in fact the calculating villain of the piece. She had seemed like such a nonentity, poisonous though her private thoughts were...

Problematic behavior in your character, on its own, isn't to be condemned. It's only when it harms your relationship with her. Be very aware of assigning negative judgment when her antics aren't directed at you. They may just be her means of coping and getting through life.

When she's deliberately and pointedly trying to wreck her alliance with you, then that deserves special scrutiny. Her time with you is supposed to be golden. She can't lash out at you the way she might sloppily do to other people in her life. You two have an understanding. You're there to support her, so in the end, any adverse action against you is really a self-harming exercise.

EXERCISE #67: IF SHE'S BEING IRRITATING...

Think about possible reasons:

- If she's annoying you, is she doing that *intentionally*...?
- Is she just venting her frustrations from other parts of her life...?
- Is she attacking you to get you to come to the fore, to really engage with her...?

Exercise 67

If she's the type to confess, to want to be pushed to share, then you'll have an easier go getting to the root of her issue. If it's truly something in you that she's railing against, hopefully you'll be willing to do whatever it takes to ease that tension through solid, open communication. Think back to what her "love language" is, so that she's receptive to your efforts.

If other aspects of her life are seeping into and straining the relationship, before asking her, try to hypothesize some ways you can help. It's lazy to put the onus (and blame) on her. Be proactive and plan ahead! Besides, if you can anticipate the cause of her unhappiness, you're less likely to be defensive and caught off guard.

Are you forcing her to change a part of herself?

Maybe you're being overly picky. Remember, flawed and quirky characters are fun to watch on screen, though, as you're realizing, not exactly fun to hang out with all the time. You can't expect the character to transform herself solely to please you. You're still early enough in the process, you can't know if everything that causes friction is really meant to be antagonizing.

You've got to be more accepting of how she thinks. Trust her and her abilities. The way her mind works out a solution may be more circuitous than the way you would consider the same facts before you. It's essential that you're open to her approach. What you think is important, but may not in fact be important to her.

It's instructive to think about how she prioritizes, what she's comfortable with letting slide, which isn't automatically classifiable as a "flaw," if she still manages to get most things done. None of us are on 24/7. She's bound to fall behind a bit in some area of her life.

Remember, as she continues to attack her goal head on, she'll struggle to balance all her responsibilities, needs, and wants, until it seems like this fight will break her.

Does this part of herself *have to change* so that she can achieve her goal?

EXERCISE #67-b: IF SHE'S BEING IRRITATING...

You ought to confine your reservations only to conduct that's standing in the way of future advancement. Bearing in mind that, while you may not like some of her habits, they could have been helpful in the past.

They may be key to figuring out:

- How she got stuck...
- Why she lost her initial fire...
- Why she may feel unable to push on...

Exercise 67-b

EXERCISE #67-c: IF SHE'S BEING IRRITATING…

- How crucial has this part of her been to who she is and to her prior success?
- Imagine a scenario where this default reaction benefited her.
- What circumstances allowed the relative success she achieved?
- If a similar situation happened today, would her default reaction garner a similarly positive result? Why or why not?

Exercise 67-c

At this point in outlining your script, you're familiar with most of her flaws. You have a sense of her past, her lowlights especially. You're basically at the midpoint stage. Three or four major characters have come into her orbit to help, confound, or surprise her. (In standard screenwriting structure, at the Midpoint, if you were actually writing your script, *all* your major and significant supporting characters would have been introduced.)

You've thought about how your character will face down some of her demons and make meaningful progress. All of her problems have been highlighted, and you know what her internal and external goals are. But perhaps she has so much on her plate, it doesn't look as though she'll be able to finish.

This is where you start to fill in the back-story. It would be meaningful for her to realize she no longer has to depend on former courses of action that would be of no benefit now. That if she really wants to earn the kind of life she thinks she deserves—and get the prize she's been dreaming of—she'll have to abandon her previous, predictable behavior.

To see why she chooses to cope in this stale manner time and again, you've got to acknowledge why it's been useful. Chances are the habituated behavior was either an unconscious decision made during an early trauma, or it might have been a conscious decision that, over a long period, became an automatic, kneejerk response.[5]

So going past these ingrained moves and committing to a new passage in her life will require her courage and determination. Even if you're sure you're only trying to help, be advised that some characters will not be receptive to your criticism and constant prodding.

Consider how close you both are to reaching a compromise and forgiving each others' faults. If you're on the verge of making headway, perhaps you need only lull her into a more open, receptive frame of mind. Returning to a scene of friendly familiarity may make her acceptance that "change is necessary" more likely. And if that doesn't work—try the opposite:

If your character's still not being very forthcoming, you may have to put her ill at ease. If you opt for a locale she already goes to with some frequency, or associates with certain memories, she may burrow into old habits. To get her to reveal some of her inner drive, call her out in a foreign space, a place where she might be more on guard. Someplace disorienting enough that it makes her re-evaluate her perspective—and yours.

EXERCISE #68: LEND HER AN EAR

When you confront her, keep the script simple. Try telling her that you've "noticed she's been under pressure." And, that you want to help, whatever form of help that might take. Then just let her take the lead. She'll either start to open up or push you farther away…

Write in a stream-of-consciousness fervor for *five minutes*. Let any random thoughts seep in. Snatches of conversation, thoughts of the character, your observations of her, how the scene feels. Even if she mentions things you've never heard before, let it flow… Trust that your character's subconscious is leading you, pointing you in a direction that could be worth exploring.

 **Exercise 68**

Pay attention to any specifics she lets drop: names, time frames, number amounts. Jot them down in a separate list to decode them in the future. Does this hint at a new urgency in her life? How can you find out more without being a pest?

> **Note:** If your relationship with your character is going well, we don't recommend using the following hardball strategems. Continue on to page 282. However, if your character is being prickly with you, you need to stir things up. You've formed a partnership with her, and if she's letting you down, then you need to question her loyalty and intentions.

EXERCISE #69: PROOF OR DARE

Come up with a list of *ten actions* that will let you familiarize yourself with the problems in her life. They must verify or contradict what you've previously picked up on.

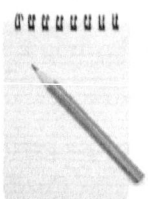

Exercise 69

EXERCISE #69-b: PROOF OR DARE

On your own, devise *three exercises* where you follow through on your list to get more information.

They can be:

- heavily observation-based, i.e., following the character, snooping in her diary, logging in her comings-and-goings.
- from the POV of the character, i.e., a letter or email she writes, a therapy session she has, a secret meeting she has with someone.
- practical games you arrange to flush out the truth from her, i.e., diverting her money without her knowing,

> letting someone know where she'll be, hiding a key piece of information from her that another character casually tells you.

Exercise 69-b

Did she cooperate and begin to unburden herself? Even without her participation, do you have enough to go on? Has your subterfuge allowed her to become more emotionally accessible? Keep in mind that there are ebbs and flows in any relationship. Little cooling off periods, where boundaries are reestablished, or life and its possibilities intrude. But persistently remote and closed characters, who are stuck in a swampland of indecision and unhelpful exile, have to want to get better. A sign of a good relationship is an easy exchange. Sparks are great, silence is not! If your character is an introvert, or unable to speak due to an infirmity, then how can you two communicate creatively?

If the previous exercise did nothing to shake info loose, brainstorm a few tactics that can force her to come to the negotiating table. Surely there's something she *needs:* advice, a loan, sanctuary, something that she's previously sought in her relationship with you, which you can now leverage.

If, in spite of your proactive efforts, the equilibrium in your relationship hasn't reestablished itself, you've got to put her under more pressure—annoy her to the point of pissing her off. Stop chasing her and make her come to you to resolve your issues.

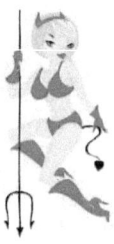

EXERCISE #70: THE PITCHFORK TREATMENT

Concoct *three ways* of blackmailing her.

    For <u>example,</u> you may warn her that you'll:

    ...contact her family because of her erratic behavior.

    ...clue in the guy she's seeing about a prior entanglement.

    ...compromise her business contacts, because she's getting in too deep.

Craft *three ways* of shocking her into reality.

    For <u>example,</u>

    ...slap down a pile of photos, waking her up to the deceptions of one of her affiliate characters.

    ...play a recording of an ally ruthlessly dissing her.

    ... show her a statement of her lover's bank balance.

Exercise 70

This is an important crux in your relationship. Think about an emotional satisfaction that may be a powerful secondary concern for you. At this point, you may have been stifling your disappointment and frustration. *Don't give yourself an ulcer. You're allowed to vent a little.* It's one way you'll prove you're serious and give her a taste of the unvarnished intimacy that you both need. Your audience won't have the patience to follow someone who doesn't reward our attention with some real, involving shred of herself.

Consult your *DYC* journal and write down your frustrations. Don't let yourself get stuck in a quagmire of unexpressed disappointment, rage, or despair.

Note: ...If you've managed to pry out some of the character's reasons for her actions, and have skipped the previous couple of exercises, now is the time for you to jump back into the *DYC* system.

EXERCISE #71: SETTING EXPECTATIONS

- Make it clear what you expect from her:
    What does she *have to share* with you?

- Show her how invested you are:
    What do you *have to offer* her to renew the relationship?

Exercise 71

You'll begin to make inroads into some major plot points in her journey and start to fuse all these obstacles together into tightly constructed scenes, after understanding the rationale behind her seemingly self-destructive behavior.

For the sake of dropping her in a sink or swim situation, put her in some kind of crisis where she's forced to sacrifice an advantage. The clashes you'll create in the scenes below, if they don't yet exist, should be directly transferable to your script. And if you're working off a draft or a collection of scenes, they should be deepened when you walk through them again with the exercises' directions in mind.

As the story progresses, you must unleash a wave of fury that gains momentum…

Getting to the heart of your character requires extensive work from both of you. However, what if she's been humoring you up to this point? How do you show her that you're serious and can be a real support to her? Demonstrate how well you know her, as well as underline your commitment to her, by stating your assessment of her progress.

She may have pushed you back at times, but even if it hasn't been a struggle to recruit her into cooperating, she may have secretly felt you were yet one more obligation in her life. If so, how can you take up some of her burden? That would require a concrete outline of objectives that you promise to help her achieve. You want to be upfront with how you can empower her: to tell you what she needs and how you should be accountable, sort of like a pre-nup states what will happen with the dissolution of a marriage.

You're not limiting the growth of your relationship. You're making it less nebulous. Clearly stating what your mutual expectations are and how the relationship will fit into the rest of her life. As you've gotten familiar with her rituals, her schedule, it's disingenuous to continue operating in the "creative cloud" as her theoretical friend. Now you're more like her secret weapon...

In view of her knowing you'll be there through thick and thin, the process should be less push-pull, and more of a real partnership. She won't see your assistance as a handout or something she's going to have to pay for later in some unwanted way. Also, by dividing up the labor that will get her into shape for her journey, in objective terms, you'll be ceding control to your character. She'll be setting more of the agenda.

MOVING IN TOGETHER

She can now stand on her two feet and make herself heard. She has enough of a voice to shape the conversations you have, and you have hints of the richness of her life in the time she spends away from you.

In real time, it's probably been two months into your relationship. Theoretically, you and your character have known each other six months in *DYC* time. The next phase, feasibly in dating hyper-speed, would be to move in together. If you point out all the positives in favor, she may come to recognize how it could be constructive.

Cohabitation is a big step, requiring trust and a general comfort level to build upon. The arrangement has to have the promise that it could be mutually beneficial. You have a different POV that sometimes makes her problems clearer and its potential solutions more expedient. You enjoy your conversations and have become part of her inner circle. You've been supportive, when you needed to be.

You can help her make definite the most salient aspects of her goal. She may assume there are certain parts of the goal that she needs to attain in order for her to feel victorious. But she may have to reassess what's essential and what can be disposed of. How does she decide what is crucial and what isn't?

You can be with her when she's not "performing" for you— not just on her down time, but on her off time. You can see how she mostly spends her days, and therefore what she values and relies on. Realize that, as she becomes sure of her next steps, she's going to need to spend more quality time with her affiliate character(s). You can still be a part of her life without being the focus of it.

So what are the drawbacks? *You can't leave your dirty socks on the floor.* You have to be considerate. You can't just lash out at her when she disappoints you. In fact, by staying at her place, you're being given more opportunity to study her human frailty. How she copes with setbacks, big and small.

In letting you move in, she is acknowledging your positive influence on her. But you're not the puppet-master. This relationship is not Svengalian. In fact, it's more co-dependent. Because without her, *you* have no story. If she gives up during the writing process, *you* have no story. If she freezes you out and doesn't tell you what's in her heart, you have a flat character—and no story.

You two have to decide what a "shared future" looks like. You're there to help her achieve her dreams. So what will your responsibilities be to her and vice versa?

EXERCISE #72: SETTING BOUNDARIES

- What do you want it to encompass?
- Where do you want it to go?
- What is expressly off limits?

Exercise 72

> **_DYC_ Example:**
>
> Keeping in mind the protagonist we used in Exercise #66, the "Pet Peeves" exercise, what would you want in a relationship with the surly, no-BS psychic?
>
> *What do you want it to encompass?*
>
> If you want to see an up-close view of how she preps behind the scenes and what she does during a session, would she insist that she do a reading with you as a sort of background check?
>
> Would she prefer you to accompany her on her house calls, as opposed to touring her office?
>
> Would she want you to be on call 24/7 as a way of demonstrating your earnestness?
>
> *Where do you want it to go?*
>
> What would you endure to be taken into her confidence? How curious are you about the origin of her gift?
>
> If you want to be involved, how deeply would she let you actively participate? Would you have to prove your belief in her?
>
> Privately? Publicly?

Would she treat you as an employee? Would she haze you? Would you ever be expected to drum up business?

What is expressly off limits?

If you want to see what toll her work takes on her, would she prevent your inquisitiveness from crossing the spiritual realm and into the personal?

What if she wanted to involve you in her problems? Would you allow yourself to become complicit in something illegal? Would you stand in the way of her sharing a damaging premonition that could possibly wreak havoc on a vulnerable client?

If the accuracy of her readings are called into question, would she be able to tolerate your doubt?

If after all this, you uncover the fact that she *is* a *charlatan*, but a very good charlatan, what would she do if you find out how she gets her intel beforehand?

Can you continue to support her? If you're willing to meet her expectations or demands on the surface, can you help her in deeper ways?

How would you bargain with her to keep you around?

Or, would she bring you deeper into her scheme?

Would you be in physical danger? If so, who could be the threat? If one of the affiliate characters learned the secret would that person also be targeted?

As you've seen, these questions can be helpful in narrowing down the specifics of the working nature of your relationship, but your response may have been even more exacting. Perhaps you came up with bullet-pointed factoids detailing potential scenarios of conflict and areas where you've both already compromised so you could move forward.

If you're not there yet, how can you feel you're a part of her life? Not just some distraction or phantom of her imagination, but someone with a gravity of your own? How do you go beyond good intentions and provide the presence (daily, semiweekly) that her timeline requires?

Think about how she spends her day and which pockets of it you can occupy...

> **EXERCISE #73: PICKING UP THE DRY-CLEANING**
>
> What minimally intrusive little favors can you provide to keep her going towards her goal?

Exercise 73

> ### *DYC* Example:
>
> - Maybe she needs you to prepare the meals at the end of the day.
> - Maybe she needs you to stop her from pressing the snooze button in the morning.
> - Maybe she needs you to "join her" as she gears up for her next test, helping her learn needed new skills.

> ### EXERCISE #74: IN THE LOCKER ROOM
>
> If your character wants to change up your routine together, then commit to the new customs. Take this opportunity to clearly define how you plan to aid her in her quest. Develop a schedule of your activities and times, so that you both start to take your responsibilities earnestly. Be sure and document her level of abilities when she starts, so that you, as her coach, can chart her progress along the way.

Exercise 74

EXERCISE #74-b: IN THE LOCKER ROOM

Devise *two instances* where you're involved in preparing her for the next step in her journey. For each, think about the logistics and the motivating techniques required to get her to show up and fully commit.

Motivation:

- How do you put her head in the game?
- What kind of attitude and sense of readiness do you have to show up with?
- How do you help her reshuffle other areas of her life so she can prioritize this goal-centric activity?

Logistics:

- Do you have to reserve a space beforehand?
- How much set-up time do you need?
- Do you need to get special equipment?

Exercise 74-b

EXERCISE #74-c: IN THE LOCKER ROOM

Spend *a page* describing:

- What she's doing.
- What you're doing.
- Her attitude throughout—both during that first day and during the first few sessions of this new conscious, training effort.
- How this working partnership is different from how you used to spend time together.

Exercise 74-c

You may have to continually coax more effort out of your character. Praise her when it's deserved. Brush aside, if you can, any of her misgivings. Don't downplay them, put them in perspective. It takes sensitivity to show a little faith, while telling her the unvarnished truth. When two people are fumbling around and trying to connect, their words often take on a strained poignancy and immediacy. When you're writing, dialogue is best composed *verbally*, particularly in strained situations.

> ### EXERCISE #75: PEP TALK
>
> Audio record your side of a conversation with her. Imagine that she's not threatened by the suggestions you're offering and is interested enough to hear you out without interruption. But, even if you're trying to be helpful, you can't expect her to remain receptive while you're pointing out her faults.
>
> Make your speech build, so that when she has to swallow the bitter pill of criticism, she knows that you have her best interests at heart. She can't feel you're taking advantage of the situation to vent and get back at her. It's got to come from a pure place.
>
> She's probably already aware of what she does well, so she may brush aside any flattery, but if you come up with some words of well-deserved praise they'll be the spoonful of sugar to make the medicine go down.
>
> Plan on talking into your recorder for *four* or *five minutes*.

Exercise 75

EXERCISE #75-b: PEP TALK

In turn, <u>write</u> down everything she says back to you. She's had plenty of time to soberly assess your points, so she'll probably have the upper hand in her response.

As she's writing, she can be as emotional or angry as she wants. She calls the shots. Just as you were allowed to go on without pause, your thoughts shouldn't mesh with hers.

Her letter or email should cover about *two typed pages*. If she's a PowerPoint type of woman, then *ten*.

Exercise 75-b

Depending on her personality, a little pep talk could be a harmless way of galvanizing and streamlining her intention. But what if more than motivation is needed for her to press on? If your character is really meek, and already thinking of seriously bowing out, how can you get her to stand on her two feet, while also taking on some of her stress? It's a delicate balance and all depends on who you're dealing with.

You can't treat her like a damsel in distress, even if she may want you to. She has to do the heavy lifting. But you can buy her a *Special K* protein drink and bark out reps as she works to sculpt her physique. When you point out who else is depending on her to succeed, maybe her sense of purpose will be renewed.

EXERCISE #76: ON THE ROUNDED *SHOULDERS OF ATLAS*

- Who is the most important person in her life?
- How involved is he/she in her end goal?
- How will he/she be impacted if her actions misfire?
- How will his/her life be improved, if she is ultimately successful?

Exercise 76

This must be her journey, not anyone else's. Even if she's partly fighting the good fight on others' behalf. If you can figure out a way to help her improve upon her weaknesses, that's a targeted means of being of service without taking responsibility for her meeting her goal. After all, at this stage, you two are equals. This is no longer an amusing proposition, an experiment she halfheartedly signed up for extra cash, "insight," or free medical testing.

If she's in it for the long haul, some things may have to change. You can't expect your novelty to last. She's going to expect some maturity in your relationship. Maybe she figures she's owed more than you've given.

To demonstrate your staying power and usefulness, pretend as though you're signing up for a task the protagonist herself has to accomplish. Think about it in all its practical dimensions. After you thrash out this theoretical situation, walk through a couple of the set-piece challenges she'll face, becoming aware of the beat-by-beat breaths in those scenes.

EXERCISE #77: PROVE YOURSELF ALREADY!

Take the following hypothetical dilemma and tease it out in *ten steps*.

You have to save money... (x)

(You can ignore the letters in parentheses at the end of each line, as well as the designation "set-piece." We'll discuss what these mean at the end of the exercise.)

Make sure it follows the rough shape of a swoosh, as below:

DYC Example:

(Does the money have to be in a foreign currency?) (p)
  (Does that money have to be laundered?) (q)
    (Does that involve working for a sketchy character?) (r)
      (Do you have to do something stomach churning?) (s—set-piece)
        (Do you have to avoid being caught?) (s—set-piece)
          (If you are, how do you get out of it?) (s—set-piece)
        (Does that mean getting an advance from somebody?) (t)
      (How will you work that off?) (u)
    (How time-consuming is that?) (v)
  (What gets left by the wayside?) (w)

Here's one for you:

You have to lose weight... (x)

It doesn't have to generate conflict as in the above example. It can

Dating Your Character

> be a walk-through, where you're fully enmeshed in the attitude, skill, funding, time constraints, and other essential conditions that define what's about to unfold.

Exercise 77

> **EXERCISE #77-b: PROVE YOURSELF ALREADY?**
> Now do the same branch-out of *two* real, risk-riddled *situations* that could most likely occur for your protagonist in Act Two.

Exercise 77-b

In the above exercise, each letter is a branch in a tree. If a character can't get "x," then "y" doesn't happen. If she doesn't have "y," then her end goal is even farther out of reach.

Sometimes your character won't get "x." Or "x" will be snatched from her. She'll have to come up with a nifty solution,

"x^2," to eventually find her way around to "y" and "z."

To give you a rough idea of the possibility for signature action scenes within the tree, it's reasonable to figure that two or three combined scenes could form a **"set-piece."** A scene that is primarily action-based is a set-piece. Tension in previous scenes has been building for a while, resulting in necessary action that brings about a final release. But, as mentioned in Chapter Four, this explosion can also be found in a "block comedy sequence" of visual gags that provide a madcap eruption.

The swoosh exercise forces you to clarify each step involved in the chain of events (and the potential for complication in the set-piece) that will all bring about a change in your character's focus. When distilled, that list should result in three big dramatic plot reversals that only compound the danger for her.

In the example above, a couple of those moments for "you" are in the set-piece (s). When "you have to do something stomach churning" that implies it's not in your wheelhouse and/or compromises you in some way. So, the risk has just been ramped up. Then, even if "you avoid being caught," which is a whole other world of hurt, what's going to be the cost? Missing an important meet-up? A debilitating physical injury?

The third instance where there's a difference in the story equation's threat-level is when "you" take a hit (w). At this point, you have to realign "x," what you've been after all along. Remember, "x" is the encompassing need you're trying to satisfy.

Eventually, you'll have to react on the fly and improvise with "x^2," which is why you're willing to get drawn into the orbits of (r) and (t).

FILM EXAMPLE

In the 2011 Justin Timberlake film *In Time*, his character is gifted with 100 years of life to spend as he wishes. This is a world in which time is the currency of life and where most citizens have a prescribed expiration date of 25 years. But Will has been accused by the police, "the timekeepers," for robbing and killing his benefactor.

When he and his girlfriend/hostage, Sylvia (Amanda Seyfried), are robbed of their time by a local thief (x), it makes their escape from the timekeepers (z) on their heels nearly impossible. With certain death looming, Will decides to "ransom" Sylvia (x^2). When her selfishly principled father refuses to pay up, Will and Sylvia form a Bonnie and Clyde-type duo and knock off time banks (y).

Will's latent hostility to the status quo is now expressed as both a practical life-giving tool for himself and a rallying cry for the time-impoverished citizens of the area. Their flashy crime capers are the set-pieces that the previous plot points have made imperative. Will's original goal of living the life he was given to the fullest, and evading the police who want to confiscate his time property (and thus his life), has morphed into something bigger.

You need to make sure there are links in your outline that directly lead from one course of action to the next. Think about all the drawbacks inherent in trying to attack one of those goals, (one of those letters)...Do they feed into a couple of key adrenaline-laced circumstances? Consider how your genre and tone of attack impact these choices and the progression within the movement from point to point.

> ### EXERCISE #78: MURPHY'S LAW
> List at least ~~ten ways~~ three of those steps in your script or outline can go wrong...

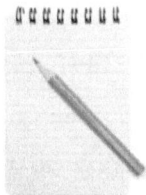

Exercise 78

This opportunity for conflict is what powers your plot and reveals your character. Don't shy away from complications, as long as the main goal of the character is affected by these dilemmas. Of course, maneuvering out of these quandaries requires a hardiness of spirit. Even the stoutest characters stand in need of encouragement, now and then.

Having proven your usefulness and integrity time and again, you've become a vital cog in her operation. As you forge ever closer bonds, it'll probably be easier to have more serious and open-ended conversations. Since you're in proximity to one another more often, you can take advantage of the convenience of sharing each other's thoughts in a less formal, event-oriented atmosphere.

You two have been through a lot, so arrange a "home date" that lets you catch up and decompress. It's an opportunity to enjoy spending quality time with her. You don't want her to see you as only being around for the lighter stuff.

EXERCISE #79: THE HOME DATE
Write her a note telling her you want to make some time to talk. Let her know you'll cook or pick up a meal. Sign off that you hope to see her at the time you've designated.

Exercise 79

The discussion is meant to be deeper than the ones you usually have. Really weigh her responses. Especially, what she's holding back.

This exercise will ask her to think on three levels:

- How she appraises her life at the moment.
- How honest she is with herself.
- And, at this stage in your relationship, how forthright she is with you.

It will also require her to gauge your support in a practical way. It'll force her to determine her end goals and the tangible steps that have to occur for her to eventually get there.

You'll take on some of her pre-planning for a few of these tests. You'll get past acting as a functionary—chauffeur, masseuse, whatever—since you've demonstrated that you have a handle on the ins and outs of a couple of the feats that will challenge her.

Dating Your Character

> ### EXERCISE #79-b: THE HOME DATE
>
> At the "home date" ask her:
>
> - What's bothering her—about your relationship and about life in general…?
> - How can you be of help…?
> - What *two* concrete *tasks* or actions would give her some relief…?
>
> This exercise should take you about *an hour* to complete and generate about *five* or *six double-spaced, typewritten pages*.

Exercise 79-b

Your character has to let you in. She has to be willing to constantly recalibrate her plans. If she's stubborn and doesn't want to modify them, then at least she has to be open about what's motivating her and why she thinks she's on the right track, contrary to her results so far.

Chances are, even after this encounter, she won't have spilled her guts entirely. You'll have to put in a bit more time and work. Anything that's worth doing well requires attention and practice. So one magical exchange can only light the way. And know that you can't solely rely on a few choice rendezvous to reveal more to you.

Remember this relationship can't always be about getting what you want—information. Though you've shown her that you're serious about your relationship, you've got to appreciate her and demonstrate that gratitude. *As a reward for trusting you, a simple shoulder rub or foot massage goes a long way.*

On days where special efforts aren't made, you're both bound to fall into bad habits, petty acts of indifference, or other selfish maneuvers that can prove divisive if they accumulate. This may not even be conscious. Nerves or tiredness can overcome your best intentions. But being authentic takes energy.

If you can take on the responsibility of gearing her up for her future confrontations, you'll lift some of the pressure off her shoulders. She'll be the one going into battle. But because she has you to share her vision, someone who understands the sacrifices it will demand, that will ground her and transcend any moments of doubt. She'll be annoyed that you're asking so much from her. And in order to unmask her, you might have to piss her off.

We're launching into the next *DYC* phase, **The First Fight.** For her to get what she wants, she's going to have to come clean with what she needs—that secret agenda under it all—that will allow her to complete her transformation. But, if you've done your homework and exercised your truth-seeking muscles, something surprising can happen as you approach the first big explosion between you.

GO ON TO CHAPTER SIX.

THE FIRST FIGHT "BACK HALF OF ACT II"—STEP SIX

IN ALL THE preceding chapters (Steps I-V), focusing on and investing in the writer-character relationship has yielded a number of benefits. You feel like you know her and can motivate her effectively. You've helped her up the stakes, even when she initially didn't want to. And you've found a way to keep the Second Act lively, using the complex machinery of your character: creating instability in her status quo, escalating strife, and increasing the hazards in her story.

In *DYC* terminology, this entire eight-step process is about creating a relationship, dimensionality, and genuine stakes so your audience can experience her as a walking, talking breathing "iconic" representation of a human being.

Don't shy away from philosophical and emotional clashes. We guarantee there will be some sort of tension on the horizon from petty arguments, your barrage of questions, her worries for the future, and the constant pressure you're both under. But rising conflict with her will be necessary to stoke her to a boiling point. If you aren't sure what will fire her up, how will you recognize how much she's willing to do to retrain her mind, body, and spirit?

EXERCISE #80: PUTTING ON THE SCREWS

Devise *two* awkward sets of *circumstances* that will threaten her success. Construct your dilemma for her in *three stages*. With each stage, exert more pressure on her at regular intervals. Describe her likely state of mind as things heat up, threatening her relationships, her place in the world, and even objects that may be sentimental or have value to her. This should take about a *page and a half* for each scenario.

Exercise 80

How much is she in danger of crumbling? How far does/can this set her back on her journey?

> **EXERCISE #81: FORCING THE ISSUE**
> Construct the run-up to such a scenario. Then, play out the scene itself. Your ratio of action to dialogue is up to you. Each of your *four scenes* should take about *three pages*...

 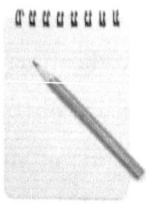

Exercise 81

> **EXERCISE #81-b: FORCING THE ISSUE**
> Using the same *three-stage* technique, devise *two* dangerous (for her) sets of *circumstances* that will threaten her very survival.

Exercise 81-b

Going forward, you'll recognize opportunities to exacerbate the pitfalls you've already designed. All types of conflict are useful in helping you figure out what she's desperately <u>trying to *avoid*, what she's *afraid* of...and that will help you refine what she *needs*.</u>

DECONSTRUCTING NEGATIVE REACTIONS TO CONFLICT

Negative reactions can take many self-defeating forms, namely, denial and despair. So is surrendering your integrity, by choosing what's easiest, what's safest. In short, selling out to be less than you are. Some of these detrimental emotional beats will go a long way to making your character more relatable and relevant.

FILM EXAMPLE

In *Hotel Rwanda*, Don Cheadle's character, Paul Rusesabagina, desperately hopes someone—or some nation—will come to the rescue during an ugly Hutu uprising. Rusesabagina, based on a real person, is friendly with Col. Oliver of the UN's peacekeeping force and puts his faith in him. But Col. Oliver and his heavily armed troops are there strictly to observe. It's gut-wrenching to watch the crude, machete-wielding, genocidal wave of Hutus prepare to slaughter the Tutsi power elite.

Even though Hutus are already stationed outside the perimeter of the luxury hotel he manages, Rusesabagina clings to the belief that its wealthy international clientele will quickly draw the attention of many news agencies. But there's not much of a public spotlight to dampen the bloodthirsty enthusiasm of the Hutus, reporters and cameras only trickle in.

Rusesabagina is a man whose social skills have made him smoothly effective. He's not someone accustomed to violence and atrocity firsthand. However, as any real promise of help fades away, he comes to the grim conclusion that he's the lone hope for the people in his hotel. He's clever, someone whose gift of anticipation, which made him such a top-notch manager, now allows him to imagine each coming threat. At every turn, his ingenuity saves the day by the slimmest of margins. But he goes above and beyond trying to protect his family, which is his primary motivation. Deeper in the script, he repeatedly puts himself at great risk for the sake of his guests and staff.

FEAR AS FUEL—THE DUALITY OF YOUR CHARACTER'S ULTIMATE DRIVE

Fear often manifests in your character making bad decisions, but acting out of the *belief* that she's moving somewhere away from the fear… Fear propels her rapid movement forward or fear drives her to retreat safely backward. But, as in the example above, fear can bring out positive attributes, like a brave selflessness that protects someone weaker.

Though his initial actions are justifiable, Rusesabagina ends up severely beating the attackers who breach the hotel and come after his family. If even this cultured man can let a primitive satisfaction leak through, superseding the brutality that's absolutely necessary, we can see how reacting from <u>fear</u> and resorting to violence can shatter your character's core.

<u>Fear</u> is the tightly wound coil within your character that springs her into action. The longer you're afraid, the more likely you'll hit a point where you surely have to retaliate. Unexpressed or repressed emotions operate as if in an echo chamber, amplifying in magnitude over time.

Note, though, that <u>fear</u> is a response to something *specific*. It's not paranoia, because your character's already felt some of the effects. The danger's out there and has already struck more than once.

AVOIDANCE/ DENIAL

Fear is not an overwhelmingly miasmic sensation, but is directed to a specific person or group, in marked difference to the state of "<u>denial</u>." <u>Avoidance</u> also recognizes a definite subject, but is a null action, because it flees from confrontation.

<u>Avoidance</u> is a traditionally early emotional response, which goes hand-in-hand with <u>denial</u>. If <u>denial</u> is the state of mind, <u>avoidance</u> is the "action." Besides your own role in complicating her life, what duties, people, and outcomes is she <u>trying to avoid</u>?

EXERCISE #82: LIFE IS "GREAT"

- Does she seem to be more available to you? When and how is her behavior different?
- What behavior is she demonstrating that leads you to believe she's avoiding life?
- Is she ducking you, avoiding phone calls, not answering texts?
- Is what she's normally on top of turning to shit?

Exercise 82

EXERCISE #82-b: LIFE IS GREAT

- What is she doing instead?
- Who is she hanging with?
- Are her actions supporting her quest or derailing it?
- Is her community behind her or trying to redirect her energies?

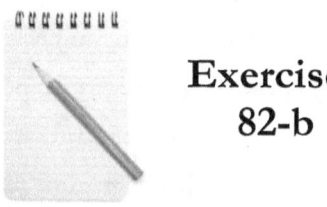

Exercise 82-b

FILM EXAMPLE

The First Act, in many cinematic examples, is generally when a character wrestles with <u>denial</u>. The character has not yet chosen to act, and this is often where we see the slow bankruptcy of spirit.

In the Sarah Jessica Parker/Matthew McConaughey rom-com, *Failure to Launch,* Tripp (McConaughey) seems to be content with his life. He's got a cool pad/maid service, (his parents' house/his mom), an easy, part-time work routine, and a goal comfortably within reach (restoring a boat). He has fun with the ladies and really isn't bummed out by the fact that he can't maintain a serious relationship. It's only when lovely Paula (Parker) comes into his life, appearing to accept his living arrangements, that he seriously reevaluates the appropriateness of how he's been functioning.

Though <u>denial</u> is usually present very early on, it can waylay someone at any point in the story. But contrary to the prolonged, willful ignorance of people in <u>denial</u> in real life, that can't happen in filmed entertainment. Screenwriting convention doesn't allow for the character's passivity for long, especially if the factors that pile up and cause a character's paralysis happen deep in Act II. Though life's spinning out of control, and it's tempting to just disappear under the covers, your character can't wait for a freak asteroid to put her out of her misery.

As a writer, you've got to regard any case where your character may be unable to move, as simply the calm before the storm. There had better be underlying tension, and/or a decision that we have invested in, hanging in the balance.

While you're required to be true to your character, your most important job is to help shape the arc of her story. She has to come up from under the covers and *do something.* Build a shelter, invent a new type of camera, take over behind the wheel and drive, attack the alien horde, maybe bring down an advanced civilization or two. She may indeed be frozen, or temporarily revert to some throwback pattern of behavior, but in 99% of stories (even a tragedy), your character will pull herself up and at least face her last challenge. She'll engage and do battle with her inner and outer nemeses, even if the outcome isn't certain...

Film is a visual medium after all. If she never comes out of her funk, there probably won't be much to see. She can still make mistakes—disastrous mistakes—but her hiding from life is not an option.

How then can she overcome her inactivity to begin fighting back with renewed strength and determination?

DEVISING ACTIVE AND PASSIVE REACTIONS

From about page 30 on, your goal is to see that almost all your character's actions are active. Actions and reactions are really just the alternating beats and rhythms in your story's musical composition. She does something, and someone else hits the "story ball" back.

Shifts, turns in the road, surprises are all part of the volley back. She then can make the same swing, move to hit it, stop playing against that competitor, or even step aside from that particular game. Contrary to what is commonly thought, reactions can be "active" as long as your character continues to plan, move, and grow *pari passu* with escalating hurdles.

So what's the difference between passive and active character resolutions?

A passive policy involves the character farming out the hard work to someone else or waiting for someone to come to the fore. While natural in real life, films don't often celebrate this kind of enervating normality. Your character has to start volunteering for heavy duty, recruiting likeminded allies, and coming up with inventive moves to overcome her debilitations!

Dating Your Character

> **EXERCISE #83: FROM PAWN TO QUEEN**
>
> Without changing the abilities assigned to your character in these exercises, come up with *three ways* to make her decisions active.
>
> - Your character is on a strict diet, but must taste-test a number of wedding cakes for a demanding, but unavailable, client.
> - Your character has a marked limp, but has to scale a three-story wall in order to disable a security camera for her part in a museum heist.
> - Your character is deathly afraid of water and never learned to swim. A child has fallen into a swimming pool and has gone under. Your character calls out for someone else to dive in and save him. But the only other people around are a couple of passed out teens in the house.

Exercise 83

Consciously making active versus passive decisions inherently involves more risk. The character may be unaware of what the particular consequences could be and her potential for failure. Even if she's successful on her set course, the reactions from other characters could be just as dangerous for her. And, an insight into what fully awaits her may induce her to reassess, compromise, and walk away from the fight. So, keep in mind that a sliver of delusion may allow her to persevere.

But if she's been shielding herself all along, living in a bubble, why hasn't she acted before?

- Out of laziness?
- Not enough personal investment?
- Not feeling that she's the only one who can and will come through it in the end?

Beyond the inertia and excuses, how else has she been lying to herself?

EXERCISE #83-b: FROM PAWN TO QUEEN

Without resorting to reviewing your notes and scenes, recall the times when your character has lied.

- What was she trying to protect by lying?
- Was she protecting a relationship with someone else or an idea of herself?
- What is she afraid could happen if she told the truth?
- What does she accept as the reason she resorted to deception?
- And what unacknowledged motivation is there within her choice to fib?

Exercise 83-b

For any character to be relatable, she has to match human proportions. She has to be crafted with flaws, foibles, and daunting idiosyncrasies. She must be perfect in her imperfection.

It's not just the world that's trying to bring her down. She'll undoubtedly compromise her higher purpose time and again, and may make less than honorable accommodations calculated to ease her journey. And those less-than-perfect choices only end up sabotaging her efforts.

You've been thinking about how your story arc will resolve her flaws, wrestling with the personal and wider fallout from her errors in judgment. But you probably haven't given much thought to your character's manipulative, darker side.

- Does she ever knowingly act in a manner that's certain to hurt other characters?
- Does she do this for their own good or for selfish reasons?
- What would cause her to take that surprising, or not so surprising, shadowy turn?

Perhaps neither of you saw it coming, but as Yoda would say, percolate out into the open it did. And frankly, until this untapped pollutant oozes up from her unconscious, the character may feel flat and lacking in dimension.

Light and dark elements add to her compelling complexity.

EXERCISE #84: SHRINKING HER DOWN TO SIZE

Think about occasions where your character's cowardice, inadvertent misleading statements, omissions, or surprising bad behavior have caused a painful reversal for another character.

- How did she cope with that awareness later?
- Was there a debt she owed that played out, unexpectedly, in a subsequent plot moment?
- (If there aren't any, try and come up with *three or four examples* for her story.)

Exercise 84

> **EXERCISE #84-b: SHRINKING HER DOWN TO SIZE**
>
> How many reasonable "cop outs" can you concoct to make her appear less than heroic?

Exercise 84-b

We all Photoshop our mental picture of who we are, partly, to conform to modern society's ideas of morality, self-worth, and beauty. Your character's most likely also sculpting her identity. How people arrive at their vision of themselves is more emotional than you might think.

First, let's attune ourselves to the forces at work that shape personal and popular opinion in general. People who are trying objectively to look at topical subjects outside themselves still seem to fall into certain predictable habits.

According to recent research commissioned by the BBC for their 2014 documentary *Scotland Decides*, while debating about whether to remain a part of Great Britain or become an independent, sovereign country, those on the fence didn't try to refute the views they tentatively held. Commonly, people tended to only consider arguments put forth by the side they were already biased toward.

As you'd expect, images played a huge role in helping these voters come to a conclusion. After the Unionists realized previous weeks of fear-mongering was riling the public, its iconography strove to reinforce a message of enduring loyalty and tradition, which they hoped the undecided would cherish nostalgically.

The Scottish National Party also plucked at the heartstrings. One of its political flyers featured a blue-painted face, which recalled Mel Gibson's blue-streaked *Braveheart* rendering of hero William Wallace, who fought for Scottish independence in the 13th century. With an undercurrent that stoked long-nursed notions of thwarted destiny, the SNP offered a striking, bold, blue world that seemed limitless, but also unknown.

The Unionists' successful campaign eventually relied on a visual environment that was self-consciously cozy, British. Both sides ended up waging a sentimental battle more than an analysis of an independent Scotland's administrative upheaval, economic viability, and the European Union's probable position on its membership.

Why are emotional arguments so persuasive?

Basically, there are three channels of varying consciousness that contribute to making a selection that can significantly impact your life. Advertisers have made an entire industry out of the interplay of the conscious, unconscious, and subconscious.

According to Freud, the "unconscious" mind has cravings of its own that are thankfully invisible to the conscious mind. It's where taboo desires, traumatic memories, and shameful emotions are stored. Through accessing the eruptions of the unconscious during dreams "ideas of feeble potential...[can] reach a degree of intensity which enables them to force their way into consciousness."[6]

Though he would disagree about the existence of yet another stratum, the "subconscious," the psychologist Pierre Janet argued that "underneath the layers of critical thought...lay a powerful awareness that he called 'the subconscious mind.'"[7] Because there is a limit to the information that the mind can be aware of, it's composed of your knowledge and prior experience. According to brain research, the mind clocks 40 pieces of information at any given moment consciously, but records something like 40,000 pieces of information in the unconscious.[8]

When there are important issues at stake, it's up to you to judge how compliant or suggestible your character is. For you to gain entry into her mental machinery, you'll need to get more comfortable with these and other elements that feed into her thought paths. If there are choices she sometimes opts for that aren't objectively logical or seem counterproductive, they'll have stemmed from some recess of her psyche, where it does in fact make a kind of cloudy sense to her. Maybe, out of a subconscious need to excise the guilt she has from some of her actions.

If you find you need to complicate her progress, it's crucial to be able to break down her system of moral equivalency and self-determination.

In *DYC* screenwriting terms and execution, the three parts of the decision-making process are:

- the **OVERT PLAN**—an openly shared goal that she announces to the world broadcasting what she's about to do…(ego-invested conscious)
- the **COVERT INTENTION**—a private goal that is never stated and kept within…(intuitive subconscious)
- the **UGLY WELLSPRING of ACTION**—what she actually does that goes outside the scope of her plan. This action comes up during stress and usually confounds her and surprises you. This is a private hunger that is emotionally charged when it surfaces. It can turn the direction of the story on its head…(manifested unconscious)

While your character may not ever be privy to the interplay of the wheels spinning in her head, if you can be more clued in, you'll be able to tap into the more hidden parts of her nature. Your invigorated awareness will allow you to step aside and let her be truly responsible for her actions.

EXERCISE #85: GOING BEYOND THE BLUEPRINT

- Describe in utmost detail the nature of one of her most comprehensive plans.

- How can you muddy her intentions so that she errs on the side of excess, indulging in a less than heroic satisfaction?

Example from Elizabeth:

My priest/activist character wants to confront the biggest outpost of the recently privatized Brazilian hydroelectric energy industry. He's a vocal supporter of indigenous peoples' right to territory and sovereignty. But he knows that these large companies have mercenaries on their payroll. They've also managed to "incentivize" the local fishermen, who have lost their livelihoods through the damming of a major tributary of the Amazon. My character **OVERTLY PLANS** to train the youngest warriors of the Volta Grande to booby-trap the cheap, wooden forts and slick, muddy trenches that have closed them off to their ancestral land.

The *Xingu* and other tribes' very survival are on the line, because they are unprepared for a life that doesn't conform to the rhythms of the rainforest. Those from other tribes, who have already accepted money to be moved off their lands, have become severely depressed in the big city of Manaus.

My character, Jorge, learns to throw poison-tipped spears from the small tribe of *Taino* Indians he embeds with. He's been practicing ostensibly to ward off predators in the jungle. But he exaggerates the design of his *yekuana* whip-spear to lengthen its trunk and curve. Now, the curve no longer allows for a straight trajectory. It actually favors a gracefully arcing descent, something useful if your prey isn't in a tree or slithering on the ground in front of you, but standing at human height some distance away. His **COVERT INTENTION** is not to cripple the industry or make a political statement. It is to draw first blood, which will create carnage: of mixed-race *pardo* and Amerindian alike.

The **UGLY WELLSPRING of ACTION** he takes is to row a dugout canoe-full of the modified weapons under the guise of self-defense. While he and some of the more daring tribesmen use the spears to attack, those setting up snares on the front lines will receive the bulk of any retaliation. He's so wrapped up in his righteous fantasy, I don't know how consciously culpable he is at the end of the day. He's also probably not factoring in how quickly the repercussions will become deadly from the violence he's stoking. He has no idea of the suffering he has wrought, while trying to save them. The hydroelectric cooperative has the money to pay professionals to wage a precise, high-tech war, while keeping the media largely at bay.

Exercise 85

FILM EXAMPLE

In Christopher Nolan's *The Prestige,* two junior magicians, Robert (Hugh Jackman) and Alfred (Christian Bale), have a healthy competition to see who will go forth from their mentor's shadow and become a headliner, himself. Robert is a gentleman magician, who doesn't have the drive that Cockney Alfred does. The Inciting Incident in *The Prestige* happens after Robert's wife, who's part of the act, is killed when she can't pull off a Houdini-esque escape. Robert blames Alfred for making it impossible for her to have released her bound hands.

In order to ruin Alfred's prospects, Robert embarks on a solo career with new urgency. His dilettantism is no longer possible. He's been cruelly concussed out of his comfortable apprenticeship and must approach life with a single-minded obsession. He **OVERTLY PLANS** to eviscerate Alfred with the only tool available to him: magic. But his quest for retribution grows in brutality. When all is said and done, Robert really **COVERTLY**

Dating Your Character

INTENDS to avenge his wife's horrific death in as approximate a way as he is able, committing the murder of Alfred publicly…and getting away with it.

Through the **UGLY WELLSPRING of ACTION** he takes, his vengeful path not only poisons their professional rivalry until it becomes absolutely rancid, it results in multiple deaths. Before engineering Alfred's lynching, combining both his flair for the dramatic and his desire to best Alfred, he even manages to outdo his signature trick.

If your character's intentions are her *most private deliberations*, then getting her to openly admit them to you *requires trust*. She has to believe there is some reason to compel her to do so. This is not something friends ask of each other. This kind of driving force may only be shown the light of day in a therapist's office. She has to recognize that she'll be closer to her goal if she does so: that she can craft a final goal that will deliver satisfaction on several levels, if she can be honest with herself and with you…

It's important that she make her final corrections and preparations dutifully. Regardless of her confidence or lack thereof, she should be able to clearly articulate the rest of her game plan and the measures she's taking to emerge victorious. Or, if at the end, she's destined to fail, then at least she'll have marshaled the strength to give it a serious go.

> **EXERCISE #86: SUBMARINE SANDWICH**
> - How many interior goals would have to be met?
> - What kind of poignant breakthrough would satisfy her?
> - What action or skill would allow her to demonstrate this new emotional awareness?

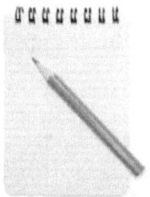

Exercise 86

> **EXERCISE #86-b: SUBMARINE SANDWICH**
> - What kind of relationship is she repairing?
> - Does she have to quash one of her natural gifts in order to give someone else a chance to shine?

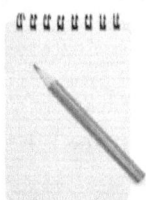

Exercise 86-b

FILM EXAMPLE

In *Rachel Getting Married*, for which Anne Hathaway was nominated for an Oscar as Best Actress in a Leading Role, her character, Kym, has to stop telling lies. That's got to be at the top of her inner to-do list. It's the only way she'll get any benefit out of the rehab program she's in. Instead, she regales the other in-patients with stories of family tragedy that turn her into a victim and a saint. The painful truth is as dramatic, but that doesn't satisfy the storyteller in Kym. She's in denial about her guilt, the pain she caused her whole family, and her inability to make any kind of meaningful atonement.

Secondly, Kym has to gain greater perspective. She was to blame for the death of her younger brother, Ethan, by a traffic collision she caused. But her mother Abby (Debra Winger) was also partially at fault for letting her daughter, who was inebriated at the time, take charge of Ethan. She needs to take control of her life and regain her sobriety. Even before the accident, she's been dulling the aches of impending adulthood. But if she can trust that by owning up to what she did, she'll be able to live a life of real connection and feeling again.

Thirdly, after Kym decides she doesn't want to hide from her past anymore, she creates a public spectacle of herself by crashing into a tree... On the day of her sister Rachel's (Rosemarie DeWitt) wedding, naturally. It's perhaps too neat a symmetry, but it symbolizes that she's willing to face the truth, even if it hurts.

In coming out in the open by showing she understands the damage she's done, and also the toll it's taken on her, she's managed to make a start at patching up her relationship with Rachel. But the fight that followed Kym's confrontation of her mother's shared responsibility in the accident is just the first step. She'll have to take many more to forge a path of honesty that may lead to forgiveness.

As you've seen, a moving emotional development isn't always a soft and cuddly moment of acceptance and vulnerability. Kym's reconciliation with herself is violent, solitary. But a demonstration of love and affection sometimes demands steely self-sacrifice. If this kind of generous action isn't one your character would even have contemplated earlier on, why is this the only action she can take now, and why is it the "right" one?

Being capable of enduring such an ordeal calls on reserves of strength that almost defy comprehension. In general, it requires seeing the big picture and altruistically balancing the welfare of others against the character's own. That isn't something most mortals are blessed with.

> **EXERCISE #87: AEGIS OF HONOR**
> - Who is she saving/protecting?
> - What is she preventing?

Exercise 87

What allows her to do this? What distinguishes her from everyone else? Even from likeminded friends and comrades?

Why doesn't she seem afraid, or act afraid, like anyone would be?

At this point in your story, your character may not, in fact, be exhibiting this fearlessness. If so, if she's wavered, she'll have to regain her composure. As discussed, fear can be a way-station reaction until a character involuntarily responds or decides how to reply. Deep in the Second Act, if she makes a self-defeating choice or succumbs to inertia, she's got to bounce right back. There's no more time for detrimental action.

Nevertheless, it might be helpful to look at the various ways her old self might have reacted in these latter situations to gauge how far she's come. You've got to stand back and be objective. You've always been on her side, so maybe you've exaggerated her progress. You've got to feel comfortable tracing a true arc in her story.

> **EXERCISE #88: STARING DOWN THE LION**
>
> Without referring to past episodes that you've defined as "traumatic," think about *two occurrences* that may be in your outline, or in your responses to previous exercises, that show her afraid.
>
> - What caused her to be anxious?
> - How did she handle that nervousness?
> - How will she confront a similar event in the story and rewrite her destiny?

Exercise 88

Isolating her former reactions to this primal catalyst has other benefits. Besides providing a parallel you may wish to incorporate in your script, if she's the stoic type, it's an opportunity for her to show you fear. Likewise, it's a technique to distinguish her from the other souls doing battle in the story: her family, friends, and the strangers who come into her path.

If her prior method of handling fear has been unorthodox, clumsy, or off-putting, you can now frame it. Not as a means of rehabilitating her, but in further backing the specificity of her choices in counterpoint to how the others react. (However, more than likely, that will allow you to supply a waffling, flawed, or distasteful character with added appeal.)

After all, her friends may be encouraging her, but no one's experiencing the onslaught to the degree she is. And, irrespective of their best intentions, they won't be as stout-hearted. If she's accompanied by other characters at a really stressful stage, one or two of them may just bail on her.

If that's the case, she'll never feel more alone...

So what differentiates her from these friends and fellow combatants? What's that soul-piece in her inner compass guiding her? Without that, whatever it is, like them, she'd be able to fade into the background. She wouldn't have to bear the brunt of all the slings and arrows herself.

Each of these other supporting characters is basically a chance to contrast your protagonist's true feelings in any awkward, difficult, or dire situation. Certain affiliate characters may be more on her side, while other minor and major antagonists exist to compound the discomfort of her journey. They all conspire to push her to make choices. She can agree and go along with everyone else, or resolve to take a stand. Though, in Act I, she would probably just stew and hold her reservations inside.

Don't look on the more trying characters with annoyance. They're there not only to make your character look good in contrast. They'll force her to improve and become more of a substantial force to reckon with. But, if your protagonist is coming up against cliché or boring baddies, her eventual triumph isn't going to be that spectacular. So spend time studying who they are, too, and activate them in ways that are fresh and novel.

> **EXERCISE #89: KEY FRIENDS, FRENEMIES, AND FOES**
> - What are their *one* or *two traits* that are oppositional to the protagonist's?
> - How do they offer support in scenes where she's under duress?
> - How are they unknowingly leveraged to put even more pressure on her?

Exercise 89

Not every character has to function in direct proportion to the protagonist. Just realize and take advantage of the fact that in the complex, lengthy equation of your screenplay, no one is a plain "0" stock character and no one—not your antagonist, or your protagonist (even in Act 3)—is "∞ (infinite)." Like people, they come from diverse backgrounds, have individual goals, and varying ratios of good/bad in them.

If you think of the mechanics of how your story moves, and how your character flourishes and is thwarted, it's not solely specific events that bring this about. It's also about the other characters who have attempted to engineer dicey situations favorable to them. Which characters can mirror and challenge her awakening at every step?

FILM EXAMPLE

While there were many different Batman incarnations, the Christopher Nolan film franchise set the stage for one of the most memorable dynamic hero-villain pairings: the sparks fly between Batman (Christian Bale) and his nemesis the Joker (Heath Ledger). In the second film, Ledger's goofily grotesque Joker finally taunts Batman with the question, *"Why so serious?"*

Writer David S. Goyer's line irritates Batman. The words resonate with comedy and pathos. They target his Achilles Heel—his over-amped sense of responsibility. The Joker, a creepy, intuitive psychopath, knows Batman cares deeply about stopping crime—*all* crime. Because Batman cares so much, The Joker's able to set him up to take a fall. Just like Pavlov's habituated dog, when the Caped Crusader gets the call to help, he responds to the signal immediately.

Batman goes through a painful awakening process and surrenders to a point of view larger in scope, more disinterested. That compelling truth—that life can be arbitrary and meaningless—and his struggle with it—is the glue that keeps audiences coming back. (Not to mention spectacular stunts, special effects, and some award-worthy performances.) Out of that "dark night of the soul" strides forth a new "dark knight."

DYC's Phase 6 is dedicated to fomenting and releasing this kind of impending implosion due to the tension between your character's inner and outer self. In life, there may be many competing drives within a character. In art, we simplify and magnify to focus the thrust of a story. Art is not life, but life pushed to an illogical extreme. If you're successful, your audience will see themselves reflected in your character's portrayal and her journey.

Those competing drives—dual opposites—power your story like a plus-minus battery. Your script will need to have two components: an active form of denial juxtaposed to an evolving, progressively active form of awareness. Some truly skillful writers can defy the dual approach and design a complexity that defies description. If you're having trouble organizing the oscillation of your character's course, this dual engine is a very efficient way to move your character through, like a little caterpillar that scrunches its body to propel itself.

An internal conflict may grow from a trauma that shaped her, but isn't necessarily consumed with it. Especially, if the pain's been buried deep within her. Her internal conflict is with smaller, more pointed and direct issues, which make attaining her goal near impossible. She vacillates in choosing what the best method is, whose advice to listen to. She's trying to decide which defeats are flukes and which have lessons worth learning from.

Yes, the wounded part of her will dictate how she initially pursues her goal and will block her attempts. The damage she's sustained in the past has had time to grow and warp the character. It's taught her how to behave, like a cult leader who brainwashes his followers with the hope of a better future, if they totally cede their lives to his care. Inside her core, a lie is working its way out like a splinter.

But we're going to concentrate on the more practical war she's waging inside herself and how others' goals and approaches to a similar dilemma will affect her.

EXERCISE #90: YOUR CHARACTER IS THE SUN

- Boil down the essence of your character's plan to achieve her goal in *three paragraphs*.
- Draft a list of the other characters' concerns, justifiable and not, that are tearing apart the feasibility of that idea.
- Now, list your *ten* most important *characters*.

(If you don't have ten, then that's fine. But your more limited cast means you have to spend that much more focus on developing them so they're nearly as well-rounded and full of life as your protagonist and antagonist.)

- Since we're focusing on agency, rate where these characters fall on a "1" to "10" range of goal attack. "1" represents a reactive person, someone whose decisions come from a place of fear. "10" represents a proactive/creative person.
- Your protagonist may not get full marks, but perhaps your villain may.

Exercise 90

EXERCISE #90-b: YOUR CHARACTER IS THE SUN

- In which of your proposed scenes can you hone these characters' actions to refine, define, and create a stronger spine on the major conflict?
- In what ways can their particular value systems capitalize on additional areas of vulnerability in the protagonist?

Exercise 90-b

FILM EXAMPLE

In the classic *On the Waterfront*, starring Marlon Brando as a compromised former boxer, every character falls somewhere along the spectrum of his internal conflict. That conflict is between being practical in a rigged world or following his heart and healing his pride to be an upstanding guy. And it costs a lot to be practical. His family is aligned on the side of the mob running the docks, but the girl he has a crush on is an absolutist fearlessly on the side of righteousness, especially after her brother is killed.

As Terry Malloy (Brando) explores both these moral choices during the course of the story, attempting to carve out a middle ground for himself, the audience is clearly invited into the inner workings of his world. He wants to do what's ethical, which is defend his friends, the dockworkers who are trying to form a union to bust open the mob's control on the job lottery.

Previously, Malloy already had a chance to stand on his own in the face of mob pressure, but he caved. He threw a fight at the suggestion of his brother, who is the right-hand man of the corrupt boss of the local dockworker's union.

Out of grudging respect for his brother, Malloy's been recently working as a stool pigeon to stop any regular organizing among the longshoremen. Dutifully, Malloy reports back that his pal Joey was one of those present at a meeting. The next thing he knows, Joey's been pushed off the top of a building.

When the Waterfront Crime Commission steps in to get to the bottom of the violence on the docks and the murder, Malloy's torn. He cannot volunteer information, because of his brother's strong-arming and the supposed debt he owes the union. But the investigation hinges on someone coming forward. After he shares what he knows with the Crime Commission, he finds his precious pet pigeons slaughtered.

On the scale of enterprising activity, he's right in the middle—at a "5"—with the potential to go either way. Down to "1" or up to "10." The stakes continue to rise as more people are killed…

Interestingly, if you look at all the ancillary characters in this incredibly well-crafted movie, written by Budd Schulberg and based on waterfront diaries, as they each work on Malloy they pull him like a yo-yo between his two possible choices. It's a good demonstration of the dual-engine in action.

If "10" is "doing the right thing, reporting the murderer and standing up to the mob," then the sister of the murdered man, Edie Doyle (Eva Marie Saint), is a "7." She's pure, good-hearted, and virginal; she's passionate about justice, and in a movie about injustice (most crime films), she represents absolute good. But she doesn't do anything on her own, she pleads for Malloy to act with her. And then, reverses herself at their darkest hour. Remember, this is not a scale of good and evil. It's about taking action, come what may, versus letting someone else do the heavy lifting.

Next to her on the spectrum at "8.5" is the priest Father Barry (Karl Malden). Even though he's a more pragmatic character, he's galvanized early on into siding with some of his parishioners. Intent on keeping the mob dogs from his door, he nevertheless rallies and tends to the dockworkers when he can.

Johnny Friendly (Lee J. Cobb) is the slick union operator on the docks, instigating mob violence when necessary. While he never directly gets his hands dirty, he gives his commands to his chief enforcer, Charley the "Gent" (Rod Steiger), Malloy's brother, who carries out every last stinking order. Friendly is ultimate evil, he has no conscience in pursuing his agenda to its deadly ends. He's a "10."

The Gent is a "6," because he does try to look out for Malloy, but for his own selfish reasons. He knows what he's doing is wrong, but there's no way he can back out.

This was an intensely personal film for both director Elia Kazan and writer Budd Schulberg. They were pressured to name Hollywood creatives aligned with the Communist party during Sen. Joe McCarthy's witch-hunt in the 1950's. To save their own skins, or perhaps because their political leanings agreed with the purge, they complied. Those who were blacklisted were driven to leave the country and write under pen names for years afterward. Kazan, himself, mostly rehabilitated his reputation through the making of this film and its critically acclaimed reception. The film won eight Oscars.

Malloy's largely a hollow character, not that in he's uninteresting or cliché, but that he's empty inside. He's already sold his soul once before. So chances are he'll do the same again. If he was willing to cheapen his dream, what could persuade him to choose a noble path on behalf of others, when his own brother is urging him to choose what's safe? Nevertheless, seeing him tragically suffer, and try to become the man he's always wished to be, is incredibly moving. His famous line to his brother, when he knows all is lost is movie-dialogue history: "I coulda had class. I coulda been a contender. I coulda been somebody, instead of a bum..."

Just like Malloy, your character's despair will be running at an all time "high" throughout parts of the Second Act. It's how you both deal with it that matters. Your character may say she's sick and tired of your probing questions. It's true she's been through a lot, so you may have the urge to give her a break. You might buy into her protestations and indulge her.

Well, allowing a little "staycation" is fine, but when she does resume the pursuit of her goal, she's gotta go at it hard. It's meant to be an uphill climb, something she needs to be developing stamina for. *Though, honestly, she might breathe easier with you gone. After all, you add a load to her already burdened shoulders.* But that's the burden of being a hero! She has to take up the slack of others and carry more than her fair share…

On the other hand, if she's distancing herself from you, maybe she's being swept along by momentum and in no mood to contemplate the last few scenarios with any meaningful depth. Perhaps she feels like she no longer needs you.

While you just want to make sure her recent string of successes hasn't gone to her head, she might be pissed off because she doesn't think you actually believe she'll triumph. *You're not letting her do her thing. You're in the way. You're not going to be the one there weighing what to do in the moment.*

Will it get ugly, as she tries to slough you off?

Normally, people avoid confrontation altogether. But what if your character only feels "seen" when she's confronted, interrogated, or attacked with probing questions? For her, the passion behind your inquiry could be proof of your deep, emotional investment. When you argue for something, you're defending a principle, an action you took, or maybe another person. We don't endorse physical altercations, and verbal fights are certainly draining, but perhaps at a choice moment, like this one, you two should get your egos stirring and blood pumping.

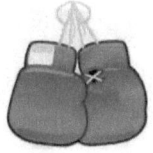

EXERCISE #91: GETTING IN THE RING

- What's still not happening as it should?
- Does she have to get on board with the last step of her new regimen, so that she can prevail over her obstacles?

Exercise 91

Dating Your Character

It's juvenile that it's come to this, exchanging blows in a ring. She's obviously sick and tired of all the rounds she's got to fight and the interim titles she has to win to be conditioned and rate an HBO-televised bout in prime-time. She's also stressed and hungry to prove herself. Having to go toe to toe against you is just that much more provoking.

You, yourself, may feel that you're going to have to push through, no matter what, (alone, even) to reach the end of your script. "Bull your way through" might strike you as the only way to approach this. But is this the best way? Bulling your way through, you'd be "bullying" your character. Unfortunately, you could end up with Act II and III being plot-heavy and character-thin.

Leading up to this moment, you've guided her to develop the chops she needs for her ultimate push. But you're anticipating once you get to the Second Act Turning Point, her final crisis—she may turn back. She could have a meltdown. She's throwing a tantrum now…

She's been making it all about you: you're the one who's seriously messed up. She might even be defending her slow-down by hurling accusing questions your way: *What's the big deal? Haven't I gotten better on nearly everything? Do you even see what I've accomplished in this short time?*

She might even be prepared to walk away—booking a vacation and conveniently forgetting to buy you a ticket, too. To ensure that she doesn't use you as an excuse to surrender, you've got to shake her out of her paralysis. Force her to come to grips with the full scope of what she's set her mind to do, if she's to fulfill her destiny.

Hopefully the following exercise will root out a pervasive hidden secret, truth, or problem at the bottom of the character's heart that's still holding her back. You'll know it when you touch down on it, because suddenly you'll feel a surge of emotion in response.

EXERCISE #92: "WHAT'S THE PROBLEM?"

Grab an imaginary chair. Put your character in the chair beside you. Your character's angry about something: pissed off at you or at her situation. Either way—angry, depressed, stalled, impatient, in avoidance. Tap into a strong emotion. For the purposes of the exercise, it doesn't matter if it's passive or aggressive.

Get your implement: a pen, computer, tape recorder, or a friend who acts as the interviewer-prompter. You'll be writing down answers to the same question, over and over...

Repetition works to peel away the layers that cover the truth. Sanford Meisner uses this technique within his work with actors, where the idea of repetition helps allow something authentic to pop out after boredom. There's a remarkable power in asking this simple, little question.

- What's the problem?
- Why is that a problem?
- Exactly, what's the problem with that?
- What's the problem, again?
- Okay, got it. And what's the problem?
- I need to know, exactly—what's the problem?

Exercise 92

EXERCISE #92-b: "WHAT'S THE PROBLEM?"

- Jot down an "aha" thought that strikes you...
- Now knowing what's underneath all her reservations, what's the kind of thing that would be a beneficial surprise to her?
- What would bring her down even lower?

Exercise 92-b

Example from Devo:

I'm using an example from an outline for a feature:

- What's the problem?

Carolyn, a scientist, can't figure out what the code is on an invitation left at the murder scene.

- Why is that a problem?

She's been trying to figure it out, and is stumped and ready to give up. Her assistant is dead. This whole ordeal has triggered her earlier feelings about the world not being a safe place.

- Exactly, what's the problem with that?

If she stops, she won't find out who murdered her assistant. She will let down his family and the other people counting on her.

- What's the problem, again?

If she doesn't find out who murdered her assistant, she won't find out who stole her formula. She'll be unable to reinstate her good name in the scientific community.

- Okay, got it. And what's the problem?

If she doesn't find out who stole her formula, she'll be ostracized from the community of her peers and give up her life's dream. She will not please her dad, i.e., keep her word to her dying father by becoming a successful doctor.

- And what's the problem?

If she gives up her life's dream, she will have nothing left to live for. It will destroy her.

- I need to know, exactly—what's the problem?

Okay, she finally tells me, albeit exasperated. Secretly she feels she would rather die than go on living with this defeat. The shame and humiliation will undo her, because of the loss of her dream.

- My "aha" moment:

So underneath all my character's verve and determination is dread (and maybe a bit of shame at her feeling of inadequacy). Carolyn fears her whole life will mean nothing. And, if that were the case, she would rather die. Her self-esteem is hinged on curing an illness. The value she puts on her life is tied to her success and

> identity as a scientist.
>
> - Potential surprises:
>
> Is there a test subject who is taking her drug and is suddenly helped? Is she suddenly invigorated? Or the opposite, does someone who depends on her, die... Does that motivate her? Does she have to reach down and find an even deeper well of resources? Or does something the dying person says actually crack the very code that leads to the antagonist/murderer?
>
> - Feeling even lower:
>
> She's probed as deep as she can into her soul—with you watching, no less. She knows she'll never bury her hurt or accept being hurt in that way ever again. But it's clear she has some unresolved anger. So what the problem probably boils down to is: she's feeling defeated.

And you have to present her with something in the story to give her courage—enough hope—to go those final steps. She has to take a leap of faith. She has to find a reason to risk it all, something that's worth gambling her life away. She can't just be fixated on what her victory might look like. The promise of glory and riches is shiny enough to inspire the dream. But, for her to make it through to the end come what may, she's got to feel a need in her bones—that she really has no other choice.

Talking to someone older and more experienced, who knows what's at stake, can put her conflicted POV in perspective. This elder lived through what it was like before things turned to rot and became even worse. And, yet, if he's managed to retain some glimmer of hope, then surely your character can find the wherewithal within her to persevere.

FILM EXAMPLE

The iconic swashbuckling archeologist Indiana Jones (Harrison Ford) is an incredible example of a character mastering his fears over a number of films; however, in the final installment of the initial trilogy, Indy finds himself on a precipice (literally) with his intimidating professor-father (Sean Connery).

Indy repairs an old emotional break with his father, whom he'd long ago felt abandoned by, and that leads to a life-changing view on trust. He once lacked faith in others, and faith in the world, but he discovers the courage to seek out the most faith-based object that has eluded humanity. He learns that sometimes you can only trust in those things you can't see. This is metaphorically reinforced by his having to cross on an invisible plank leading to the Holy Grail.

The key to Indy is located in the dueling forces within him, an engine creating a movement from "faithless to faithful." This is the "under everything" that actors, directors, and producers intuitively search for in a character. What's your character fighting against, and what's she fighting for?

If you're stymied in your relationship, soft words of encouragement may get her out of a stall, which will help you and your character advance the story's plot. There have already been positive signs that show you're both committed to her moving towards this long-awaited, ultimate goal and moment of enlightenment:

- You've been seeing each other frequently (regular writing sessions)
- You've met her family, friends, and some adversaries.

But, perhaps because of this exhaustive work, you may still meet with some obstinance from her. If so, try gently coaxing her back into your life. She can't up and disappear on you or stay in her funk. You can't just let her be on the periphery, looking on at the puzzles you're constructing. You can't be purely hoping that she'll figure a way through them. She can't be a bobble-head, nodding as you do your part while she pretends like she cares. You both have to keep watch over each other. If either of you is feeling a slow-down, it could be stemming from an aversion to commitment.

Commitment is a fraught word. To make a gross generalization, it's something that women reach out for and makes men recoil. Beyond its statement of permanence, women often imbue it with the added value of safety and loyalty, which men merely see as added responsibility and an end to excitement. That bipolar characterization's a staple of the old *Men are from Mars, Women are from Venus*, part of a commonly accepted lexicon.

Since it goes against our nature to embrace stereotypes of any kind, we chose not to introduce this depiction earlier, because of the temptation to oversimplify distinct differences that derive from personality, not gender. However, if you believe there's been a gender-based barrier to an increased understanding of your character, perhaps resulting in miscues and misinterpretations, the following exercise may be helpful.

Nevertheless, we feel that 95% of our tactics and exercises work equally well for female and male characters—and with a little re-working, for children, too. What follows is a basic activity that could lead you both toward greater emotional clarity.

EXERCISE #93: BLUE OR PINK?

If your character is male:

Your male protagonist might be inclined to play a bit of emotional hide-and-seek, because he's still exploring his agenda with you. Just give him a little space. Try taking a day or two off.

- Write him a little note and leave it out for him to find. Something along the lines of: "Taking a couple days off. Think you're the best character ever and appreciate that you have a lot going on. Talk when I get back. Looking forward to anything you want to share with me."

You can expand your research on some of your ancillary characters and pose more questions to them.

If your protagonist is female:

She's probably loving the increasing intimacy of your relationship and your willingness to please her. But maybe she's started taking advantage of you. Has she flown off the handle lately or been flaky?

A little positive reinforcement and acknowledgement of what she's going through will go a long way to repairing the disconnect and her fear of fully activating change.

- Have her continue the sentence:

Dating Your Character

"To feel more comfortable about the next few steps, I need you to:"

_____

_____

_____

_____

_____

Exercise 93

Example from Devo's Karisma character in *Santa Fe 7*:
"Hi!! I'm really glad you asked, but at this moment, I'm seriously running on empty emotionally. I don't think I can keep up the pace and the pressure. And I wish I could tell you why, but I just don't know. Really. But I know you want me to tell you what I need.

Maybe just remind me about why I can do this? Why me? Sometimes, I just want to give up. Maybe you could tell me all those things that make me the right person for the job, if you know what I mean. And I'm getting that you don't trust me.

And I know this isn't important, and a really low priority, but you know what? It'd help for you to tell me that I'm beautiful—as I am. Because it's so hard to know if I really am. I don't have the flash and sophistication of other girls. I get super insecure around the ones who are really put together. And Alexandra…is a *model!* So whenever she's around, I just want to disappear. But I need her help, and I don't want her to sense how awkward I feel around her now… It's not like when we were kids.

Anyway, it's all going fine and I'm chipping away at the mystery. Just stop pushing me already! We've found some fantastic clues about what could have happened. Going through some of RF's old papers has also revealed some more of who I am. It's gotten some of my personal stuff out into the open. So you should be *happy*, right?

It's all coming together, now. If I get too comfortable telling you what's going to happen, I might spill the beans to the others.

Anyway, just trust me. I need to be trusted and to trust myself to do the right thing.

Dating Your Character

The "Second Act Sag" is where many scripts collapse under an industry reader's scrutiny. The reader's evaluation might tersely say "pace is off." Maybe you've not yet found a way to up the tension, and there are one or two missing pieces of the puzzle. With all the potential for drama in the Second Act, perhaps you're experiencing fatigue from the twists and turns.

And when you freak out about all the impending curves in the story, you can lose sight of the most vital driver of your story. You can get too caught up in trying to make things happen without tapping into the telling emotions of your character. In fact, she's the one who's actually making those things "happen." So, pay attention and listen to her. While she marches ahead, she has to authentically rise to the stakes and have primacy over them.

If you feel under pressure in your story, conversely, the problem could be that you haven't put enough pressure on your protagonist. Look to create additional conflicts for her from other characters and within her environment, which directly tie into the likelihood of her fulfilling her goals. This is what can constitute a compelling portrait of a character in crisis; because that's what's going on, she's in crisis.

You should be much farther along in your understanding of her emotional universe and her current predicament. Enough to know what the most vulnerable parts of her are, how she's grown in tenacity, and which other characters can significantly alter her orbit.

In CHAPTER 7—MAKING A COMMITMENT, you'll be able to see how the "piston-like movement" of her inner and outer goals generates a constant flow of energy and movement for your character…

MAKING A COMMITMENT "ACT II TURNING POINT"—STEP SEVEN

THE PROTAGONIST'S POV, or point of view, is basically how she rightly or wrongly sees the world. What's bothering her, what she wants to see happen, and how she comes in contact with people. For her to change, she has to change how she sees herself and how other characters see her. It's how she evaluates everyone and everything through this particular mental sieve.

POV is a character's values as expressed in her world view. She might have an opinion about world politics or religion, but that's not her POV. Therefore, POV is established through an extended series of actions and dialogue that show her standing for something.

You've pinpointed why *you* want to tell this story (Chapter 1) and, by homing in on what's motivating the character (Chapter 5), you know why she's willing to take so many risks to create a shift in herself and in her world. You've also recently identified a dual nature to her and she's confided her fears to you (Chapter 6). But has she communicated this urgency in the scenes you've started to explore?

> **EXERCISE #94: THIS IS WHY!**
> Go over the snatches of scenes you may have scribbled in your journal or are already part of your script's current draft. If any of your responses to *DYC* exercises stand out, include those, too. *Circle* where she shows not only how she's feeling…but why.

Exercise 94

> **EXERCISE #94b: THIS IS WHY!**
> Does it come through in one line? Is it a part of a brief argument with an affiliate character? Does a scene wholly consist of this rant?
>
> Come up with a list of other ways she can exemplify this attitude or world view.

Exercise 94-b

Example from Devo's teen mystery:

She looked at me and laughed, and then snorted, covering her mouth.

"I guess with that horse laugh, maybe you have it worse," I added.

"How do you *survive* at this school?"

"I don't just survive, I thrive," I said.

"O*kay*..." she said. "It looked like you were praying or meditating or—"

"Anyway..."

"Nice to meet *you*...?"

"Karisma..."

With that the bus lurched over anther hump and we were in the Albuquerque high school parking lot. I'd have to tell Aaron, my brother, about her later. We keep up the ritual—tradition—of sharing our "RF moments." When our mind tells us to watch out for this one or that one. I had the feeling this girl was going to play heavily into something. Not that I had any specifics. She was funny, but I suspected she didn't know that.

I trundled across the yard and picked up a couple pieces of trash off the school lawn. The ravens were out in droves and some misguided, squawking seagulls also poked around. I looked at the overstuffed trashcan and crap spilling out all over the sides. I hated the lazy-assed kids who just threw their wrappers on the ground.

It seriously bugs me how unconscious we are. I'm including me, "because me is we."

Karisma isn't my main character, but she's an important member of the ensemble. When flipping through my script, I circled lines in scenes where she butts in and voices her opinion, even though she's the shy, sweet one. But while a reader would know she's the one person who's most invested in keeping the commune family together once they've gone their separate ways, there aren't really places where it's clear why she's like that. I have to find out why she, of all the characters, is desperately trying to hold onto a time that was largely confusing for them.

So, I went with the flow and let Karisma interact with someone other than one of her childhood friends. I decided to let her prowl around on her first day of "normal" school. Then I kept going, wanting to stay in her head, seeing how she moves in a strange, modern world.

I was able to zero in on her sense of humor and her loneliness. She even seems cut off from her brother, because it sounds like, if not for the "RF moments," they don't really talk. I understand how isolated she must feel. If she doesn't know current music, I think that's another way to show how out of touch she is. Since she had few possessions on the commune, it

> would be interesting to think about what she chooses to hang onto and what she's going to get rid of for this new way of life. If she's having trouble connecting, what still provides that sense of self for her?
>
> What I found most intriguing was the quote "because me is we." Even though Karisma's off the commune, its tenets have still stuck to her. I don't know if she believes in them or if it's just an automatic response. I'll play around with more slogans. Some that truly convey a certain wisdom, others that sound really phony and should be on a cheap t-shirt. I want to know how much of a devotee she was.
>
> This is a prose exploration and maybe only a couple of paragraphs will turn up in my script. But not limiting your thinking to script format and the inevitable constraints of that kind of writing can be very helpful.

Regardless of your character's mood in the previous exercise, most examples of POV come from a place of anger, hurt, guilt, or righteousness. But you may be having trouble pinpointing the exact nature of why she's upset and why she's fighting. Perhaps a way to back into the cause of her distress and dissatisfaction may be to look at why a certain setback hits her so much harder than any of the other characters who have experienced a similarly crushing event. Remember, your character may be part of a team, but the degree to which she is impacted, what moves her, and the course of action she takes is unique to her. POV tethers the audience to the character.

POV's the needle and thread that stitches together the scenes of the plot. Stuff can't just happen to the character, with the character vowing and acting to shake up her world in turn. We have to know why she's going about things the way she is. We have to know what shaped her current outlook and what could test that privately held worldview. POV dictates the kind of character-rich scenes the plot can provide. It also goes a long way to making your character sympathetic, or at least her actions more understandable.

It can be especially fascinating to take an intimate look at a seemingly normal character with a hidden side. In those instances, it's really POV that does the heavy lifting. If, on the surface, not much happens, we have to have access to the character's internal world to see what she really thinks, because that's where most of the action is, a la *The Secret Life of Walter Mitty*. But let's take a look at a really strong film in the Woody Allen oeuvre that almost wholly leverages its tension from POV.

FILM EXAMPLE

In the psychologically astute, existential murder mystery *Crimes and Misdemeanors*, the main storyline features an arresting performance by Martin Landau (Judah) as an intelligent, worldly, and emotionally available patriarch. He's beloved by his family, as well as by his circle of friends and colleagues. But when his flighty flight-attendant/mistress (Anjelica Huston) threatens the perfect life he's made for himself, he considers killing her.

While this narrative thread is unspooled, the B storyline features Woody Allen's perennial nebbish (Cliff) as a failed filmmaker, who feels he's selling out by making a documentary on a fatuous TV producer. We're treated to the moral debate between producing art from pure impulses versus creating with an eye to appeal to some level of commercialism. Cliff, of course, stubbornly sees this as a black and white issue.

But nothing in *Crimes and Misdemeanors* is that simple. Judah's brother Jack (Jerry Orbach), a working stiff with vague ties to the mafia, offers to handle the arrangements. The idea is anathema to Judah, but still…he lets himself flirt with the possibility.

As Judah steps ever closer to crossing the line, he can't believe how easy it will all be. It's only after he makes the transaction that he's filled with racking doubt. He'd never really thought he'd actually be able to go through with it. After he finds out he's capable of contracting out such a monstrous deed, he loses his sense of self. When he decides he's endured enough self-recrimination, and feels that he'll never recover if the assassination is carried out, he tries to cancel the hit. But there's no going back, Jack tells him.

The movie indulges in private V.O.s and hushed confessions. Actually, its dramatic conflict is solely derived from Judah's moral wavering. And his thoughts are completely accessible to the audience. Over the course of the movie, he becomes nervous, indecisive, brittle, pushing his family away. He feels like a walking fraud, losing the easygoing authority he once had.

This is a dark look at a character whose defining core is his weaseliness. Judah isn't a James Bond villain, but a master equivocator. It's his vacillating cowardliness that makes him bearable. He's very much an everyman, who gives into temptation…and drives a Jaguar. We sympathize with the boredom he feels, with the lack of meaningful connection he has with his wife (Claire Bloom). He's a decent, likable guy compared to the B story with phony entertainment types. He's the last guy you'd want to punish.

But for all Judah's pretense at empathy with his patients, his girlfriend, and his family, his non-negotiable trait is that, at heart, when it comes to momentous life decisions, he'll reliably choose what will benefit him and his immediate family. Even when that means distancing himself from his financially strapped brother who idolizes him.

Of course, when talking about POV, the writer's own can provide another thematic overlay. Allen's own storyline allows him to skewer Hollywood, New York intellectuals, and the nature of integrity. In fact, if not for Allen's big canvas approach to evil, selfishness, and the moneyed elite, this story might have seemed too insular and lacking a balance.

In typical Woody Allen fashion, the ruling class avoids retributive justice here; no blasphemous or murderous act Judah commits is apparently big enough to warrant legal or eternal damnation. Judah, the former moral relativist, who was self-aware enough to take responsibility for his actions, becomes an amoral rationalist who finds his getting away with murder reason enough to spite God. His experience with murder, done by proxy, by no means makes him a born-again killer. But, oddly, he can look back on the whole episode, including his fear and self-hatred, with something akin to condescending fondness.

Judah's wickedly awakened character is tightly connected to his POV. Without that, we wouldn't understand why he determined his mistress had to die. Why he felt guilty and withdrew from his family. We could have seen him take these actions, but without benefit of his thoughts and private conversations, we would have had to guess about his compunctions. We could certainly have made grand, overarching generalizations, but that would have robbed the film of its power. Its success rests on us following the twists of his mind, the nature of his internal monologue. Otherwise, it's just a morality tale without a moral.

LOCATION AND POV

Location can tell you about the protagonist's POV or that of someone else in your story. You're able to pick up on what their perceptions of themselves and others are, and maybe what they're planning on doing. You can learn what a character is capable of, what they want, and even in some instances what formed them…

FILM EXAMPLE

If heavily featured, it can become more than a color or tonal shift, it can evolve into a character in its own right. *French Kiss* is a delightful rom-com starring Meg Ryan as Kate, an uptight teacher, and Kevin Kline as Luc, a rakish French thief. When Kate's journey starts, she's in the claustrophobic quarters of a plane before being thrown into the aloof cacophony that is Paris. We witness her control-freak ways and how utterly unprepared she is for this kind of adventure.

We sympathize with her clueless American, because most of her requests are reasonable. Paris doesn't co-operate; the city doesn't allow her to fall in love with it. It's gray, rainy, and full of petty predators, who ruin the romantic experience that tourists have come to expect.

Luc, himself, sticks to her like Velcro, because he's smuggled something in her bag. But it's not jewelry or drugs, or anything callously fungible like that. He's stowed something incredibly fragile—a lone, tender sapling. He demonstrates such a moving protectiveness for Kate (and her bag) that we initially attribute it to a quirky solicitousness of his as a benevolent, if gruff, Frenchman.

He hopes to graft the baby plant onto his family's native grapevines. It's finally through the vineyard itself that we truly understand Luc's rationale for the string of cons he's run. That Luc's humble dream rests in such a perishable treasure evokes a sympathy and understanding for his character, when he could have been seen as incredibly manipulative.

As the story progresses, it's the trek through the glorious French countryside that returns the sense of amorous emotional possibility to the story. When they stop in the small village of La Ravelle, Kate's enchanted by its quaintness and lack of stuffiness. She starts to appreciate everything around her in all its natural glory. It's a huge contrast to her first introduction to France, which came via the cold haughtiness of Paris.

The location is an immense selling point for both the film and for Luc's character. Though Kate's later impressed by Luc's knowledge of viticulture, her heart seems won over as much by Marseilles as by him. It's the potential in the vineyard that finally makes what seemed like a pipedream feasible at last. She eventually sees that he has a real, loving regard of the nuances in the soil. The vineyard also allows him to show her that he's capable of planning for the future and sacrificing for that future.

EXERCISE #95: LANDSCAPE AS REFLECTING POOL

- What do your ideas for your final set-piece symbolize?
- How can physical features be extrapolated, so that we can infer something of the character's inner self?
- How can you sprinkle clues elsewhere in the story, so that attentive readers/viewers will be able to pick up on her changing mindset and emotions, in action and subtext, through other similar landscapes or objects?

Exercise 95

FILM EXAMPLE

In *Chinatown*, a multiple Oscar-nominee that won Best Original Screenplay for writer Robert Towne, water is the precious resource that's rained down great fortunes to those who've harnessed it and redirected its energy. Starring Jack Nicholson, Faye Dunaway, and noted film director John Huston, the film is a labyrinthine maze through the halls of power. It's also a noir history lesson on the birth of modern Los Angeles and a sordid example of family authority carried to an unnatural extreme.

Water has made possible the city of Los Angeles' growth, transforming its arid geography into an expanse of happy orange groves and bright green suburban lawns. But the water barons, who bestowed the property and water rights they picked up for a song to the newly established Metropolitan Water District, have also dammed it up and choked it off from others; only the protected interests of the great and good have experienced a boom in development and resource availability. These neglected areas, some on the outskirts of reservoirs, have been consigned to the dustbin of history and progress, bypassed.

A current of corrupt politics and cruel, ham-fistedness runs through the main storyline of murder and betrayal. The issue of water rights will spring up as but one of the motivations for the murder of the water department's chief engineer, Hollis Mulwray, who also has a wealthy portfolio of his own. At almost every location, water signifies something directly related to a future plot point or lets the audience in on a character's status, frame of mind, and emotional register.

Location is more than a **metaphorical**[*] example of your character's motivation. It provides a panorama and spectacle that can heighten all of the doubt and excitement that the character's walking into in order to achieve her goal. It can clearly state characters' value systems and private fantasies. It can show the symbolic or literal imprint a character is capable of making on her physical environment. If a location manages to reveal all of these textures, it can be a motivating force, if not a character itself, as it is in the previous example.

How do you frame her reasons so that we understand where she's coming from without holding a round table session where everyone explains what their thoughts are? First thing's first.

---

[*] A **metaphor** is often visual proof of the nature of the problem she's facing externally or internally. But it doesn't always have to be something directly observable. It can also be a narrative anecdote with an obvious or implied moral. This quick narrative tangent can foreshadow what will happen in the story, ferret out subtext, sum up what has happened, or be used as an ever-changing touchstone for the truth.

Dating Your Character

EXERCISE #96: RAINBOW OF THOUGHT

Make a list of the *POVs* of 5 major characters.

Study your notes, outline, or script and under each character's name, list the scenes that are clearly a reflection of that person's POV.

If you're working off a draft of your script, you might find it helpful to color code each person's POV in every scene where it's expressed. Go beyond indicating how often certain characters appear in the story. It's more important to gauge how accurate and character-centric their interactions are.

Exercise 96

EXERCISE #96-b: RAINBOW OF THOUGHT

Slice and dice the complementary POVs to see how they differ.

- Where is there an overlap?
- Where is there an alliance of sorts?
- How do characters' POVs result in direct conflict?
- Where do they fall on the "1-10" scale of your theme?

Exercise 96-b

EXERCISE #96c: RAINBOW OF THOUGHT

If characters had their way, how do we know what the consequences would be? We have to know what their dreams are, the unintended outcomes, and why the protagonist's view is infinitely preferable.

For each character's vision, craft an "ideal" ending, a "likely" ending, and an "unlucky" ending.

Exercise 96-c

Use these alternative universes to think about all the different permutations of your story that are possible. Some may pose intriguing challenges for your character to overcome. Others may help you become clear on what exactly your character's fighting for. And what happens if she's unsuccessful. This is how you starkly represent the true stakes of the story…

Dating Your Character

Remember, films thrive on visuals. You have to craft concrete actions that demonstrate the contrasting constraints of each character's views.

> **EXERCISE #97: STOKING CONFLICT**
>
> - Come up with *three examples* of direct conflict...
> - Come up with *two examples* of indirect conflict...

Exercise 97

> **EXERCISE #97-b: STOKING CONFLICT**
>
> Regardless of how long the characters have known each other, generate ideas for unresolved conflicts that could have arisen in their back-story.
> - How can these be reawakened and complicate your character's progress?
> - How do they help the protagonist hone her own notions?

Exercise 97-b

> **EXERCISE #97-c: STOKING CONFLICT**
> Just like past traumas shaped your character's outlook, how else were prior experiences crucial in forming her perspective?
> - What did she witness?
> - What idea kept being reinforced that she could never fully go along with?

Exercise 97-c

What if your character's basically a loner, with only one affiliate character for her to bounce ideas off of? You don't need a group of people in order to test what your character holds true. What's important is to fully comprehend the limitations of her beliefs and what could challenge them.

Her POV equips her for these set-tos. It seems to predestine her eventual embarkation on the journey and her future success, because of the experiences she's had and her rare reaction to them. Your character may be part of a like-minded group of friends, but there is enough of a personal variation on the value system they share to render her unique. She sees something that no one else seems to see or grasp with the same conviction. It makes it inevitable that she would elect to go on this quest and be the one fighting for what they all believe in the final scene.

In the ramp up to the end sequence of your script, how do the other characters pose difficulties for her? Even if she's been roughly on her own for the Second Act, she'll undoubtedly face a crowd in the Third Act.

EXERCISE #98: PIE IN THE FACE

Imagine your character's standing against a wall about to face a firing line. You're going to "hurl" a bunch of pies at her. Each represents a threat: actions that characters will take…

Pitch between *10-15 pies*.

DYC Example:

For a raunchy rom-com, the last sequence might involve the following "pies":

 Out of jealousy, the protagonist's best friend wants to get the fiancé to call off the protagonist's wedding.

● The fiancé wants the protagonist to bear a larger share of the wedding's cost.

● Hoping to steal the spotlight and humiliate her ex-husband, the protagonist's mom wants to show up with a young stud in tow.

● The protagonist's immediate supervisor is planning on switching over a major account to a new vendor, while the protagonist's on her honeymoon, so she can put new policies into place without the protagonist's input.

● The protagonist's dog will systematically chew all her shoes, eventually nabbing the box storing her wedding shoes at the back of the closet, because he's felt ignored over the past few weeks.

● Another dog, the protagonist's fiancé, will have been getting together with an attractive, taut, athletic woman over the same past few weeks, before resigning to a manageably short window of exclusivity pre-negotiated with the chubby protagonist.

 The lesbian Unitarian minister officiating the wedding

Dating Your Character

will sabotage the protagonist's limo, so she arrives late, stressed, and in need of comfort and wisdom from her old college pal/experimental fling.

- The protagonist's bohemian sister is going to sublet her place to pothead friends during the honeymoon.

- Her first love will organize an unofficial reunion of her ex-lovers, as a kind of alcoholic counterprogramming event, at the banquet hall across from the church.

- Before declaring bankruptcy, the protagonist's travel agent will book the honeymoon and keep the funds.

Exercise 98

EXERCISE #98-b: PIE IN THE FACE

- Do the threats and difficulties point to one specific person or entity?
- Are they emblematic of one kind of POV?
- Does she shift her POV under pressure?
- Do any affiliate characters become emboldened?

Exercise 98-b

EXERCISE #98c: PIE IN THE FACE

- What is the general nature of these struggles? Physical? Political? Mental? Spiritual? Emotional?
- What has she had to go up against so far? Make a list of all the confrontations she's made in your exercises, your existing scenes, and that you've outlined for possible scenes.

Exercise 98-c

Make sure that she is tested on multiple levels. She may be an amateur athlete training for the Olympics, so most of her trials require physical discipline. See that she also struggles with her tactics, as well as in her personal relationships. If you can combine these battles for even more desperate scenarios, you'll create more tension.

Let's say your athlete has a big qualifying track meet coming up. She'll be vying in the 1500 meters against an old friend, who until recently has been training with her. The relationship with the friend provides added stakes, but the drama has been primed within the set-up of the stakes. Unless she's a last-minute write-in for someone else who's "scratched," you haven't surprised the character. You have to allow the potential for chaos. What develops unexpectedly while she's there? Is she hiding a hairline fracture, which could jeopardize the team, should she get further injured?

> **EXERCISE #99: EVERYTHING INCLUDING THE KITCHEN SINK...**
>
> Use the hypothetical of the Olympic hopeful. Let's call her "Portia." Come up with *ten complications* that could mar the meet that aren't specifically physical challenges.

Exercise 99

Her parents arrive, even though she didn't even tell them she was going to be competing? A professor she has a crush on shows up with his wife?

It may feel overwhelming to aim and launch projectiles at a character. After all, what you're really doing is thinking about the specific means by which you can hurt her. It's important to think about how she'll be negatively impacted, because it brings home to you that what she goes through doesn't happen in a vacuum. Even in those scenes where she's on the whole triumphant (roughly half), there always has to be some fallout that debilitates her progress, because that can afford the opportunity to not only waylay her, but provide a fork in the road.

In taking the hypothetical character from above, what if, in addition to the relationship and political types of challenges

"Portia" faces, her body does, in fact, struggle substantially?

- She trips, breaking her ankle.
- She's out for the season, totally sidelined.
- She can't honor the discipline of regular workouts that's been the mainstay of her schedule for nearly ten years.

So how does Portia channel her competitive drive?

She becomes a coach to someone else on the team, who has no chance in hell of moving up and supplanting her in the long run...

- She gets to look like an evolved, generous person, while remaining close to the action around the track.
- Having never taken it upon herself to watch tape before, she now learns crucial info about the technique of her rival.
- She believes her archrival has some blindness in her right eye, which can be exploited.
- So now to test an idea she has, she instructs her "protégé" to make a risky move that could force her to sacrifice an inside lane in order to put pressure on the runner's right side, which, in the 1500, could be viable, since it's more of a middle-distance race of endurance than strict sprinting speed.
- She becomes something of a miracle worker for her protégé, and both start getting local press...

She's also had more time and energy to devote to her studies, so what was a horrible setback is now a stealthy temptation. Why should she force herself to accelerate her painful physical therapy, if her life's looking up right now? All the while she's thought she'd just been killing time, when she's actually been making headway of a different kind...

Unexpected complications aren't always negative. They can be tantalizingly attractive near-equivalents that the character couldn't be blamed for accepting. You're challenging her frame of mind by these changes in fortune. She has to analyze what it is she really wants when comparable opportunities are open to her. These may satisfy the root of her needs but not in the way she imagined.

ANTAGONISTS

When contemplating the dangers that await your character, you may not realize how vulnerable she is to perils that can originate from unexpected places. All her relationships are potential minefields. Start to view them through that lens. Look at the relationship risks that your character will have to take. Understand that her small successes will be alternating with the collateral damage she incurs. It's this roller coaster ride that, in effect, provides the plot. All hazards, by this point, have to become as specific and real for you and the character as they'll ever be. It's time to name names and figure out where the most pressing threats are coming from.

For your character to react and strategize, she has to have

particular, progressively more difficult targets. If there are several antagonists opposing your character in different areas of her life, and there probably are, who's the most dangerous?

> **EXERCISE #100: COMING THREAT**
>
> In order to up the ante, make a list of supplemental characters who don't yet exist in any of your notes or outlines. Imagine these people have already harmed, are thinking about harming, or will indirectly harm your character.

Exercise 100

> **EXERCISE #100-b: COMING THREAT**
>
> - When do we first meet them?
> - Choose *three* potential *spots* before and during the timeframe of the story.

Exercise 100-b

> **EXERCISE #100-c: COMING THREAT**
> Rank them according to the level of damage they have, will, and may wreak…

Exercise 100-c

The difference between "known" antagonists and "unknown" antagonists is that these new characters are most likely motivated by more than a proximity to your character. They aren't annoyed by her habits, don't have an axe to grind from childhood, or see her as a peer by whom to measure themselves.

Philosophical in nature, their antipathy almost starts impersonally. Their goals aren't petty, they arise out of a mirror image POV rooted in *how* your character is arriving at her own objective, which could be…

    1) …virtually the *same* thing.
    2) …the complete *opposite* thing.

That these new potential antagonists will elect to direct some of their energies at her is a mark of her partial success or notoriety. What this helps you do is refine how and why the protagonist goes after her "swoosh" goals:

- Why she's okay with certain trade-offs…
- What she's absolutely not okay with…
- Why she doesn't see herself in the wrong…

If you're sparked by the prospect of heightened conflict that these characters can bring, consider attributing some of their impulses and actions to one of your existing characters. You may feel that these newly imagined characters are much stronger choices than one of your other characters. If you do make a swap-out, ensure that any new character not only delivers on what she seems capable of, but also subsumes some of the useful traits, and action beats, of this "fired!" character.

Remember, the character who's being cut from the team was originally drafted for some reason. What purpose did she have? Transplant as much of that essence as you can into this fresh character, so she's working double duty and more than merits her place in the lineup. This shouldn't be an equal substitution or one agreed to out of fatigue, boredom, or fickleness. Really analyze the value of any new characters to see if an existing character can assimilate what they're contributing with similar effect.

EXERCISE #101: TARGETING YOUR CHARACTER

Now, look at the new character who ranked highest as a threat. In her potential back-story, how many times has she ruined something for your character—inadvertently, and deliberately?

- How has this character mostly operated?
- By hiding behind someone else's actions?
- By disguising her motives so that suspicion falls on someone else?

Exercise 101

Dating Your Character

EXERCISE #101-b: TARGETING YOUR CHARACTER

Come up with another *five ways* this new antagonist could trip up your character, from a series of minor inconveniences to a major life blow.

Exercise 101-b

EXERCISE #102: AFFILIATE CHARACTERS AS TRUE RIVALS

Now experiment by assigning these despicable acts to the characters who already populate your story landscape. If need be, give them more schooling or another personality trait to make this action credible.

Exercise 102

This automatically amplifies the security risk other characters can pose. By fleshing out the hidden motivations of people who were previously regarded as "safe," characters there to aid the protagonist or comment upon her actions, you now show how fragile and cutthroat her ecosystem really is.

> **EXERCISE #102-b: AFFILIATE CHARACTERS AS TRUE RIVALS**
>
> Compound the damage these newly adorned affiliate characters wreak. Take *two* of your newly proposed *reversals* and make the fallout more pervasive.
>
> ### *DYC* Example:
>
> If your character's blamed for a huge amount of missing money, how can there be consequences on the home front?
>
> *With your character forced to go on the lam, would her family be put in danger?*
>
> *Would they be taken hostage?*

Exercise 102-b

This is all leading to gaining a foothold in understanding the ethos of her key antagonist. Someone who may not even immediately see herself as directly in competition with her, but who later commits to bringing her down. Before you besmirch this person with foul traits, consider that most antagonists have a shred of reasonable justification.

TV EXAMPLE

In creator Aaron Korsh's cult-favorite USA network show *Suits*, there are weekly legal battles in which ace attorney Harvey Specter and his wunderkind associate Mike Ross have to deftly maneuver. Their worthy adversaries—defense attorneys, arrogant CEOs, crusading Department of Justice attorneys—come and go. But there are a couple of omnipresent threats who hover around the fringes, intrude when most inconvenient, and have the power to split up the dynamic duo of Specter and Ross: their boss (for many seasons) Jessica Pearson and her deputy taskmaster Louis Litt.

Jessica is a savvy, and sometimes ruthless, power broker, who values the firm she built over any personal entanglements. When evaluating a dilemma, her logic is infallible, even if that means she has to cut a former friend to his knees. Harvey, the right-hand man that she personally groomed, is as ambitious and charismatic. Because Mike is what Harvey used to be to Jessica, Harvey involuntarily identifies with Mike and sometimes twists himself into knots to protect his protégé, while skirting the law.

Though they work in the same firm and are ostensibly on the same side, Harvey and Mike kept Jessica in the dark about Mike's lack of formal education for many years. Though she sensed a deception, they always delivered, so she backed off.

If she knew, absolutely, the firm's liability in letting Mike practice law without having gone to law school or passed the bar (under his own name), it'd be her legal obligation to fire Mike. So, though Harvey and Mike mislead Jessica on this sensitive issue, which sometimes comes to the fore, Jessica isn't villainous for not wanting a gifted charlatan practicing law at the firm where she's managing partner. But she is the antagonist. If you're writing a film, your antagonist would have to be more than a sometime work threat, since you don't have the ever-revolving door of weekly perils that provide most of the tension in TV shows.

Just realize that your antagonist's POV is not necessarily "evil." His actions may be vile. But his thinking, while possibly too simplistic in its outlook, or too cruelly rational, stems from a reasonable conjecture that has been taken too far. Most importantly, he has a purpose!

Perceiving what motivates the antagonist humanizes him and clarifies why he and the protagonist are waging war. Just as you don't want your character's behavior to appear random, you don't want her clashing with an out-and-out megalomaniac, unless we rarely see him. Depending on your genre, if you're writing about a super-villain type, we might only hear about him and feel his influence through his underlings, rather than have access to him up-close.

Generally, as the character's tested through her interactions with the antagonist, repulsed as she is by everything he stands for, she's also perversely galvanized. She only fights harder for what she knows is right. She may profess to hold a certain outlook, but when her opinions collide with those of people she respects, that can test her resolve.

Winnowing your character's POV from similar opinions helps narrow down her wants from her needs. She has to do this to enable you to construct scenes that force her to make difficult choices, the most moving of which are usually the "lesser-of-two-evils" type. Where she isn't happily trotting towards more growth and confidence, but has to make sacrifices that are not only personal, but also feel as though they may derail her eventual progress.

Part of the "fitness" regimen she's on concerns her mental preparation. Before going into combat, she needs to reconcile herself to the various losses she may have to suffer. Just as commanders have to brace themselves for inevitable troop sacrifices, she has to already know what she's willing to cede. She can't decide that in the spur of the moment. If it's at least crossed her mind, the shock and guilt won't devastate her.

> **EXERCISE #103: THE MATHEMATICS OF SUCCESS**
>
> Ask her to imagine life without certain possessions, relationships, or accomplishments. What positives and negatives does she come up with?

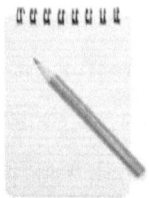

Exercise 103

> **Example from Elizabeth:**
>
> This was a more difficult exercise than I imagined, because my character starts from a pretty spare place. He's already surrendered his worldly goods, except for a small measure of vanity: a weekly trim and shave from the local barber. He left his friends and his profession behind to go on a primal, Herzogian quest to completely remake his life.
>
> My character is still rather proud, but deservedly so. There's nothing he can't do or learn, once he puts his mind to it. For him to discount his expertise, in order to feign ignorance and take

someone into his confidence, would exact a personal price, but nothing insurmountable.

I know that he values his *Porfidio*. So giving up one of the last of his stash in order to curry favor would be less of a sting than a mark of respect to someone who would appreciate the smooth burn of the tequila. Or someone whose institutional knowledge he wouldn't get any other way.

Principally, he needs a renewed sense of purpose. He willingly dulled that greater calling, because he fell in love and got married. His life had felt full; he didn't have to rail against anything. But there was always something that gnawed at him. When his wife was killed by her ex-lover, there was nothing to tether him to his home or even his country.

Having rebuilt his life among a people who dearly need his sophistication and agency, he's almost assumed a parental role to the *Xingu*. He's their buffer to the world, teaching them how to navigate a civilization that no longer follows the predictable logic of the natural world.

So it would cost him to lose one of the first brave indigenous warriors who came to trust him. What could possibly outweigh such a loss? The allegiance of a larger tribe that's held out and kept itself hidden?

> **EXERCISE #104: POLYESTER OR WORM-RIDDLED SILK?**
>
> Devise a scene that starts out lightly: the character's semi-offering to give up a prized possession in order to gain entry to some person's inner circle or to learn the truth behind a troubling secret.
>
> Then, the other person either takes her up on it…
>
> …or, doesn't value the present, demanding something else…
>
> What happens?

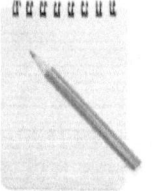

Exercise 104

EXERCISE #104-b: POLYESTER OR WORM-RIDDLED SILK?

- What's the personal cost of making this trade?
- Are there future ramifications?
- Will this bully expect more of the same?
- How does your character react to being caught off guard, in the moment?
- How does she reflect on the scene later?

Exercise 104-b

EXERCISE #104-c: POLYESTER OR WORM-RIDDLED SILK?

Fashion *two scenes* where, through no fault of her own, the surprising end result is the loss of one of her key relationships...

Exercise 104-c

The knowledge of these losses will prepare her to accept the burdensome terms of others in order for her to gain mph on the way to her ultimate goal. By concentrating on what she vitally needs, instead of what she wants or thinks she's willing to do, you'll get to the heart of the character: what's she willing to fight for and what fundamentally energizes her. And, by trimming the fat, you automatically come up with obstacles that will provide the story tinder for her to make very combustible decisions.

While your character is laser-focused straight ahead at the curves in the road on her final ascent, there's jeopardy all around. As her world changes, so do the challenges: she always has to be aware of unforeseen consequences. To sense when something's off, even when she can't put her finger on it. This authenticates her progress; it's not just something out of your imagination's bag of tricks, but a reflection of how her world works.

The unknowable dangers opposing your protagonist consist of more than rough geographical terrain or the machinations of characters who are her accepted enemies. People, who were friends and supporters, can be persuaded to commit acts of betrayal later on. The "rules" that everyone understands govern the universe may be inexplicably upended. Positives can become negatives, assets become liabilities. No future physical combat is taken away from the past survivalist champions in *Hunger Games: Catching Fire*.

Whatever the protagonist's going after, notice the ripple effect of her change in the world. It's not only about *her*...

- How are people starting to perceive her?
- How are her friends reacting to the sacrifices she's been making?
- Do they misunderstand them?

EXERCISE #105: ASKING AFFILIATE CHARACTERS

- Is she cutting them out of her life?
- Do they feel like she's leaving them behind or shitting on where they all come from?
- Is she more of a threat to them, because she's beginning to distinguish herself, and they're all after the same thing?

Exercise 105

We've briefly looked at the character net of protagonist, antagonist, and compromised affiliates, but we're going to focus right now on the other human elements that could go bad—the rest of the supporting cast who may not be treating her so well, either. Characters, like rotting vegetables left on the shelf, can shrivel up, bloat, or offer rancid toxins. When exposed to prolonged heat or overlooked in favor of some saltier, naughtier personas, they can start to ferment.

Your protagonist may have to willingly forfeit characters' fortunes or welfare for the greater good. But maybe she does so without any qualms or for her own selfish needs.

Let's look at the price of having alienated her affection:

EXERCISE #106: AXING AN AFFILIATE CHARACTER

Construct *three* key *scenes* where the protagonist *chooses* to throw one of her friends under the bus…

…because it's for the greater good.

…because it's a lot more convenient.

…because it's something she's wanted to do anyway.

Exercise 106

> ### EXERCISE #106-b: AXING AN AFFILIATE CHARACTER
>
> - How does she attempt to atone for what she's done, if at all?
> - Does someone else do so and horn in on the relationship?

Exercise 106-b

Whatever her best intentions or hard-won insights, at the end, no highly evolved person is perfect without the stain of certain actions. One way to dig into her future ability to do harm is to uncover these secrets, missteps, and indulgences from the past. But when weighing the potential for corruption in your protagonist, be aware that people hurt other creatures besides human beings; they can undermine causes; inflict damage on anything in their wake. That she may be assigning more courageous reasons to mask unseemly motivations—hatred, anxiety, and shame—shouldn't stay hidden from you, because it can blind her.

She'll have to deal with characters who will develop into hindrances once their ultimate agendas are finally disclosed. But, for this unexpected turn of events to be plausible, either the viewers have already been a couple of steps ahead, or crumbs have been left. When all's revealed, it's got to be a credible twist. We're then left to conclude there was an error in the protagonist's judgment that didn't allow her to see this affiliate character's true nature.

While we were privy to your protagonist's shortcomings, we didn't necessarily know her underlying wound had also skewed her perception. As her co-creator, even if you're intimately aware of her flaws, her fears, and her failure, how attuned are you to the holes in her perception? Lapses can stem from:

- prejudices
- being too self-centered
- a physical or mental disability
- lax judgment making her unable to accurately predict the future behavior of those around her.

These blind spots can cause real pain. They can be the root of many other complications that have befallen her. Furthermore, they're the hardest to recognize, let alone bring to the character's attention. Since their reach is pervasive, they're extremely challenging to overcome.

EXERCISE #107: UNLOCKING THE DOORS OF PERCEPTION

- How has she allowed herself to be misled by a character?
- What's been going on behind her back that she's remained oblivious to?
- Why? What has she been telling herself this whole time?
- How have her natural prejudices or blinders aided in the cover up?
- What deep, crucial mistakes can stem from beliefs she holds that are dead wrong in the face of facts or the rest of her practical experience?

Exercise 107

EXERCISE #108: 20/20 VISION

- How are your character's past memories now seen through a different prism?
- How has this weakness of character been allowed to slide up to now?
- What's the easiest way she can correct this problem of nearsightedness?
- What's the hardest adjustment she has to make to correct this gap in her perception?

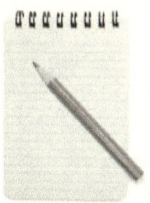

Exercise 108

THE DARKEST HOUR

Commonly, a combination of these lapses and a new awareness about her deficiency brings about the darkest moment in the character's arc, a time when she feels she can no longer go on. This isn't simply a disruption; it doesn't just put the character's progress "on pause." It's more than a kick in the gut. It's so overwhelming it upends the logic of all the incremental stages of growth before it. The fallout of betrayal and blunted hope can be depression, because it seems like her momentum's totally been stopped and can't be resumed. The character may not even have the luxury of anger to buck her up. Her life's been ripped away. Its purpose, values, the sweetness of its associations twisted and tarnished.

> **EXERCISE #109: YOUR CHARACTER'S BIGGEST FAN**
>
> Answer the question: "Do I truly care that she's suffered so much?" Make your list as exhaustive as you can.

Exercise 109

> **EXERCISE #109-b: YOUR CHARACTER'S BIGGEST FAN**
>
> - How has she earned your admiration?
> - How much heart has she shown in tackling obstacles?
> - How much do you believe in your character's purpose, in her POV?
>
> Even if it's not one you personally hold, there has to be some Third Way that allows you to empathize and be invested in what's driving her.[9]

Exercise 109-b

We've already made the point that it's not enough for your character to run through the maze, outsmarting or outgunning her foes. We have to *desperately* want her to succeed. We've got to be *outraged* when someone stands in her way or tries to hurt her.

> **EXERCISE #110: TOTAL ECLIPSE**
> - What could eclipse the importance of her journey?
> - How can you take away what she feels is the purpose of her great voyage? (a belief, or a goal)
> - How can you alter her new orbit so it gets further out of whack with the sudden ascension of another character or group?

Exercise 110

How she sees the world, and her place in it, forms the fundamental, internal gravity of who she is, without that her ability to rely on her own intuition is severely impacted. While this dark moment usually occurs just before Act III, where she has to emerge from a state of desolation and resist the overpowering urge to quit, there will be points during the last climactic sequence where she'll also have to contend with piercing doubt. She'll have to endure excruciating fear where everything's on the line and it looks like she's been outwitted.

FILM EXAMPLE

Deep in the Second Act of the 2008 sci-fi thriller *Wanted*, the protagonist, Wesley (James McAvoy), has to withstand the horrible truth about his father and why he was suddenly snatched out of his humdrum existence by a team of assassins to train and become part of their fraternity.

He shoots his father, someone he thought was an adversary. Unfortunately, with the dying man's last breath, he tells Wesley that he's being used and that the fraternity led by Sloan (Morgan Freeman) is corrupt. This news that he's just executed his father is confirmed by Wesley's mentor, Fox (Angelina Jolie), who then confides, with an evil purr, that she's been tasked with killing Wesley. He momentarily manages to escape by letting his handhold go from the train he's dangling off of, plummeting down hundreds of feet to certain death in the ravine below.

So now, besides being confused with the real nature of his purpose, the guilt of having murdered his family, and the betrayal by the seductive woman whose spell he had fallen under, Wesley now knows he's going to be hunted by the fraternity. He's in the depths of despair; he can't take them all on, it would be certain suicide. And he doesn't know who he really is without them and their guidance; they taught him how to fight, they were the ones who plucked him out of obscurity. His father was happy to let him toil like an unthinking slave in his little cubicle job, hiding his true gifts from him.

But Wesley regroups. He chooses to accept his destiny and take out Sloan. He doesn't want to hide and revert to his former mole-like existence. He decides to continue his father's mission…come what may.

When your character feels lost, if she can tap into what initially motivated her to attempt the impossible, that hunger and need will see her through. Whenever meaning has seemingly been erased, traces of it can be found in the old drive that propelled her.

It's a cinematic trope that you can "never go back"…to the good times, to what you frittered away and seldom appreciated. But before setting out on that final leg of her journey, if she makes the time to revisit her beginnings, old wounds, the origin of her deepest trauma, she can cleanse herself of any past sins or regrets that could potentially hold her back or be used against her during this culminating push to victory. It's about revisiting all the positive memories, the valuable lessons she learned, the lives of people she's touched since then. If you show her these emotional touchstones, they can ground her enough to find a way forward in her bleakest hour.

At this point in her story, she'll certainly feel the piercing humiliation of returning, not as the conquering hero, but possibly as a notable failure. So going home won't appear like a pleasant or fulfilling prospect. But sometimes a character needs to own up to what they were like in the past and to the destruction they left behind.

FILM EXAMPLE

In what is probably the toughest hole a rom-com heroine has ever had to climb out of, Birdee (Sandra Bullock) in *Hope Floats* is confronted on a Jerry Springer-type show by the news that her husband is having an affair with one of her friends and is planning to sue for divorce. She returns home to the small town she left, after she married the prom king and skipped out on any real responsibility for her adult life.

She has to endure delighted ridicule from the former high school nobodies she snubbed when she was her younger, self-absorbed cheerleader self. She must surface from a profound dejection, as her disappointed mother (Gena Rowlands) and worried young daughter (Mae Whitman) look on.

Out of the rubble of her public humiliation, she manages to recover her self-respect, get a job, and later forge a promising career as a photographer, all the while intriguing local hunk/old friend Justin (Harry Connick, Jr.), who encourages her to pursue her dreams.

What makes Birdee's transformation so satisfying is each person she has to win over. She's on a veritable apology tour, atoning for things she doesn't remember doing half the time. What she's doing is reconstructing the core of who she is, because without that she isn't any good to anybody, least of all her sensitive daughter. After the dust's settled, and she's been berated one too many times, we come to see this character is worth saving. She's trying to reform her forgotten selfishness. While we can't discount her past rottenness, she's been forced to evolve and is worth rooting for.

At this crucial stage in your character's life, she's getting rid of the last shreds of debilitating behavior. She's streamlining herself so she can take on the challenges that await her. But how will she be able to withstand the assault on her body, mind, and spirit that's coming? During those nerve-wracking moments, she'll have to find her inner strength somewhere. She'll have to channel the goodwill she's stored up from you and certain affiliate characters. Luke Skywalker had Yoda, and perversely, when Shakespeare's Scottish thane lost hope, he had Lady Macbeth to help him stay true on their path of greedy carnage.

All along, you've been her rock, that voice in her head urging her onward; she may have had a champion or a mentor who's been guiding her, too. But when she's all alone, your character will have to locate some refuge deep within herself. She'll have to find a way of centering herself. How has she built up her reservoir of resilience beforehand? By having returned to the place where she came from.

Take a trip down memory lane with your character. It's one many of us have endured, and continue to endure, on a yearly basis: the time-honored tradition of making treks over the winter months to visit with people you may hardly speak to otherwise, but who presumably provide the food, warmth, and cheer that the holidays require. Though not everyone loathes these seasonal get-togethers, chances are, to some degree, your protagonist has a less than ideal family situation.

Normally people don't point out "hard truths" to their friends or loved ones, those insights that are painful to give and receive. But, when particularly heinous nuggets do tumble out, isn't it usually at alcohol-infused seasonal gatherings? So take advantage of the close quarters, the boredom, sibling rivalry, any other kind of rivalry, and if you're of a certain class, the general desire to humiliate one another for sport.

While she may go along grudgingly, once you explain what you're after, she may be secretly interested in what her relatives and old pals say about her. If she's to grow, she has to acknowledge everything that's been holding her back. Past failures, troubled relationships, even events that were out of her control, but which she continues to blame herself for. You'll be there as a mirror showing her what she can't see and what she doesn't want to see. This is what you're here for. You're not just her shadow buddy and cheerleader, anymore.

This will probably be one of the last excruciating trials you'll be responsible for putting your character through in your "creative cloud," outside the specific demands of the story you're co-creating. You can expect it to be fraught with recriminations, petty jealousies, and old taunts. However, it's rich territory for mining the telltale faults and foibles that could have given rise to family lore. You'll be seeing her in a new light, not the one that she's been basking in from all her accomplishments thus far, but the one that puts her into perspective, one that shades in the rest of the trees in the family forest. She came from somewhere, she existed before you ran across her, and these people know her ins and outs. Even if she had cut them out of her life, they can probably still sniff out her deceptions.

Imagine you've both just finished an epic dinner at her folks' and it's been a stressful evening for you both. And now, the official gathering has broken up. Some people are leisurely revisiting their childhood bedrooms, others are retelling old stories in the kitchen, and a couple of young adults are skulking off to smoke outside. In the library, the old and the bitter have cracked open the scotch.

Encourage your character to give you the space to bond with members of her family...

Go into the library and partake. Once you weather their cranky barbs, and they sate their curiosity about you, they'll undoubtedly rake your character over the coals, too.

EXERCISE #111: THE HOLIDAY FROM HELL
What do they allude to in her personal history?
Find a corner and jot down these insights.

Exercise 111

> **EXERCISE #111b: THE HOLIDAY FROM HELL**
> The next day, address this gossip with her. If she doesn't answer, press her.
> - What does she deny?
> - What does her side of the story look like?
> - Is she even open to multiple interpretations of the same event?

Exercise 111-b

Be advised that this isn't the tenor of the rest of your discussions with your character. This is a rare moment of brutal honesty, which is too abrasive to continue, except when it's necessary to call her to the mat. She may be fuming at the skeletons you've dug up. But, if you've reined in your inner asshole, after a few days, she may feel lighter having thrown off the weight of any hidden shame.

For her to make her final ascent in the story, she has to be reborn. A figure of the new, but forged from the pain and trials of her past. Everything, no matter how discounted or ignored, has happened in her life for a reason. It's all been in preparation for the definitive encounter that will occur in the Third Act.

Be firm with her. Don't allow her to pick at the fresh crust of scar tissue. If there are still some unresolved, festering wounds, then, she can look to the Climax to lance them for good.

THIRD ACT

While not every script has a juncture late in the saga where counsel is sought, most tales will linger for a time in "the theater of doubt," a mental space outside the continuum, in a Terry Gilliam kind of place, where down can be up and you can fall through doors in the sky above to other dimensions below. It's a moment of self-reflection that epitomizes the true nature of the character's quest, a blip in real time that could last several minutes in stage time in this "theater of doubt" limbo. She realizes she'll only have the chance to right some old wrongs, and restore the natural balance of the world, if she goes on. This is the occasion when she understands fully the crisis that awaits her.

EXERCISE #112: THE DEVIL GETS HIS DAY

Looking at your own script or your outline of potential scenes and plot points, how can you increase the danger, the seeming likelihood of failure, and tap into a feeling of emotional impotence to undermine and wreck her? Stating one dimension of a setback isn't nearly enough at this point. Let whatever unmoors her bleed into as many areas of her life as possible.

- What massive reversal contributes to the protagonist's sense of powerlessness?

Think back to your work in Chapter 5 and how everything just got worse and scurried down the rabbit hole in the swoosh exercise on page 297.

Exercise 112

> **EXERCISE #112b: THE DEVIL GETS HIS DAY**
>
> Construct a complicated set-piece where *three scenes* totally obliterate her last relatively successful series of steps. Focus on a rising action that gets out of control. Alarms are going off, you can hear the rhythmic crunch of jackboots running up the stairs just outside—the whole world seems to be crumbling around her, and it's happening on hyper drive!
>
> - What topples the steady chain of building blocks she's been balancing in her crazy leaning *Janga* tower?

Exercise 112-b

SETBACKS AND REVERSALS AS EVOLUTIONARY EVOLUTION

> ### EXERCISE #113: THE NEW WORLD ORDER
> - How can the course she's been charting be re-plotted with new coordinates to align with her changed reality?
> - Does a character have to come to the fore in a last-minute substitution?
> - Does she have to tweak her idea of success in order to wrest some form of victory?

Exercise 113

As you already know, not every setback has to spell doom. Sometimes, your character can benefit from being shaken up. Perhaps, it's precisely to see vestiges of her old approach disintegrate, before she can forge a stronger identity that will enable her to carry on more nimbly.

EXERCISE #113-b: THE NEW WORLD ORDER

- Does she approach her final encounter with her chief antagonist from a completely different angle?
- Does she use a weakness he's never seen in himself...?
- How can this be a summation of "everything that's gone wrong?" In spite of her efforts, how can a last blow compound the abuse she received earlier in this sequence? (Not just another misstep or unfair roadblock—at this time, in this place—after all she's been through. But, the most cruelly ironic setback that could have befallen her...)

Exercise 113-b

> **EXERCISE #114: THE TASTE OF FREEDOM**
>
> - What does her "out of control" life look like?
> - Does she derive any benefit from the lax restrictions?
> - What new insights can be put to tactical advantage?
> - What small achievement will give her hope that she can turn all her other problems around?

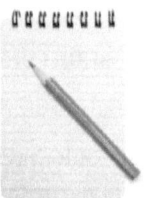

Exercise 114

WEAKNESSES AS STRENGTH

In a paradoxical twist, some part of a formerly despised trait can be leveraged to undo the antagonist in the Climax. It's unexpected, poetic, and is usually a result of the character going back to her roots to find the strength to press on. At this final moment, this secret tool used to devastate the antagonist has a full-circle richness that's satisfying. It's not a cop-out; it doesn't feel like the journey was for nothing. In fact, that's a big part of what the interlude for self-analysis is largely for. It sums up how far the character's come. How much she's learned, what she's conquered. The visible changes she's made.

So it's not as if she would have been successful all along had she only prized and reconstituted this fragment of herself. There were many steps to reaching this last, consummate goal. But in a nod to who she is at heart, the ultimate challenge is overcome because of an intrinsic "gift" that she had the wherewithal to regenerate as a powerful weapon.

FILM EXAMPLE

The following is a notable speech by a young doctor (Elyes Gabel) in Max Brooks' zombie thriller for the thinking man, *World War Z*. It's an apt introduction to the idea of using what you have, what you were born with, what makes you distinctive, even if it's not automatically seen as beneficial to you.

> DR. FASSBACH
> Mother Nature is a serial killer. No one's better. Or, more creative. Like all serial killers She can't help the urge to want to get caught. And what good are all those brilliant crimes, if no one takes the credit? So she leaves crumbs...
>
> Now, the hard part, why you spent a decade in school, is seeing the crumbs for the clues they are.
>
> Sometimes the things you thought were the most brutal

```
aspect of the virus, turn
out to be the chink in
its armor... and she loves
disguising her weaknesses
as strengths.
```

In the film, the virus that zombifies people doesn't bother attacking those that are already weak and dying, because those bodies would make weak hosts. So the key for Gerry (Brad Pitt) is to "infect" people with curable pathogens, making them unappealing to zombies. He capitalizes on the idea of weakness and frailty to render healthy populations safe to the zombie incursion.

> **EXERCISE #115: WIRE IN THE BLOOD***
>
> In the *DYC* sense, we'd like you to think about what makes your character unique, specifically those qualities of hers that are commonly misconstrued by others.
>
> - Which of those qualities is simply misunderstood or feared?
> - Which have the potential to make positive change?
> - Which, though decidedly immoral or cruel, can give the character the upper hand when she confronts her archenemy?

Exercise 115

---

* "Wire in the Blood" refers to a popular British TV show, but the original line is from T.S. Eliot's *Four Quartets*, which hints at the secret thrill and yearning for life that can be gotten after you've survived dark memories: "The trilling wire in the blood/sings below inveterate scars/appeasing long forgotten wars."

YOU ARE DONE WITH THIS STEP.

Up next is Chapter 8—HITCHED OR DITCHED.

You're now heading into the staging point, where your character will step into the arena for her final engagement: a duel to the death—spiritually or literally.

She'll either be victorious, or be tragically vanquished…

HITCHED OR DITCHED

"CLIMAX/RESOLUTION"—

STEP EIGHT

THE SETTING OF THE SHOWDOWN

IF YOU'VE DONE your work and made your character suffer, you're now primed to enjoy the final chapter of your relationship. She's earned her ending and her supreme moment of satisfaction is just around the corner.

By this stage, you've painstakingly established what's in your character's marrow. So, having exhaustively worried about how she'll act, what's hanging in the balance for her, and what ties in neatly to the plot points, you should now be able to give way and share in the sensation of these final experiences. You'll almost feel like a spectator on the sidelines as she threads the latter period of challenges and emerges triumphant.

You've done enough dreamy pre-visualization, list-making, and comparative study to be steeped in your character's world. But, if the finale seems too far away, break it down into chunks that will pay off everything you've set up. It sometimes helps to conjure up all the complex moving parts of its design.

The first step, in this last phase of your journey, is for you to inventory and size up the two most likely places where all this heightened action will take place. And within those areas, the

Dating Your Character

Byzantine warren of challenges you'll set up, which have got to become an almost organic addition to the landscape of the story. You're going to have to expose yourself, on an elemental level, to the natures of the danger that you're asking your character to confront.

In architecture, the production of scale models helps designers imagine and walk around the site of their projects from all different angles. Computer imaging even makes it possible to study the effects of light throughout the day to denote the areas that will become hot spots needing mechanical, cantilevered shades; by inputting formulas regarding use and the precise situation of the building, they can predict the ability of different proposed materials to stanch off/resist/endure weathering over time.

That kind of location-rich experience could be had in the 2010 Starz limited series *The Pillars of the Earth*, in addition to the immersive performances of Matthew Macfadyen, Rufus Sewell, and future Oscar winner Eddie Redmayne. Viewers were made privy to the tremendous undertaking of the construction of a great medieval cathedral.

You, too, will need to gaze up and around (and through) a 3-D rendering of your ending's elaborate edifice—your story's expansion joints, moveable membranes, and angled profiles—to see how the space can best frame and give rise to your characters' actions.

At this stage, the palace of rooms you erect will be the only voyeuristic and functional embellishments you'll have to offer, as the character is now fully driving the story and its outcome. But, knowing how these obstacles will constrict and challenge her is vital to illustrating how much she's grown, the new skills she's acquired, and the remnants of fear still standing in her way.

EXERCISE #116: HIDDEN SPACES

Look at where your characters can hide or crouch.
- Are there areas that are closed off from the rest of the space?

Remember, the location for her ultimate trial isn't just the final room, or maze of rooms.

It's also what surrounds this heavily guarded fortress.
Is it by the stormy Atlantic Ocean?
In the redoubtable glitz and glamour of a global financial capital?
In a sleepy Italian village on the outskirts of Milan?
- How does the nature of the materials forming the building or locale inform, impinge upon, and immobilize the abilities of the characters?

Exercise 116

EXERCISE #117: LAYING OUT THE FLOOR PLAN

- How do you ramp up to the final Climax?
- What do we know going in?
- What is held back from her view—or yours?

Exercise 117

EXERCISE #117-b: LAYING OUT THE FLOOR PLAN

- Do you parade the full glory of horrors that will be on view in the last 15-20 minute sequence? **(open view)**
- Do you give a preview of what's to come, by showing not one, but the first two hurdles that she'll confront? **(limited view)**
- How do you structure, perhaps even limit, the character's view so the audience can't anticipate the obstacles that will follow? **(closed view)**

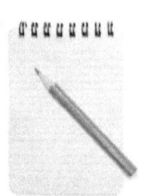

Exercise 117-b

EXERCISE #117-c: LAYING OUT THE FLOOR PLAN

So they stop floating around in your imagination as mere possibilities, study the array of pikes and spikes that will comprise the barriers to her achievement. What will they look like on screen?

- How will they convey the full dimension of the hopelessness of her cause?

Exercise 117-c

Dating Your Character

FILM EXAMPLE

Below is a sample of a page in the final chase/surveillance sequence of *The Italian Job*, the 2003 remake written by Donna and Wayne Powers. Only the barest visual cues and adjectives are used. Each sentence leads to the next. Simple, largely actionable sentences. They build with sturdy logic and clarity.

INT. MAINFRAME COMPUTER ROOM—SAME TIME

inconspicuous on a shelf, the dummy file box CLICKS into *action*. In response, the false panels on the mainframes HUM to life and in the adjacent—

TRAFFIC CONTROL CENTER

The mosaic of traffic screens SPIRAL INTO DARKNESS. The workers can't believe it. They start hitting their keyboards trying to get the system up and running again. But it's useless since—

INT. U-HAUL

Lyle controls the system now. A single mouse click loads his new algorithm into the computer and—

SERIES OF RAPID-FIRE SHOTS

All the traffic signals in Hollywood turn green simultaneously.

EXT. INTERSECTIONS

```
Cars collide into each other. A domino line of
rear-end crashes. A motorcycle tumbling over.

INT. TRAFFIC CONTROL CENTER

The stymied workers watch helplessly.
```

Incidentally, the final sequence takes about 30 pages, because there are three key converging parts that comprise it: the theft of Steve's (Edward Norton) bullion, the chase through the streets of Los Angeles, and the apprehension of Steve by some vengeful Ukrainians. The page length in Climaxes for thriller and action films commonly take up to 30 pages in length, 10 pages more than in comedies, romances, or dramas.

You don't want to safely luxuriate when playing with your train set of words, characters, and plot points. As you're constructing your elaborate array of scenes, running 15 or 20 minutes, you want to feel as on edge as your character and your audience.

Words are the tools by which we shape ideas to communicate our experiences, but they also strive for an inherent tidiness. You don't have to be transparently clear rendering all the details that comprise a scene, and what they mean. As you lay out beat after beat, you need only be emotionally logical.

Dare to be caveman-like and guttural, to make your writing more unwieldy and primal...

If you allow yourself to pare back your mental processes to give your visceral impulses authority, it will lead to a visual sensation of immediacy and quick pacing. As in the sequence from *The Italian Job*, where the spartan, active bursts of language help support the tone and pace. While action films live and breathe in quick, staccato blasts of information, you don't have to be as rigidly terse. Just note that white space is attractive to script readers. After all, it takes less time to flip a page.

Rely on your visual sense of what the final stakes will look like, leaving yourself open to more possibilities. By putting a premium on your visual eloquence, which is a primary concern at this point in your script, you'll force yourself to convey the dramatic elements of your story at its most basic level.

In the same vein of logical simplicity, before your character mounts her closing attack, we have to see how she arrived in a position to wage war. She's got to work towards this last confrontation. She can't just magically arrive. In your rush to see your character exert her newfound power, don't get ahead of yourself. All the little details matter.

We're assuming she's mortal, and if not, she must have an Achilles Heel that can be aggravated before she even shows up on the scene. Seeing how quickly she maneuvers to get herself there has to be emblematic for us to see how far she's come. Especially if your protagonist will not ultimately be victorious, it's all the more moving if we have a true sense of how far she managed to advance before succumbing to her baser instincts and weaknesses...

EXERCISE #118: THE PATH OF ARRIVAL

- How hard is it on her body for her to get there?
- Is there an emotional upheaval she barely keeps under wraps?

Did you consider the logistics?

- Travel time?
- Financial arrangements?
- Any permission she needs to get?

Exercise 118

EXERCISE #119: HER FIELD OF DREAMS

Your character having determined where her final battle will inevitably unfold, you're now ready to experience this place on a couple of sense levels: vision, smell, taste, hearing, touch...so

Dating Your Character

> that you feel less like the architect and more like one of the joint-tenants in this ultimate sequence.

Exercise 119

EXERCISE #119-b: HER FIELD OF DREAMS

Beyond the physical characteristics of the space:
- Who would be there?
- Who/what kind of character would it be surprising to
- find there?
- What's the nature of the physical feat your protagonist is going to be called upon to execute?

Exercise 119-b

Think about how you want this location to echo in the mind of the audience and throughout the film. What sort of memories will the story form in their minds? Is a different version of the final scene also the place where the character experienced a huge setback? Having her reverse a painful defeat in the same or a similar locale is tremendously satisfying. Eventual success is only sweetened by the devastation that precedes it.

EXERCISE #120: GROUND ZERO

We have to see along the way why this particular place would be meaningful to your character. Not just a place for her to win, but part of the win itself.

- What does it represent?
- Whose particular stamp has been on it?
- What similar aspects has she encountered in different locales?

Exercise 120

EXERCISE #120-b: GROUND ZERO

- After she defeats her chief rival, how does this place figure into her plans or vision of success, if at all?
- And after her efforts, what will it become in reality?

Exercise 120-b

All your *DYC* work has been leading to this final challenge. It's an opportunity to see your character conquer her demons, demonstrate her well-earned courage, and be vindicated. It's got to shape up as an extreme test of character, skill, and will. While it's a time for her to shine, it's not going to feel like a triumphal march. Remember, she'll be fighting on all fronts, unsure of the ultimate outcome.

While you may design two parallel set-pieces to play out in the same, adjacent, or intertwined locales, the protagonist herself will have to reconcile two significant problems that crop up simultaneously. She'll have almost no time to breathe during this decisive push.

FILM EXAMPLE

In the 2006 film *The Last King of Scotland*, we see a harrowing portrait of Ugandan dictator Idi Amin, which netted Forest Whitaker an Oscar for Best Leading Actor. Amin is swanning around Entebbe airport, enjoying the attentions of the world press. He pretends to broker peace between Israel and the Palestinian terrorists who've hijacked an Air France jetliner that departed from Tel Aviv. Meanwhile, Nicholas (James McAvoy), Amin's private doctor and former trusted advisor, is being tortured in a nearby airport shop, under the tyrant's personal supervision. He looks half-dead, but refuses to give Amin the satisfaction of hearing him scream in pain. He had an affair with one of Amin's wives, Kay (Kerry Washington).

Nicholas also had a perverse kind of bromance with Amin. Most of the time, he was under the spell of the charismatic, impish figure. He was intoxicated by the combination of absolute power and lighthearted frivolity that Amin first projected. He never wanted to acknowledge the barbaric murders that were sometimes happening just a hundred feet away from Amin's entourage, contrary to the government's official storyline. After turning a blind eye for so long, Nicholas wakes up to the horrors Amin's committed and his own naïve complicity by keeping the dictator alive.

When Amin shuffles back to the doting reporters to give a press conference, Nicholas is smuggled into the warehouse with the Air France hostages, managing to ignore the pain and blend in with the other non-Israeli, European hostages who are waiting to be transported out of the country. Nicholas not only withstands immense physical suffering, but is able to convince an old foe that, in saving him, he's preserving a witness to the truth of Amin's bloody savagery.

Dating Your Character

How will your character face down and endure a similar level of heightened menace and agony? How will she show us how far she's broken through her past weaknesses? What other parallel threads of resistance are meeting at this last do-or-die place? How can you aim a spotlight on an already white-hot, tense situation? How can you compound or frame the main action within an even bigger tableau?

EXERCISE #121: LOOKING DOWN AT THE SCAFFOLDING

What has the character proven she's now capable of that she was previously unable to do? How does she illustrate her new mastery?

There should be a combination of at least five different:

- skills…
- vital objects retrieved…or repaired
- relationships salvaged…that can now be:

…hazarded

…put to good use

…built upon to get even greater purchase, to vault even farther ahead

Exercise 121

> **EXERCISE #121-b: LOOKING DOWN AT THE SCAFFOLDING**
>
> - Write down what those *five assets* are on the left side of a sheet of paper.
> - Now in a crude form of storyboarding, draw *five pages* showing how those things will be placed in jeopardy or used in a surprising twist.
>
> (If you really suck at *Pictionary*, then you can log onto your computer and play with clip art. Or maybe ask the neighbor kid for some of her stickers. If you have a mind to, experiment with open-source *Celtx* software.)

Exercise 121-b

Now that you've put your character through her paces for a preview of what it'll take for her to rout her enemy(s), you have to consider how the experience will play out for your audience. They have to feel as daunted as your character does throughout her exposure to rising danger.

EXERCISE #122: HEARTBEAT BY HEARTBEAT

- How do you get the audience viscerally invested in the outcome?
- How does the character's ability to evade or circumvent crises catch the audience by surprise?
- How does she specifically snatch victory from defeat?

Write a *half page* on each.

Exercise 122

EXERCISE #122-b: HEARTBEAT BY HEARTBEAT

Once you draw up your plan, "act" it out. Say your words aloud. Even though you've probably used description, how can you hone your words so they themselves seem conversational? How do they let us know what's at stake, even on a subliminal level? Are they breathy and fragmented? Are they rat-a-tat action, spelling out the tense rhythm in a cat and mouse game?

Dating Your Character

Exercise 122-b

THIRD ACT ANXIETY ATTACK

As you wind down your story, you may be getting cold feet. What if the last sequence isn't as good as you thought? What if you don't quite know how she'll get the upper hand with the antagonist?

You might be scared that she'll bolt on you and leave you in the lurch. If you're this worried, what must *she* be feeling? How can she just throw herself out there?

She could be mauled, get lost on the way there, or be let down by someone she trusts...!

Let her know that you're not going to be that person. You have her back. After the previous spate of exercises, she's as well prepared as she can be.

Identification with her is what you worked for. In a sense, it's been your goal all along to fuse with her as if you are one.

Don't let nerves get the best of either of you.

In fact, just get it out of your systems...

EXERCISE #123: "POWER WALK"

Go on a jog. Seriously. Or just a brisk walk. Plug in your earbuds, tune out the world (as much as you can do safely). Set your phone's timer app for *20 minutes*.

Think about the last sequence. Visualize it. With each step you take, think about each step your character will take in a second of screen time. Really "feel" each second that passes by with each step. Your sense of the immediacy of "now" will be heightened.

Have you just left it at visualization? Or have you walked around and done some recon?

When you're learning something, you don't just read about it. When you're putting a math theory into practice, you don't finish your homework by "visualizing" the answer. When you're conscious of time, see how long twenty minutes is?

- Do you really think that your last sequence is going to entertain your audience for that long?
- No one's going to yawn or want to go to the bathroom?
- As you recap these final scenes in your head, are you rattling them off or do you get caught up in all the frenzy and drama they entail?

# Exercise 123

The audience can only reach a fulfilling journey by being in tune to your character's state of mind. You need them to stay in that shared dream state. Good movies, can feel just as real as dreams, they can permeate the brain.

It will require your audience to endure the same onslaught launched by your character's enemies, and suffer the same setbacks your hero does over the variety of steps she takes to attain her goals. It will allow them to feel as though they're there in that moment, inside that predicament, with her. Your supreme ambition is to let your audience approximate those similar emotions of sheer exhaustion and utter exhilaration at every leg of the adventure.

The *DYC* process is about layering onion-skin calligraphy sheets over one another to gradually add the singular features of your character over the outline, as you go deeper and spend more time with your character. This steady investigation makes it more likely you'll have a rich trove of feelings, experiences, personal issues, desires, needs, fears, and skills to call upon. Your objective is to conceptualize her frame-of-mind as she enters scenes. You'll be watching, as will your audience, as she figures her passage through them, using all she has at hand and then some.

As you've noticed, the further you get into her story, the more facilities she'll be able to draw from deep within herself. To make your character indelible, what you have to capture is the fullest expression of what she had to change internally. She's had to abandon old ways of thinking in order for her to be worthy and capable of championing the cause of her POV. In this final stage of combat, she has the fortitude to risk everything—the advantages she's gained and her life—unselfishly, conscious of the potential cost, but unwilling to act out of fear any longer.

FILM EXAMPLE

In the surprisingly dark Meg Ryan rom-com, *Addicted to Love,* her character Maggie stalks her ex-boyfriend, camping out across from his apartment in an abandoned building. Methodically, she wiretaps him, tries to undermine his career, and causes him to have a near-fatal allergic attack. All in the name of destroying his current romance and exerting revenge.

Meanwhile, Maggie teams up with a fellow "dumpee," Sam (Matthew Broderick), who adds zest to her hostile antics. And, when she realizes all her efforts are in vain, it's his company that cheers her. But throughout their escapades, while it's obvious to us, it's only after he threatens to break up their twisted partnership that she realizes she's fallen for him. In tough motorcycle-chick fashion, she pushes him out faster than he was prepared to leave. She's more afraid of admitting the truth to herself than she is of losing him.

Since this is a rom-com, Maggie doesn't have to bring down a corporation, fight a hideous monster, or uncover the identity of a murderer. Her goal is much more modest, but still a real effort for her master. She has to come to grips with what drew her to her ex, a man who's turned to a woman who happens to be the exact opposite of her. She starts off as an obstinate, rebellious spirit with a know-it-all attitude. But she spends money, time, and any remaining modicum of self respect on her mad bender of vindication. She willingly abandons her sense of individual purpose and any hope of being fit for a future relationship.

For all her leather-clad prickliness, Maggie's mushier inside than she would have anyone believe, including Sam. While his mild-mannered demeanor was persuaded to indulge in her infantile antics, he's always been right about how this would end. But her own stubbornness hasn't allowed her to digest his reasonable arguments and his growing concern for her. She has to admit to herself that, after her ex stomped on her heart, it blew out her vein of vulnerability. And that she's in danger of permanently collapsing her ability to love and enjoy life. She'll have to embrace the emotional lifeblood coursing through her or face a life of emptiness.

The revamped 2.0 version of your character, who's cowed by nothing (or at least brave enough to continue on), may be impressive in a myriad of ways. You're proud of her and your role in getting her in fighting shape. Yet she could be stubbornly resisting you, if she's in a mood to brawl. She's hyped up and may not be able to turn it off and on.

Your nerves may be jangling, too, over what will happen next. You're wondering how you're going to juggle so many story threads and built-in layers of set-ups and pay-offs, that it could feel like the wrap-up won't ever be done. Even if your writing already has velocity, how can you make sure you don't let a ball drop?

If you've used your *DYC* exercises to deepen an existing script in a rewrite process, then going through with a yellow highlighter, or creating a reverse-engineered outline to look at what is still needed, may help your character fulfill on those earlier details that stated her potential for change.

EXERCISE #124: STRINGING PEARLS

• Draft a list of your script's plot pivots...

(It's gonna be a long list.)

  • Furthermore, draft a list for each character's dilemmas...

When all is said and done, you'll probably have roughly 35 plot beats/problems that your character will be facing, and another 5 or so that ancillary characters have to sort out.

Exercise 124

EXERCISE #124-b: STRINGING PEARLS

• Do all these beats link up?

• Does a scene jump out of nowhere?

• Does a character miraculously arrive unscathed at her next destination?

Exercise 124-b

You have to show us how she got out of a scrape. That's usually the best part! Though you could sparingly, as a tease, have her step out of a car, bruised, bleeding, and rumpled, and let us guess…

Taking a slightly wider perspective, consider the tone of the script and the character's ability in the beginning versus at the conclusion. Have you contemplated how these two poles line up and relate to each other?

EXERCISE #124-c: STRINGING PEARLS

- In your Set-up and Inciting Incident, what impossible goal presented itself to the character and how did she see herself accomplishing it?
- Does the end justify the means?
- Does the denouement directly correlate to the ambitions she voiced in Act I?
- How markedly different is the character we initially met from the character who emerges at the story's close?

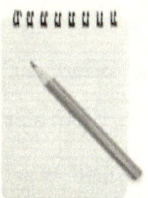

Exercise 124-c

Let's look at the resolutions that aren't centrally tied to her. The subplots of the story have probably caught the audience's interest and are also important. So, don't leave them hanging…

> **EXERCISE #125: TYING UP LOOSE ENDS**
>
> - Is another character's goal attained?
> - Does one of the other characters get a chance to substantiate an arc of growth?
> - Does the protagonist's "way of being" alter due to someone else's specific influence?

Exercise 125

While we're not tying the bow just yet on the stack of boxes containing your layers of story puzzles and character dilemmas, we are approaching the final opportunity for you to demonstrate all the ingenuity you and your character are capable of.

Our lives are filled with experiences of transformative events, people, and places. If the only constant is change, our survival and success is dependent on our talent to adapt as things shift around us. When we speak about characters changing, we're looking at a character starting out in one place and then making some monumental—(everything's relative)—metamorphosis that enables her to achieve a particular goal or desire.

As you've strived to prove, authentic, earned change occurs in all domains: physical, mental, social, and spiritual. Besides her behavior, dialogue, and actions, there are other subtler ways for your reader and audience to grok* this transformative pull. When done artfully, metaphors are a surprisingly powerful mirror of your character's inner transfiguration. Many evocations of this transformational pull can be expressed through a metaphor, a linking pattern of similar symbols, or a certain style that's only present at moments that denote her inner life. But you don't want to be so obvious with your metaphor that the audience is onto you, anticipating the next time *grandfather's watch* shows up to remind everyone that time is a- ticking.

---

* Grok means to understand thoroughly and intuitively. It was coined by Robert A. Heinlein in the science-fiction novel *Stranger in a Strange Land* (1961).

EXERCISE #126: PERVASIVE METAPHORS

• What are the specific examples of metaphor that keep popping up in your story?

This may require revisiting some of the more visceral and sensory exercises to see if there's something that repeats itself or something that stands out as a possible repeating motif.

Exercise 126

DYC Example:

A shell-shocked WWI soldier decides to give up on life after the sudden death of his mother, which he finds out in a letter six months after the fact. He becomes in thrall to cocaine and falls into a debilitating depression in the muddy trenches of the Somme.

Here is a list of possible metaphors that could be woven in from the Set-up all the way to the Resolution:

"mud" (in the trenches, sloshing in the rain on the muddy ground at the family's farm house, diving in the mud during a hard-fought football game, as a youngster making mud-pies with a girl he has a crush on)

> **"drugs"** (seeing his grandfather take drugs to cope with a bad back, taking drugs to enhance his performance in college athletics, experimenting with mind-altering drugs with friends, liking to hang out at the drugstore after school for sodas, candy, and philosophical conversations with the sweet girl he likes)

Remember, keep true to your period and fact-check your use of metaphor to resonate authentically with your character's particular lifeline. Metaphors are delicate beams for propping up the visual and spiritual canopy of your story. They're just one method we've discussed for you to codify and ornament the procession of your character's narrative and evolution.

Ideally, you've been connecting painlessly with your character most of the time. So, the homecoming or leave-taking that Step 8 most often features may be especially poignant. She'll have to make her peace with you, too, before moving on and putting herself to the task of completing her goal. Hopefully she's arrived at a new paradigm that will allow her to succeed using all the levels of her abilities.

In a tragedy, the obstacles within the world or within her core being will prove too overwhelming. But at least the audience will have developed enough of an understanding of her fatal flaw to render the tragic ending satisfying, if bittersweet.

She's about to walk away from you towards her final decisive appointment with steady purpose. (Imagine her wearing wedding-dress-white—a lab coat, a leotard and tutu, a suit of armor—it's only the color palette that's emblematic.) As she enjoys the peace before the storm, when she closes her eyes and imagines her happy ending, what does she see?

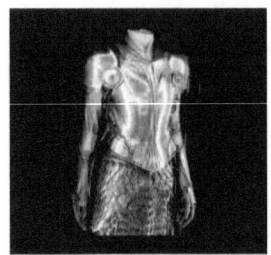

EXERCISE #127: WALKING DOWN THE AISLE

- What are all the ways the ending has to be satisfying for her?
- What set-up did you layer in during the Inciting Incident that could pay off now?
- Have you shown why this would be meaningful to her, and why she was unable to achieve this before?
- Is it, in one sense, the culmination of her dreams? But amended substantially because she's a different person?

Exercise 127

At some point of the story's final beats, you may find yourself in the same kind of suspended animation as she does. You also might feel that you're "hanging on for dear life," since the outcome isn't guaranteed. As uncomfortable as it is to be in this place…this is exactly what you want.

You want to be "in there" with your character, where you can still be astonished. Keeping yourself in the dark in the final stage can lend a freshness and velocity to the writing. So, you don't feel like you're just mindlessly going through the motions, connecting the dots. After all your weeks of hard work, you certainly don't want to end up with anything predictable and stale. The most gratifying endings are unexpected, but in their roundabout way, inevitable.

Though she may not divulge it, she still needs your support. She's more vulnerable than she's ever been at any other stage, and she doesn't know it. She probably feels temporarily invincible. You have every confidence in her, and it's up to her to make it happen. You're conscious now that you'll be saying good-bye; she's going off to battle, on *your* behalf…

How do you properly end your time together? In training for a common mission, you transcended your personal peculiarities, grew close, and even shared secrets. Commit to paper your rush of thoughts. Depending on what you're writing, you'll either compose a letter of appreciation, or she'll draft a different sort of letter to you. If your story is a tragedy, her letter will be a fond farewell.

In such a sad case, hopefully she'll be able to show you some compassion. It will be a painful letter for her to write. She'll be acknowledging an empty future, knowing, deep in her heart, that she's destined for failure. You could be cruelly stringing her along, but at this point, having intermittent doubts is a far cry from knowing in the furthermost reaches of her soul that it won't work out. For all her efforts, she won't be able to overcome the harrowing blitz in the impossible situation ahead of her.

> **EXERCISE #128: APPRECIATION LETTER/SUICIDE NOTE**
> Compose the letter…

Exercise 128

> **_DYC_ Example: The Suicide Note (the story is a tragedy)**
>
> In the following example, we envision the disappointing scenario where the character succumbs to his environment. It was simply too much to ask of him and beyond his scope to survive.
>
> Dear Elizabeth,
>
> I truly appreciate the talks we've had. I haven't been able to tell people what it's like here. The guys who are here don't need to be told. And people back home wouldn't believe it.
>
> Unless you're used to a near constant state of calm. Then crazy 5-minute intervals of gunfire. When it was clockwork, it was okay. Half an hour after first light, a short, colorful burst before dinner time.
>
> I guess they were bound to have picked up on our jokes about that. Germans are pretty smart, even if they are stubborn robots. The punctuality made their offensives ineffective for a while.
>
> But now we have to keep changing our passwords. Yesterday, two of them entered our trenches from behind. They spoke okay English, better than me. Had the right accent and everything. Sounded like officers. You know, like I been saying, that real high-pitched nasal sound the British have.
>
> They wounded a bunch of other guys and McGreavy. Then they were blown up. There was a panic before one of the

sergeants just lobbed a grenade. Killed one of his own, too. But I didn't hear the whole story, maybe he was already dyin' anyway.

When all you can think about's death, that's all you think about. I'm just stuck here. Couldn't desert if I wanted to. Not with crazy Germans breaking our line.

I didn't know him. McGreavy. I think he was the one with the cackle two trenches over, 'cause you don't hear it...

Sometimes, I don't lift my head up out of the mud, though it smells of manure. The stench in the air is worse—rotten eggs. Burns your eyes if the wind brings it close.

My body aches. I'm just so tired, and it's more of the same. There's nothing to look forward to. Ma was always with me, but I don't talk to her anymore. Somehow, she was keeping me alive, her barking at me.

"Duck, boy! That hole! *That* hole! Take it boy! It's been dug for you!"

Now it's quiet and fuzzy inside my head like Aunt Ellen's prize rabbit muffler. I watch people as they do things: run, hide, shoot. And, I just do what they do.

Don't know why, but there's talk of a charge. The officers keep looking at the sky to check the weather. Then, they point at maps as big as flags, which flap and crackle in the poisonous air. Blue veins of rivers, brown veins of roads, and yellow dots. I hate those yellow dots; they oughta be red. That's where we're

> going to go. We've been grousing about when they'd stick the next one. I don't think I'm going to make it.
>
> There's only room for so many on that dot...
>
> It's not hard to write those words. I'm not as frightened as I reckoned I'd be. But I'm disgusted confessing that to you. You've been so nice and patient.
>
> I want you to know I appreciate all you done for me. It's owing to you I made it out of that little village with the sniper.
>
> Best to you and yours.
>
> Your pal,
>
> Wallace "Maxim" Hanley, Pvt. 1st Class, 33rd Infantry, U.S. Army National Guard
>
> July 1916

Admittedly, that's agonizing. Are you dead-sure your character must ditch the dream and stay buried in a bog of muck? It's your choice...

But what if her dream was to surprisingly morph? Can you direct your energy to helping your character realize a deeper, richer, fuller kind of commitment to herself, and others, before succumbing?

Have you unconditionally ruled out a bittersweet victory, where the character attains her most important objective but gives up her life to do so? That's tragic, but it's not the sort of systemic failure that's at the heart of tragedies. (And it won't likely bum out your audience as much.)

If you're in the process of banging out your script, step away from us and spend two weeks absorbed in its final sequence. If you've been working on the exercises in *DYC* in preparation for the actual writing of the screenplay, then please continue below.

THE OTHER SIDE

Your character has experienced the Climax of her adventure. She's made it. She may be battered and bloody, but she's alive. And as a result of her evolution, you've seen her validate something that other people discounted or took for granted.

The next few exercises are here to ensure that you delivered on everything you explicitly set out to offer up for our entertainment. How persuasively has your character demonstrated a true growth and maturity over the course of the narrative?

EXERCISE #129: JANUS IMAGE

- What were her expectations at the beginning of the story?
- How has she stayed the same or perhaps used a part of herself that she was afraid to access?

Exercise 129

EXERCISE #129-b: JANUS IMAGE

- What was the value system that she was transforming?
- What did your character have to give up or sacrifice at the end?
- Looking at her future, what does she imagine she's given up forever?

Exercise 129-b

Dating Your Character

The full power of your character has been forged from a sense of cause and effect. She eventually moved from behavior that was blocking her from getting something she wanted. Along the way, she may have even put to good use some of her shadow side.

There was a build or progression that had an internal logic, which showed her embrace a refreshed, new vision—a modified POV about herself and the world. By reviewing her final decisions in the last sequence, let's see if it also contains the layers and payoffs any studio or television exec will be looking for.

EXERCISE #130: THE MAGMA OF THE EMOTIONAL CORE

Sit for a moment and write down the answer to the prompts below. Don't censor yourself, just write.

"At the end of the movie, my character made the following decision and took the following actions":

_____.

"From a character standpoint, the last scene can be best described as":

_____.

Exercise 130

DYC Sample bad answer to above:

In the last scene, the protagonist chooses not to shoot her estranged father, even though he admits to mistakenly engineering the kidnapping of her son.

My character changed for the better because she was finally able to confront her father.

DYC Sample better answer to above:

After trapping and binding her estranged father in a foreclosed home, there's a tense exchange where the protagonist gets him to confess to mistakenly engineering the kidnapping of her son. Tempted, nevertheless, she chooses not to shoot him. Instead, she passes the gun to her teenage son. He tries to pull the trigger, but he can't.

His fingers were broken when a van door was slammed on his hand during the abduction. His mother presses her hands on either side of his to steady his grip. Then, he pulls the trigger, shooting his grandfather in both hands.

My character gained a true sense of her own self-worth, after she was able to use her dogged determination and knowledge of the neighborhood to rescue her son. She was capable of operating objectively, without remorse for what might befall her father. That proved to him how she'd developed into a self-possessed woman, one who wasn't afraid of him anymore. Because of that, he eventually came around and gave up his

> partner.
>
> You see the difference. One answer is vague. The other has heightened stakes, detail, and life.

A lot of effort has gone into showing your character stretch herself and experience change. You've explored a world rife with exciting complications, moments of visual spectacle, all while staying largely within the bounds of your recognizable genre. But have you also ended your adventure in the way certain kinds of films always seem to wind things up?

GENRE WRAP-UPS

We're sure you plan to provide the scares (horror), touching moments (drama), adrenaline (action), and belly-busting laughs (comedy) for your screenplay. But for some genres, you should be aware that there are a few more added prescriptions for a proper finale:

MYSTERY/THRILLER

- The farther out your final reveal...the better. Leave it to the last five minutes.

DRAMA

- Because the explosion is such an emotionally draining one, there's a need for resolution to the conflict and a sense of what things will look like after FADE OUT.

ACTION

- After racking up a high body count, fellow soldiers/cop partners/etc. limit themselves to a stoic slap on the back or shake of the hands to signal it's a job well done and their friendship/work partnership is intact. There's also usually a tangential love interest who's reunited with her alpha male hero.

MELODRAMA

- It's common to see acceptance of the cycle of life and death. After patiently suffering along with the characters over the course of the movie, catharsis is critical. Tears have got to flow...

FILM EXAMPLE

The Fault in Our Stars, based on the best-selling novel by John Green, features the poetic odyssey of two teens suffering through treatment for cancer and falling in love along the way. It's a search for meaning and the continuation of life we all look for.

Presumably, Hazel (Shailene Woodley) dies at the melodramatic, coming-of-age tale's close. But before she does, she's just trying to come to terms with it all. She grows obsessed with a certain book, *An Imperial Affliction*, about a heroine who, at the end, dies mid-sentence. Hazel implores the book's author (Willem Dafoe) to tell her what will happen after the heroine's gone: what will happen to the heroine's pet hamster, Sisyphus? She's also worried about the future of the girl's mother and the mysterious "Tulip Man."

These contemplations replace the relentless worry about the people she loves who will survive her…her own mother and family. In the face of hearing from the author that after death, or a story's ending, there's nothing, she refutes that. She imagines the future, hoping her parents will continue on and prosper after she dies; her mom's (Laura Dern) even planning on taking some classes to embark on a career as a counselor, so she can put her experience as a caregiver to good use. For Hazel, her supreme focus on the life-death cycle ends up comforting her and makes it easier for her to deal with the inevitable.

Dating Your Character

At this point, you know your narrative, your character, your genre's final requirements, and have had your audience constantly present during your outlining/writing process. Now marketing considerations are paramount.

Let's clarify all the work you've done so far. The basic concerns of a well-written logline can be understood as part of the "cha-cha-cha" (or character-challenge-change) that your script promises. "Cha-cha-cha" helps you stay in tune to your character's rhythm and is the way she moves through life and her story.

LOGLINES—WHY ARE THEY SO IMPORTANT?

You may have created a logline to help you and your character stay on track during the writing, but once used out in the marketplace, a logline is a necessary tool for your project. You'll see that a nifty line doesn't give away the plot, but shares enough to make the reader want to read on.

> **Logline Tips:**
> Here are some vital questions that you should keep in mind when attempting to convert a 100+-page script into a 25-word pot of gold:

- **Who is your target audience and why should they care?**

  Remember the four quadrants from Chapter 2?

- **Will the people who'd want to see your movie be pulled in by your logline? What would grab them specifically?**

- **Think about other films (or TV shows) you've seen which are similar—is yours crafted for that specific demographic?**

Your logline needs to offer a fresh way into your character and her world. One surefire tactic is to take advantage of a cliché—like the "dumb blonde." *Legally Blonde* takes that cliché and turns it on its head.

The below example's also funny and light, so you know the story's a comedy:

"A dumb blonde gets into law school to win over the guy who dumped her and becomes the star student."

- **Does your title suggest scenes for the movie poster or the trailer?**

- **Does your logline bear no connection to the title of your film?**

Just as an actor's headshot should closely resemble the person who appears in front of the casting director, so should your title directly reflect what your script's really about to an audience.

Your theme should be implied in the title via a sense of irony or its specific genre-appropriate tone—mystery, humor, etc. Think of these examples and how they manage to evoke a taste of the story: *Wedding Crashers, The Hurt Locker, The Girl with the Dragon Tattoo.*

- **Is the genre clear? (No more than two mixed genres, please!)**

You want to surprise and catch your audience off guard not confuse them till they're frustrated and grumbling, "I still don't know what the hell it's about…"

- **Is your logline shopworn? Too vague?**

No one wants the feeling "been there, done that." Or, conversely, "I don't get it."

- **Is your logline too short?**

You may hear the generic, and slightly disdainful, "And then what?" Your listener doesn't want to feel like he's part of your pitch or is functioning as a straight man to your comedic gambits.

- **Too long?**

You should be able to grab people instantly in one or two sentences. If your audience doesn't gain a clear understanding of the whole HOG (Hero-Obstacle-Goal), you'll need to incorporate choice details to add intensity and definition.

If someone seems interested and you get on a roll launching

into your 5-minute pitch, even if you've dangled tantalizing tidbits, be aware that if you go on too long people may tune out. If you become involved in tangents and squander the logic of your narrative, they may even forget the first part of your spiel.

- **Is change to the character implied?**

Let's look at a poor example.

"*Moby Dick* is about a man who chases after a big whale." There aren't stakes here or much of an inherent drama, let alone a compelling reason for the protagonist.

This is better:

"*Moby Dick* is about a solitary man's quest to find purpose, after he vows to himself that he'll catch a legendary whale that's been eluding him his entire life."

The logline implies that the story's going to be a meditation on life with a macho, objective goal as well.

- **Does your logline miss the mark about the story?**

If so, think about your "cha-cha-cha." Looking more closely at your character's pay-off transformation could give you a clue about how your story can connect with its intended audience.

- **Have you encapsulated at least two of the following in your logline: the conflict, pace, stakes, and conceivable controversy?**
- **Is your logline crassly pushing some agenda?**

The current political, social, and cultural climate is something to consider as you think about boiling down your material into an exciting logline. But don't bludgeon the potential buyer with a "story-lite" rant:

"*The China Syndrome* is about the possibility of mass devastation in the rush to nuclear energy."

There's an ounce of political snideness there.

This version is without judgment and offers more specifics about the hysteria that could ensue tied to plot:

"A whistleblower brings attention to the weak override system in a nuclear power plant by holding the engineering corps hostage."

Notice how clever the title is. It's gravely portentous and uses an obscure scientific term that's meant to pique your interest.

- **Is your logline more of a teaser?**

A logline is a reliable litmus test that answers the basic question—"Do you have a story?" If you can't describe your movie in 25 words or less, some vital element is missing.

This logline for the comedy *Tootsie* isn't good enough:

"A man must become a woman in order to become a better man."

This is a crucial life lesson that Dustin Hoffman's character utters in the film, and it's a great line. But it's not a logline.

At face value, if you don't know the movie, it doesn't make

sense, and there's nothing funny there. So, you need to add in some adjectives and a little less philosophy:

"A failed actor finally nails a juicy part in a daytime soap...after he auditions as a frumpy woman."

EXERCISE #131: LOGLINE POLISH

"A suicidal cop partners with another cop on the eve of his retirement."

In the 80's, that was a fresh twist on the prototypical good-guy cop who's an honorable protector and hero.

How could you update the Mel Gibson movie *Lethal Weapon* for today?

- How have the expectations within the genre of the crime thriller changed?

Exercise 131

EXERCISE #131-b: LOGLINE POLISH

Test drive the logline for your script with *10 people*.

But be careful who you share your gem with. We suggest you seek out regular folks outside the business, your audience, to not only safeguard your idea, but play it out with your potential ticket-buyers.

If the consensus is "boring," or anything short of genuine enthusiasm, then go back to the drawing board…

Exercise 131-b

As we wrap up our *Dating Your Character* guide, we thank you for going on this journey with us. Taking seriously the role of character creation, you've matured as a writer. You've celebrated your imagination as a space for you and your character to bond in a genuine writing partnership.

You've both come full circle. You know who she is—enough to have anticipated some of her moves—but were still surprised by her actions and choices.

We want to encourage you to continue to read scripts and study human behavior. Your writing will be the better for it and its commercial prospects even further enhanced…

—Marilyn, Devo, & Elizabeth
xxx

DYC INDEX: BOOK/CELEBRITY/FILM/TV REFERENCES

Chapter	Page #	Title – Book/Film/ Publication/TV	Celebrity/ *Character*
1	15		Kenneth Branagh
1	15		Emma Thompson
1	15	Film: "Dead Again"	
1	25		Tom Hanks
1	28		John Steinbeck
1	28	Book: "The Grapes of Wrath"	
1	32		Barbara Walters
2	35		Billy Wilder
2	35		Neil Simon
2	35	Film: "The Odd Couple"	
2	35		*Felix Unger*
2	35		*Oscar Madison*
2	38		Jodie Foster
2	38		*Clarice Starling*
2	38	Film: "Silence of the Lambs"	
2	38		*Hannibal Lecter*
2	42		Terrence Malick
2	42	Film: "The Tree of Life"	
2	43	TV: "CSI"	
2	44		Spike Lee
2	44	Film: "The Inside Man"	
2	45	Film: "Romancing the Stone"	
2	45		Michael Douglas

Chapter	Page #	Title – Book/Film/ Publication/TV	Celebrity/*Character*
2	45		Diane Thomas
2	47		*Clarice Starling*
2	48		*Spock*
2	48	Film: "Star Trek"	
2	55		*Lara Croft*
2	58		Alex Kurtzman
2	58	Film: "People Like Us"	
2	61	TV: "The Good Wife"	
2	61		Julianna Margulies
2	62		Francis Ford Coppola
2	62	Film: "The Godfather"	
2	62		Al Pacino
2	62		Marlon Brando
2	62		Andrew Bujalski
2	62		The Duplass brothers
2	63	TV: "Togetherness"	
2	63		Scott Rubenstein
2	71		Marc Forster
2	71	Film: "Stranger than Fiction"	
2	72		Emma Thompson
2	72		Will Ferrell
2	72	Film: "Ruby Sparks"	
2	72		Paul Dano
2	72		Zoe Kazan
2	77		Agatha Christie
2	77	Film: "Murder on the Orient Express"	
2	77		*Hercule Poirot*

Dating Your Character

Chapter	Page #	Title – Book/Film/ Publication/TV	Celebrity/*Character*
2	78	TV: "Zen"	
2	78	TV: "Wallander"	
2	78	TV: "Rosemary and Thyme"	
2	78	Film: "Traffic"	
2	78	Film "Ocean's 11"	
2	78	Film: "Butch Cassidy and the Sundance Kid"	
2	78		Katharine Ross
2	81	Film: "Inception"	
2	81		Leonardo DiCaprio
2	82		Humphrey Bogart
2	82	Film: "The African Queen"	
2	82	Film: "Sleepless in Seattle"	
2	83		James Mangold
2	83	Film: "3:10 to Yuma"	
2	83		*Dan Evans*
2	83		Christian Bale
2	84		Russell Crowe
2	84		*Ben Wade*
2	86		Joel & Ethan Coen
2	86	Film: "Miller's Crossing"	
2	88	Film: "Fast and the Furious"	
2	88	Film: "Jane Eyre"	
2	88		Charlotte Bronte
2	88		*Jane Eyre*
2	89		*Edward Rochester*

Chapter	Page #	Title – Book/Film/ Publication/TV	Celebrity/*Character*
2	89		Michael Fassbender
2	89		Cary Fukunaga
2	89		Mia Wasikowska
2	91		Danny Boyle
2	91	Film: "Trainspotting"	
3	95	Music: "Baby Einstein"	
3	96		Josefina Lopez
3	96	Film: "Real Women Have Curves"	
3	97	TV: "On Story"	
3	97	Film: "Thelma and Louise"	
3	97		Callie Khouri
3	105		Spike Lee
3	105	Film: "Do the Right Thing"	
3	105		*Mookie*
3	105		*Pino*
3	105		John Turturro
3	105		Danny Aiello
3	105		*Jade*
3	107		Aristotle
3	107	Book: "Poetics"	
3	114	Film: "The Shawshank Redemption"	
3	114		*Andy*
3	114		Tim Robbins
3	114		*Red*
3	114		Morgan Freeman
3	128		Charles de Talleyrand

Chapter	Page #	Title – Book/Film/ Publication/TV	Celebrity/*Character*
3	141		Sam Mendes
3	141	Film: "Road to Perdition"	
3	141		Max Allan Collins
3	141		Richard Piers Rayner
3	141		Jude Law
3	142		*John Rooney*
3	142		Paul Newman
3	142	Film: "The Godfather"	
3	142		Conrad L. Hall
3	142		David Self
3	142		Tom Hanks
3	142		*Sullivan*
3	142		*Michael*
3	142	Publication: "USA Today"	
3	142	Film: "Road to Perdition"	
3	149	TV: "Unforgettable"	
3	149	Book: "The Rememberer"	
3	149		J. Robert Lennon
3	150		*Carrie Wells*
3	163	Film: "The King's Speech"	
3	163		David Seidler
3	163		*Bertie*
3	163		*King George VI*
3	163		*Edward VIII*
3	164		Everett Freeman

Chapter	Page #	Title – Book/Film/ Publication/TV	Celebrity/*Character*
3	164	Film: "The Secret Life of Walter Mitty"	
3	164	Film: "Back to the Future"	
3	164		*Phil Connors*
3	164		Bill Murray
3	165		Colin Firth
3	165	Film: "Pride and Prejudice"	
3	165		*Lizzy Bennet*
3	165		Jennifer Ehle
3	165		*Darcy*
3	166		Jane Austen
3	166	Book: "First Impressions"	
3	166		the *Bingleys*
3	168		*Bran Stark*
3	168	TV: "Game of Thrones"	
3	168		George R. R. Martin
3	172	Film: "Gladiator"	
3	172		Russell Crowe
3	174	Game System: "Oculus Rift VR"	
4	187	Film: "L.A. Confidential"	
4	187		*Bud White*
4	187		Russell Crowe
4	187		*Lt. Exley*
4	187		Guy Pearce
4	188		Kevin Spacey
4	189		Meryl Streep

Chapter	Page #	Title – Book/Film/Publication/TV	Celebrity/*Character*
4	194	Book: "Field Guide to Birds of the Desert Southwest"	
4	195		*Snoopy*
4	197	Film: "Back to the Future"	
4	197		*Marty McFly*
4	197		Michael J. Fox
4	197		John Huston
4	197	Film: "The Maltese Falcon"	
4	197		Humphrey Bogart
4	197		Dashiell Hammett
4	200	Book: "The Five Love Languages"	
4	200		Gary Chapman
4	202	Film: "Romancing the Stone"	
4	202		*Joan Wilder*
4	202		Kathleen Turner
4	202		*Jack Colton*
4	202		Michael Douglas
4	205		*Erin Brockovich*
4	205		Julia Roberts
4	206		Susannah Grant
4	211	Film: "Blue Jasmine"	
4	211		Woody Allen
4	211		Cate Blanchett
4	215		Ang Lee
4	215	Film: "The Ice Storm"	
4	232	Film: "Departures"	

Chapter	Page #	Title – Book/Film/ Publication/TV	Celebrity/*Character*
5	244		John Steinbeck
5	244	Book: "Grapes of Wrath"	
5	251	Book: "The Last Ride of Caleb O'Toole"	
5	257		Carolyn Myss
5	257	Book: "Archetype Cards"	
5	258	Film: "Leave Her to Heaven"	
5	258		*Ellen*
5	258		Gene Tierney
5	258	Film: "Laura"	
5	258		Cornel Wilde
5	269	Film: "Six Degrees of Separation"	
5	270	Film: "Notes on a Scandal"	
5	270		*Barbara*
5	270		Judi Dench
5	270		Cate Blanchett
5	270		Patrick Marber
5	270		Zoe Heller
5	300		Justin Timberlake
5	300	Film: "In Time"	
5	300		*Will*
5	300		Amanda Seyfried
5	300		*Sylvia*
5	300		*Bonnie and Clyde*
6	309	Film: "Hotel Rwanda"	
6	309		Don Cheadle

Chapter	Page #	Title – Book/Film/ Publication/TV	Celebrity/*Character*
6	309		Paul Rusesabagina
6	309		*Col. Oliver*
6	313		Sarah Jessica Parker
6	313		Matthew McConaughey
6	313	Film: "Failure to Launch"	
6	313		*Tripp*
6	313		*Paula*
6	319		*Yoda*
6	321	TV: "Scotland Decides"	
6	322		Mel Gibson
6	322	Film: "Braveheart"	
6	322		William Wallace
6	323		Freud
6	323		Pierre Janet
6	327		Christopher Nolan
6	327	Film: "The Prestige"	
6	327		*Robert*
6	327		Hugh Jackman
6	327		*Alfred*
6	327		Christian Bale
6	327		Houdini
6	330	Film: "Rachel Getting Married"	
6	330		Anne Hathaway
6	330		*Kym*
6	330		*Ethan*
6	330		*Abby*
6	330		Debra Winger
6	331		Rosemarie DeWitt

Chapter	Page #	Title – Book/Film/ Publication/TV	Celebrity/*Character*
6	331		*Rachel*
6	336		*Batman*
6	336		Christopher Nolan
6	336		Christian Bale
6	336		*The Joker*
6	336		Heath Ledger
6	336		David S. Goyer
6	337		Pavlov
6	340	Film: "On the Waterfront"	
6	340		Marlon Brando
6	340		*Terry Malloy*
6	341		*Joey*
6	341		Budd Schulberg
6	342		*Edie Doyle*
6	342		Eva Marie Saint
6	342		*Father Barry*
6	342		Karl Malden
6	342		*Johnny Friendly*
6	342		Lee J. Cobb
6	342		*Charley the "Gent"*
6	342		Rod Steiger
6	343		Elia Kazan
6	343		Sen. Joe McCarthy
6	348		Sanford Meisner
6	352		*Indiana Jones*
6	352		Harrison Ford
6	352		Sean Connery
6	354	Book: "Men are from Mars, Women are from Venus"	

Dating Your Character

Chapter	Page #	Title – Book/Film/ Publication/TV	Celebrity/*Character*
7	365	Film: "The Secret Life of Walter Mitty"	
7	365		Woody Allen
7	365	Film: "Crimes and Misdemeanors"	
7	365		Martin Landau
7	365		*Judah*
7	366		Anjelica Huston
7	366		*Cliff*
7	366		*Jack*
7	366		Jerry Orbach
7	367		*James Bond*
7	367		Claire Bloom
7	369	Film: "French Kiss"	
7	369		Meg Ryan
7	369		*Kate*
7	369		Kevin Kline
7	369		*Luc*
7	371	Film: "Chinatown"	
7	371		Robert Towne
7	371		Jack Nicholson
7	371		Faye Dunaway
7	371		John Huston
7	372		*Hollis Mulwray*
7	392		Aaron Korsh
7	392	TV: "Suits"	
7	392		*Harvey Specter*
7	392		*Mike Ross*
7	392		*Jessica Pearson*
7	392		*Louis Litt*

Chapter	Page #	Title – Book/Film/ Publication/TV	Celebrity/*Character*
7	399	Film: "Hunger Games: Catching Fire"	
7	409	Film: "Wanted"	
7	409		*Wesley*
7	409		James McAvoy
7	409		*Sloan*
7	409		Morgan Freeman
7	409		*Fox*
7	409		Angelina Jolie
7	411		*Birdee*
7	411		Sandra Bullock
7	411	Film: "Hope Floats"	
7	411		Jerry Springer
7	411		Gena Rowlands
7	411		Mae Whitman
7	411		*Justin*
7	411		Harry Connick, Jr.
7	412		*Luke Skywalker*
7	412		*Yoda*
7	412		Shakespeare
7	412		*Lady Macbeth*
7	417		Terry Gilliam
7	419	Game: "Janga"	
7	423		Elyes Gabel
7	423		Max Brooks
7	423	Film: "World War Z"	
7	423		*Dr. Fassbach*
7	424		*Gerry*
7	424		Brad Pitt
7	425		T.S. Eliot

Chapter	Page #	Title – Book/Film/ Publication/TV	Celebrity/*Character*
7	425	Poetry: "Four Quartets"	
8	428		Matthew Macfadyen
8	428		Rufus Sewell
8	428		Eddie Redmayne
8	428	TV: "The Pillars of the Earth"	
8	432	Film: "The Italian Job"	
8	432		Donna & Wayne Powers
8	433		Edward Norton
8	433		*Steve*
8	434	Film: "The Italian Job"	
8	438	Film: "The Last King of Scotland"	
8	438		Idi Amin
8	438		Forest Whitaker
8	439		*Nicholas*
8	439		James McAvoy
8	439		*Kay*
8	439		Kerry Washington
8	442	Game: "Pictionary"	
8	442	Software: "Celtx"	
8	447		Meg Ryan
8	447	Film: "Addicted to Love"	
8	447		*Maggie*
8	447		*Sam*
8	447		Matthew Broderick
8	453		Robert A. Heinlein

Chapter	Page #	Title – Book/Film/ Publication/TV	Celebrity/*Character*
8	453	Book: "Stranger in a Strange Land"	
8	469	Film: "The Fault in Our Stars"	
8	469		John Green
8	469		*Hazel*
8	469		Shailene Woodley
8	469	Meta-book: "An Imperial Affliction"	
8	469		Willem Dafoe
8	469		*Tulip Man*
8	469		Laura Dern
8	471	Film: "Legally Blonde"	
8	472	Film: "Wedding Crashers"	
8	472	Film: "The Hurt Locker"	
8	472	Film: "The Girl with the Dragon Tattoo"	
8	473	Book: "Moby Dick"	
8	474	Film: "The China Syndrome"	
8	474	Film: "Tootsie"	
8	474		Dustin Hoffman
8	475		Mel Gibson
8	475	Film: "Lethal Weapon"	

LIST OF WORKS CITED, BUT NOT GIVEN ATTRIBUTION IN CONTENT:

In Chapter 3—The First Date:

[1] Clark, L.V. *Effect of Mental Practice on the Development of a Certain Motor Skill.* Research Quarterly 31.4 (Dec. 1960): 560-569.

[2] Wloszczyna, Susan. *Power Trio Hits the 'Road'.* USA Today, July 12, 2002.

In Chapter 4—Serious Dating:

[3] Morrison, Jackie. *Biography of Meryl Streep.* Hyperink Celebrity Bios, 2012.

[4] Wedding, Danny, Mary Ann Boyd, and Ryan M. Niemiec. *Movies and Mental Illness: Using Films to Understand Psychopathology.* Cambridge: Hogrefe and Huber, 2005.

In Chapter 5—Moving in Together:

[5] Finley, Guy. *The Secret of Letting Go.* Llewellyn Publications, 2007.

In Chapter 6—The First Fight:

[6] Freud, Sigmund. *The Interpretation of Dreams.* NuVision Publications, 2009

[7] Ellenberger, Henri F. *The Discovery of the Unconscious: History and Evolution of Dynamic Psychiatry.* Basic Books, 1981.

[8] Buonomano, Dean. *Brain Bugs: How the Brain's Flaws Shape Our Lives.* W.W. Norton & Company, 2012.

In Chapter 7—Making a Commitment:

[9] Bobbio, Norberto. Trans. Allan Cameron. *Left and Right: The Significance of a Political Distinction.* Chicago: The University of Chicago Press, 1997.

DYC Chapter Exercise List

Exercise	Chapter	Page #	Description
1	1	8	**Character Check-Up** – your character's one non-negotiable trait.
2	1	9	**What Do You Really Know?** – spontaneous writing; highlighting "must-haves."
3	1	11	**Character POV** – writing from her POV.
4	1	18	**Smelling the Roses** – using one of the 5 senses to write about location.
5	1	22	**Rip & Snatch** – the kinds of people and places she would gravitate to.
6	1	26	**Look in the Mirror** – how your writing process will make you happy.
7	1	30	**Personal Logline** – your realistic writing commitment.
8	1	32	**Be Your Own Barbara Walters** – your audience's ideal reaction after the lights come up.
9	2	36	**Iconic Characters** – making a list of favorite movie characters.

DYC Chapter Exercise List			
Exercise	Chapter	Page #	Description
10	2	40	**Native Son** – where your character could have grown up.
11	2	50	**The See-Saw** – how characters learn about each other while tackling goals.
12	2	53	**Ladder of Conflict** – 5 obstacles that can get in the way of a must-do goal.
13	2	55	**The Personals** – write a catchy ad.
14	2	57	**Bird of Prey** – what her usual haunts are.
15	2	59	**Workplace Recon** – how the details of her workplace fit in with her essential components.
16	2	64	**Bar Metaphor** – chatting up your character or her sidekick.
17	2	69	**Meet Cute** – "accidentally" bumping into your character.
18	2	73	**Weight-Bearing** – the multiple ways a personal obstacle can affect other areas of your character's life.

DYC Chapter Exercise List

Exercise	Chapter	Page #	Description
19	2	79	**Public/Private Detective** – 5 ways personal problems intrude.
Chart	2	85	**Genre Checklist** – a list of the most common genres.
20		87	**Genre Checklist – Tone** – matching descriptions with genres.
Chart	2	90	**Genre Checklist – Demographics** – understanding the audiences for certain genres.
21	3	98	**Review at a Glance** – more info on non-negotiable traits.
22	3	100	**Taking Inventory of The Meet Cute** – does she want to see you again, what are the contact details?
23	3	102	**Location Scouting** – finding a venue that fits her basic likes/dislikes.
24	3	104	**Comfort Zone** – the kind of place that will put her at ease.
25	3	106	**People Watching** – the kinds of people she'd expect to show up at this

DYC Chapter Exercise List			
Exercise	Chapter	Page #	Description
			place.
26	3	109	**First Date Field Trip** – comparing and soaking in the atmospheres of 3 potential venues.
27	3	113	**Date Planner** – the level of difficulty getting her to agree to meet you.
28	3	119	**Taking Your Character's Temperature** – sensing the level of her anxiety.
29	3	122	**Managing Expectations** – how to satisfy the protagonist with the basic elements of the date itself, regardless of how you two mesh.
30	3	123	**Escape Hatch** – the character's alternatives, if the date is a bomb.
31	3	127	**Use Your Words** – say something 3 different ways.
32	3	129	**First Date Patter** – pushing for 3 awkward reveals from her.
33	3	133	**Lie Detector Test** – dispelling fears and roadblocks.

DYC Chapter Exercise List			
Exercise	Chapter	Page #	Description
34	3	137	**Five Minutes Before** – what she was thinking right before showing up to meet you.
35	3	145	**Soak Up Your Surroundings** – absorbing a new place.
36	3	146	**The First Date** – the first official meeting with her.
37	3	147	**Scene Evaluation** – gauging the level of reality of that scene.
38	3	150	**Carrie Wells Memory Walk-Through** – focusing on the atmosphere; her perspective.
39	3	152	**Charting the Arc of the Scene** – studying the flow of conversation.
40	3	157	**Hanging Out** – watching her in her element.
41	3	158	**Bubbling Up** – having her talk to you.
42	3	160	**Random Weather Pattern** – the confluence of events that can push you to make a life-changing decision.
43	3	161	**Rocking Her World** – unnerving her.

DYC Chapter Exercise List			
Exercise	Chapter	Page #	Description
44	3	170	**Broken Flush** – what she's willing to gamble on.
45	4	182	**Adventure (Reboot) Date** – interacting with a difficult character; practicing "letting go" with some control.
46	4	186	**Glamour Date** – pulling out all the stops to wow her.
Chart	4	190	**Coverage** – a look at all the factors that are used in judging a script.
47	4	194	**Making Space for Her "Shit"** – which possessions make her feel comfortable.
48	4	196	**Genre-Specific Hidden Clues** – adding a genre tinge to one of her possessions.
49	4	199	**Trust Walk** – getting a visceral sense of her place.
50	4	201	**DYC Love Language Quiz** – how she prefers to accept affection.
51	4	205	**Pressure Point** – developing one of her weaknesses.

DYC Chapter Exercise List			
Exercise	Chapter	Page #	Description
52	4	209	**Emotional TNT** – characterizing her most important disappointments.
53	4	214	**Character Liability Claim Check** – when she was emotionally traumatized.
54	4	215	**Activate Your Protagonist**… finding ways to embolden her; downsizing an impossible task; finding a character who can galvanize her; changes in that relationship because of her new daring.
55	4	217	**How Bad Is… Bad?** – differentiating between humiliations and emotional traumas.
56	4	219	**Court Reporter** – confronting her vagueness with nitty-gritty details.
57	4	221	**The Price of Admission** – dealing with unexpected reversals; making sacrifices.
58	4	226	**Afraid, Me… Really?** – fears that could get in the way of her goal; the worst that could possibly happen.

		DYC Chapter Exercise List	
Exercise	Chapter	Page #	Description
59	4	229	**Compatible Neuroses** – impulsive drives that can have a negative impact; any overlay between your issues and hers; unexplainable attraction to one of her more dissonant traits.
60	4	234	**Mirror, Mirror** – gauging her insecurity; her arrogance; one of her dreams; her attitude to work.
61	5	242	**Mapping Personality Pitfalls** – studying your history of writing snafus.
Writing Aid	5	244	**Writer's Block: Nifty Trick** – talking up what excites you about her and her story.
62	5	246	**Romantic Roadblocks** – dissecting any pattern of romantic disconnection.
63	5	247	**The Relationship Rainbow** – evaluating your relationship with her; dealing with her contradictions; areas of conflict with her.

DYC Chapter Exercise List			
Exercise	Chapter	Page #	Description
64	5	255	**Drumbeat** – noting the involuntary pacing of spontaneous conversation.
65	5	259	**Take Her, or Leave Her to Heaven** – acknowledging any of her repulsive or frightening traits.
66	5	261	**List of Pet Peeves** – her traits that drive you up the wall; how to embed problematic emotional responses in situations that could already prove difficult; constructing character-based obstacles; realizing she has other options.
67	5	271	**If She's Being Irritating…** her efforts to deliberately provoke you; dealing with the fact that you can't change everything about her; identifying key areas where she has to transform herself; thinking about how old emotional responses which were beneficial in the past are hurting her

| DYC Chapter Exercise List ||||
Exercise	Chapter	Page #	Description
			now.
68	5	276	**Lend Her an Ear** – let her take the lead in your interaction.
69	5	278	**Proof or Dare** – following up on clues dropped; trailing her to find the truth; designing 10 actions that will force her to reveal problems in her life.
70	5	281	**The Pitchfork Treatment** – getting her to cooperate; shocking her into reality.
71	5	282	**Setting Expectations** – clarifying mutual expectations.
72	5	286	**Setting Boundaries** – allowing her certain limitations; everything else you want to know about her is fair game.
73	5	289	**Picking Up the Dry-Cleaning** – doing practical favors for her as a show of support.
74	5	290	**In the Locker Room** – developing a schedule for your shared activities and also the separate tasks that

Dating Your Character

DYC Chapter Exercise List			
Exercise	Chapter	Page #	Description
			have to get done; indicating her level of ability in the beginning to chart her progress; motivating her; tackling the logistics of an obstacle; the changing nature of your relationship into a true working partnership.
75	5	293	**Pep Talk** – offering objective criticism of areas that need improvement; letting her voice her frustrations.
76	5	295	**On the Rounded Shoulders of Atlas** – the person who might make all her sacrifices worth it.
77	5	297	**Prove Yourself Already!** – taking a hypothetical and breaking it down into a 10-step dilemma with a set-piece.
78	5	301	**Murphy's Law** – complicating already difficult situations.
79	5	302	**The Home Date** – your first serious conversation about your relationship and her life in general; how you

DYC Chapter Exercise List				
Exercise	Chapter	Page #	Description
			can take some pressure off her.
80	6	307	**Putting on the Screws** – deliberately aggravating her progress in a scene to make it look more impossible for her minute by minute.
81	6	308	**Forcing the Issue** – writing 4 scenes that are rife with conflict, loaded with danger, and at risk of compromising her relationship with an affiliate character; amping up the stakes so her very survival is in question.
82	6	312	**Life Is "Great"** – the behavior of denial; avoiding her commitments to you; what she's doing on the side; the efficacy of her secretive actions.
83	6	316	**From Pawn to Queen** – making her decisions active; the benefits of self-delusion to help her get through the messiness of life.

DYC Chapter Exercise List

Exercise	Chapter	Page #	Description
84	6	320	**Shrinking Her Down to Size** – her bad behavior results in painful reversals for another character; acknowledging the cop outs that make her more human than heroic.
85	6	325	**Going Beyond the Blueprint** – muddying the nature of her comprehensive plan to achieve a noble goal with excessively selfish inner goals.
86	6	329	**Submarine Sandwich** – what a total victory at the end of the script would look like on several levels; repairing a relationship with another character in the process.
87	6	332	**Aegis of Honor** – a character she's willing to lay her life down for.
88	6	333	**Staring Down the Lion** – facing fears.
89	6	335	**Key Friends, Frenemies, and Foes** – other characters' agendas; the potential for mirroring her.

DYC Chapter Exercise List

Exercise	Chapter	Page #	Description
90	6	339	**Your Character Is the Sun** – the essence of achievability of her goal; ranking other characters' personal stances on her spectrum of proactive/reactive choices; mining these others' POVs to provide additional conflict in the main storyline and reveal deep vulnerabilities within her.
91	6	345	**Getting in the Ring** – plugging the remaining chinks in her armor; correcting residual bad habits.
92	6	348	**What's the Problem?** – pushing her to give up her last hidden, crippling doubts; putting a positive twist on one of her reservations; taking advantage of one of these primal fears in the final climax of the story.
93	6	355	**Blue or Pink?** – giving male protagonists space and female protagonists support, so your character

DYC Chapter Exercise List

Exercise	Chapter	Page #	Description
			comes to value you.
94	7	361	**This Is Why!** – refining her own POV; ways of expressing that in your scenes.
95	7	371	**Landscape as Reflecting Pool** – symbolic possibilities of the final set-piece; linking similar locales to changes in her emotional temperature.
96	7	374	**Rainbow of Thought** – 5 major characters' POVs; forming character alliances; others' ideal visions of the future.
97	7	376	**Stoking Conflict** – direct/indirect conflict; conflicts in back-story; her conflict with the status quo.
98	7	378	**Pie in the Face** – targeting her from all sides; others' shifting POVs.
99	7	383	**Everything Including the Kitchen Sink…** adding 10 complications to a field that's not her primary focus of concern.

| DYC Chapter Exercise List ||||
Exercise	Chapter	Page #	Description
100	7	386	**Coming Threat** – imagining added characters causing harm.
101	7	389	**Targeting Your Character** – her biggest threat; the spectrum of pain he could cause.
102	7	390	**Affiliate Characters as True Rivals** – amplifying the risks others pose.
103	7	395	**The Mathematics of Success** – what a pared down life looks like.
104	7	397	**Polyester or Worm-Riddled Silk?** – making tough sacrifices; losing a key relationship through no fault of her own.
105	7	400	**Asking Affiliate Characters** – feedback about how they view her.
106	7	401	**Axing an Affiliate Character** – throwing a friend under the bus.
107	7	404	**Unlocking the Doors of Perception** – how she has been misled.
108	7	405	**20/20 Vision** – seeing her memories through a different prism.

DYC Chapter Exercise List

Exercise	Chapter	Page #	Description
109	7	406	**Your Character's Biggest Fan** – how much you believe in your character.
110	7	408	**Total Eclipse** – taking away her sense of purpose.
111	7	415	**The Holiday from Hell** – digging up family dirt.
112	7	418	**The Devil Gets His Day** – complicating a set-piece.
113	7	420	**The New World Order** – getting the jump on the antagonist; having her world crumple around her.
114	7	422	**The Taste of Freedom** – benefits from being out of control.
115	7	425	**Wire in the Blood** – misconstrued qualities that can be of benefit.
116	8	429	**Hidden Spaces** – looking at the manmade-scape of the final scene to see where characters can hide; utilizing the natural features of the landscape to pose additional obstacles.
117	8	430	**Laying Out the Floorplan**– ramping up to the final climax; obscuring

Exercise	Chapter	Page #	Description
			the full array of final hurdles from her and from your audience; how these hurdles will specifically derail her and make all her attempts look futile.
118	8	435	**The Path of Arrival** – the physical and emotional toll on her just to get to the gate barring entry to the final sequence; the logistics themselves.
119	8	435	**Her Field of Dreams** – feeling the dimensions of the final battle's location in the same way she will, not as an intellectual puzzle; an affiliate character who will accompany her; another affiliate character whose presence is a surprise; the physical features of the feat she'll have to perform.
120	8	437	**Ground Zero** – why the final location is meaningful; the character whose influence can be felt here; the echoes of the specific quality of these last obstructions, as seen in

DYC Chapter Exercise List			
Exercise	Chapter	Page #	Description
			previous hurdles; what the site will look like after the end of the fight; if it will represent her victory, in part.
121	8	441	**Looking Down at the Scaffolding** – she shows off new mastery of skills she didn't have previously; she employs objects/tokens earned; she puts to good use relationships salvaged; storyboarding how these assets will come into play in scenes.
122	8	443	**Heartbeat by Heartbeat** – writing beat by beat with the audience in mind; making description sound informal, conversational.
123	8	445	**Power Walk** – putting yourself in her headspace, visually and viscerally experiencing what the final assault will be like for her; judging the non-stop drama of the final sequence.
124	8	450	**Stringing Pearls** – linking plot pivots to one another; ironing out illogical

Exercise	Chapter	Page #	Description
			character entrances, too-sudden jump cuts; clearing up subplots.
125	8	452	**Tying Up Loose Ends** – analyzing her impossible goal and how she ended up accomplishing it; tracing the noticeable character arc that allowed her to succeed; how meeting her goal alleviated other pressures or conversely put other areas of her life out of balance.
126	8	454	**Pervasive Metaphors** – extrapolating applicable metaphor patterns for deeper insight into her, her goal, and her world.
127	8	456	**Walking Down the Aisle** – making sure the ending completely satisfies her; reversing her setbacks in the inciting incident; noting the evolution of her goal to fit the earned maturity of her POV.
128	8	458	**Appreciation Letter/Suicide Note** – an opportunity to come full

Table title: **DYC Chapter Exercise List**

| DYC Chapter Exercise List ||||
Exercise	Chapter	Page #	Description
			circle, congratulating her on how far she's come; recognizing the insurmountable flaws in her that will most likely make her victory incomplete, allowing for the full expression of her soul to lend a bittersweet dignity to what will be her end.
129	8	463	**Janus Image** – how her beginning expectations differ from the actual resolution; noting the hidden parts of herself that she accessed to realize her goals; reflecting on the changes to her values; observing the sacrifices she's made, honoring those permanent losses.
130	8	465	**The Magma of the Emotional Core** – summing up her end decision; providing the context and back-story that makes it a mark of her transformation.

DYC Chapter Exercise List			
Exercise	Chapter	Page #	Description
Chart	8	468	**Genre Wrap-Ups** – expected tried-and-true formulas for final scenes.
Writing Aid	8	470	**Logline Tips** – how to encapsulate the genre, the thumbnail of your protagonist, and the promise of a major twist that will upend the world of the story.
131	8	475	**Logline Polish** – updating a classic genre logline.

www.ingramcontent.com/pod-product-compliance
Lightning Source LLC
Chambersburg PA
CBHW021846230426
43671CB00006B/289